HOLY TOLEDO

To Lorraine

Go A's!

Ku Kran

Cover illustration: Mark Ulriksen

Cover and title page lettering: Mark Matcho

Back cover painting: Bill King

Book design: Alvaro Villanueva

Photos on pages 94, 144, 206 and 218 courtesy of Michael Zagaris,

page 120 courtesy of Bob Arnold, all others courtesy of Bill King's family.

HOLY TOLEDO

LESSONS FROM BILL KING: RENAISSANCE MAN of THE MIC

By

KEN KORACH

THE VOICE OF THE OAKLAND A'S

WELLSTONE BOOKS

2013

CONTENTS

FOREWORD

BY JON MILLER

've always been able to remember the day, May 12, 1975, when the Golden State Warriors won their first and only NBA championship, for that was the day I first met Bill King. How we met underscored the divergent paths of our careers just then. I was twenty-three years old, traveling back to the Bay Area with the San Jose Earthquakes soccer team after broadcasting the Earthquakes versus Toronto Metros-Croatia game in the North American Soccer League that afternoon in Toronto. Bill, meanwhile, had just broadcast the Warriors' clinching victory over Washington in the NBA Finals!

In a very cool twist of fate, both teams ended up on the same connecting flight out of Chicago that night, heading back to the Bay Area, where thousands of revelers were already partying, eagerly awaiting the triumphal arrival of coach Al Attles and his underdog Warriors, including Rick Barry, Phil Smith, Jamaal Wilkes and Clifford Ray. Having been turned into a huge Warriors fan by Bill years earlier, I was startled to see Bill, Champagne bottle in hand, standing near Rick Barry by the opening into the first-class section. Trying not to rudely crash their party, I timidly moved forward from the coach section wanting to introduce myself to Bill.

I needn't have worried, for Bill was an inclusive kind of person. He welcomed me with an airline cup and immediately filled it with

Champagne! At which point Bill, Rick and I toasted the champion Warriors. Bill introduced me to several other Warriors on that plane, and we toasted with them as well! I had a hundred questions about that day's championship game, but Bill wanted to know the ins and outs of broadcasting soccer and from which countries the players came. When he found out our goalkeeper was a Russian-American, Bill insisted on being introduced.

"Bill," I said, "meet Mike Ivanow, goalkeeper of the Earthquakes."

Bill shook his hand, offered him some Champagne and asked, "You don't pronounce your name ee-*von*-off?"

For the next twenty minutes, Bill spoke Russian with our goalkeeper (as it turned out, he spoke much more of it than did Ivanow). They also had a fascinating discussion about Russian literature, music and poetry. When Bill found out that some of Ivanow's distant relatives from the old country had known Rasputin, he became further entranced. Bill knew a lot about Rasputin and grilled Ivanow about family stories, the kind not written in any histories.

I remember thinking, "How many points did Rick Barry score today?" But there was Bill King, on the day of an ultimate Warriors triumph, entirely in the moment, engrossed in something completely different.

A few years later, I actually had the honor of working Warriors broadcasts when Bill had conflicts with Raiders football. On one such occasion, I met the team in Chicago so I could watch that night's game, which Bill would work, then travel with the team in the morning for the next game, where I would sub for Bill. As I was checking in to the team hotel, Bill came strolling through the lobby, saying he had just been to a great pre-Columbian art exhibit at the Art Institute. Putting on my totally false "I know all about that" aspect I asked, "Name one great modern pre-Columbian artist!" Bill's laugh was one of life's great pleasures (and hey, he liked pre-Columbian art humor!). As you'll find out from this excellent book, Bill loved to laugh and he loved life. A night out with Bill was always memorable and usually fascinating as well.

My wife, Janine, and I have been married for twenty-six years.

When we were preparing to marry, in 1987, Bill found out she was an artist and sent her several of his favorite art books. Come to find out, Bill wasn't just a verbal artist on the radio, painting word pictures of the game as it happened. During the 1980s he became a full-fledged, self-taught oil painter, as you can see on the back cover of this book. Yes, that's a Bill painting of the San Francisco skyline as seen from near Bill's home in Sausalito. Ken explores Bill's love of painting in a chapter called "An Artist of the Airwaves."

The same man who had once urged me to catch the Pissarro exhibit in Boston was now creating lovely landscape oil paintings of his own! He had to be coaxed, but over dinner, he would grudgingly share photos of some of his latest work. (By the way, he would never sell one to me. Nor to anyone else. Bill was a purist and he felt that his celebrity as a broadcaster would take away from the work itself.)

For me, Bill was the ultimate NBA and NFL radio play-by-play man. In that way, Ken Korach and I had the same experience regarding Bill in our young lives as sports fans, an experience Ken brings alive beautifully in his chapter "Growing Up With Bill." In 1975, while I was being interviewed for the Cincinnati Reds' TV play-by-play job (I didn't get it), Reds GM Dick Wagner asked me if I knew Bill King. I told him Bill was the best football and basketball announcer ever.

"Bill's best sport is baseball," Wagner told me in no uncertain terms, having been with a minor-league team for which Bill had once broadcast. "That's the game he should be doing."

When the A's hired Bill and Lon Simmons as their broadcast team in 1981, I was so excited about this blockbuster booth with two Bay Area play-by-play legends, I called my friend René White in the Bay Area and asked if he would record the A's Opening Night broadcast because it was just so *big*! René came through with a recording of the A's hitting five homers and winning 16–1! Those cassettes reside in my home office with others of Red Barber, Mel Allen, Russ Hodges, Vin Scully and many of the great "Voices of the Game."

Bill captured so many remarkable moments in Bay Area sports

history, like the Warriors winning the championship, and the "Sea of Hands" and "Holy Roller" plays, and Rickey Henderson setting the all-time stolen base record, and Dave Stewart's no-hitter — I could go on, but there's no need to: They're all captured here by Ken, his longtime broadcast partner, a great way to revisit those moments now. In this book I'm confident you'll get to know the man who inspired and taught many of us young broadcasters how to do radio play-by-play. But even more, you'll get to know Bill's voracious love of life. That's why I miss him so much and why I'm so happy with this book in which you'll perhaps be inspired, as we were, by Bill's passion for living.

CHAPTER 1

GROWING UP WITH BILL

To not be able to verbalize is almost crippling to me. And people would probably say, 'I know, you never stop.'

I first met Bill King in the mid-1960s. He didn't meet me until years later. Our introduction came over the airwaves when he was calling San Francisco Warriors games on the radio and I was a kid in West Los Angeles. Even then I was fascinated by radio. I soon learned that a signal carries better at night and I could pick up Warriors games in L.A. Some nights it was clear and some nights it was staticky, but Bill's voice was so distinctive that it didn't matter. It was a magical experience, having a game four hundred miles away come out of the little box next to my bed, and Bill King made me feel like I was sitting courtside with him.

Pulling in games from faraway places was a hobby of mine from a very early age. I'm not sure what came first, my love of radio or my love of sports, although I have to imagine it was the latter, because I am the son of a coach. My dad coached basketball and baseball in high school and junior college for twenty years. During the last year of World War II, stationed in England, he coached his team to the United States Strategic and Tactical Air Forces (USSTAF) basketball championship for all of Europe. He reminds me now, only half-jokingly, that we were playing catch before I could walk. My mom was a UCLA grad and my dad graduated from USC after World War II and they were big football fans. Every Saturday during the season was spent at the L.A. Coliseum. I look back now and wonder if my parents thought it odd that I sat there during those games and hardly said a word. I was announcing the games to myself. I did the same thing at UCLA and USC basketball games and of course whenever we took in a Dodgers game, first at the Coliseum after the Dodgers moved to L.A. in 1958 and later at Dodger Stadium.

Even though I had to wait until it got dark to tune in the Warriors, I listened to Bill as much as Chick Hearn, the voice of the Lakers. (Baseball season meant Vin Scully, the voice of my summers.) There was something enthralling about Bill. I would listen to him one night and then immediately start looking forward to listening to him again to try to figure out what made him unique and also, of course, for the sheer enjoyment of seeing a game through Bill's eyes. Bill aficionados have long referred to his staccato rhythm and his incredible attention to detail. He could tell you what was happening away from the ball better than most play-by-play men could describe the action with the ball.

"The thing I learned sitting next to Bill was he was the first person I knew that broadcast away from the ball," Hank Greenwald remembers now. "I had never seen anybody do that before. Instead of just Smith passes to Jones, he could see guys setting screens on the far side of the court, and he knew the play was developing. He knew the ball was eventually going to the guy coming around. He would lead you, and I had never seen that before."

Bill had amazing court vision and a feel for how the game developed from second to second. His mind was so focused, and he had such a visceral connection to the action that was unfolding before him, he really seemed to know what was coming before anybody else did. "Seconds before it would even happen he would say, 'A guy coming off a screen,'" my friend Pat Hughes, the radio voice of the Cubs, remembers from his own childhood fascination with Bill. "I don't even think the other coach could see it, but he could see it."

"It was instantaneous," Rick Barry recalled. "He had the ability to see a game, a basketball game, and express what was happening in eloquent terms, at times instantaneously. When he was saying something, it was happening,"

Bill had the tools to bring that vision alive. I had never heard anyone who could match his vocabulary — and still haven't. I've always thought he was the most erudite and articulate announcer ever. The words that came out of his mouth were ones that often sent me to the dictionary when I was listening as a kid — and for years to come. Even though Bill never went to college, he studied the language and made expanding his vocabulary part of his preparation; he would write a few new words in his scorebook before a game and then try to work them into a broadcast.

It wasn't just that Bill studied words; it was as if the language was sacred to him. A lot of broadcasters find themselves throwing out extra words from time to time waiting for their thoughts to catch up with the flow of the action. Bill never did this. Each word was chosen with precision, savored as he was forming the word. "I get a tactile feeling on my tongue," he once explained to the *San Francisco Examiner*. He took pride in his connection to words and it irked him to no end when the language was abused or disrespected. He could go off on a rant over something like the misuse of the word "flounder." He took this as a personal affront. Especially galling to him was when an announcer would say, "The team is floundering."

"Flounder is a fish," Bill would say. "The word is 'founder.' The team is foundering."

But for all his verbal gifts, for all his hard work and commitment to his craft, the thing that set Bill apart to me was his passion. He poured his heart and soul into every broadcast. Night after night his voice would carry excitement and energy, like a jazz saxophonist commanding a room with a solo that built to a crescendo. *"Holy Toledo!"* The way he held that first syllable, drawing it out for impact, but always with a fine sense of rhythm, was more than a trademark, it was an instantaneous signal to his audience that something really important had just happened.

"I remember lying in bed listening to Bill and without ever having seen him I thought he was like a jazz musician," sportscaster Gary Radnich, who grew up in San Jose, told me. "I could just tell he was cool by listening to him talk. And then when I met him in person years later, he was just as cool. He's one of the few guys who really did do it his own way."

Bill cared about every play of every game in a way that transcended mere professionalism. He loved calling a game and loved doing right by it, and the passion he brought to the airwaves was, as I would find out, a passion that he brought to all of his pursuits in life, from sailing the seas to going to the opera to painting landscapes. Each broadcast was a tour de force of precise, rapid descriptions and was also a showcase of intense, emotional involvement, so much so that his railing at the officials was legendary — and became fodder for some of the best of the Bill King stories.

Bill didn't have a classic radio voice. I think it deepened in timbre over the decades he worked games, but in the years when I first listened to him, his voice lacked the booming bass notes of some of the classic broadcaster voices. But I always loved his sound; it was distinctive and all his own, and like all the great ones he was able to use his voice as an instrument, to go from conversational to excited without any hint of contrivance. In his self-deprecating way, he called his voice "tinny" when he compared it to the resonance of Lon Simmons', but Bill's voice was seasoned and very pleasant. It was *his* voice. Nobody sounded like Bill and nobody could use their voice to crystallize a big moment like Bill.

I feel lucky to have grown up as part of the last generation to fall in love with sports by listening to games on the radio. The televisions of the day were primitive, barely in the same category as the wall-sized, high-def marvels that sports fans now accept as a given. If you did watch a game on television, you were staring over at a little box with a fuzzy picture that you often could not make much sense of one way or another. When the batter swung, that told you there had been a pitch. Nowadays you can see every stitch on the ball. That's great, but I preferred the experience of being tethered to a single voice, a member of the family in a way, whose role was to inform and entertain but also to fire your imagination and a full range of emotional responses to the drama of a given game.

Working on this book, I have been blown away to realize just how many of my generation have indelible memories of listening to Bill do Warriors games, and the Raiders starting in 1966, precisely because the power of radio was king then. Radio was the dominant medium and the perfect match for Bill's ability to become the eyes and ears of the audience. If you wanted to follow the Warriors, you had to listen to the radio. Same with the Dodgers in L.A. When I was a kid, the only televised Dodgers games were the nine every year in San Francisco. So you had to listen to Vinny on the radio.

You were connected to the action in a way that was more immediate and more intimate and it gave you the chance to conjure your own images. With all the technology today, very little is left to the imagination. When the imagination is fed, the mind has a chance to grow.

"I've had this thesis for a long time that television actually damages the fan's understanding of the game because of the mindless way you are coached," former A's president Roy Eisenhardt told me for this book. "You are watching what you are told to watch. They want to cut to this or cut to that. You have no choice and the announcers are usually talking about where they had dinner the night before. With radio you are required to visualize the entire field. Radio inculcates into people a much stronger sense of the game than television does. Your job as the announcer is to help me use my imagination."

That was especially true for me when I was young, listening to Bill King calling the Warriors. Maybe it was in part because there were nights when I had to fight through some static to tune in Bill's voice, but for me there was always something mysterious about listening to Bill. When I saw black-and-white pictures of him with his beard and handlebar mustache, I found myself wondering more and more about just who this guy was.

Born Wilbur D. King — he could not abide "Wilbur" and hated being called that — Bill grew up on a farm near Bloomington, Illinois. He was the only child born to an older couple, Ivan and Helen, who were wed when both were twenty-five, relatively well along in life for the time. They did not have Bill until more than ten years later, on October 6, 1927. The family was well established in the area. Bill's father's father, the youngest of four boys and given the Old Testament name Zephaniah, was born in Illinois in 1854. Zephaniah's father, William King, was prominent in the community after having moved from Pennsylvania (where *his* father, Bill's great-great-grandfather, was born exactly two weeks after the Declaration of Independence was signed).

According to an account of McLean County, Illinois, published by Chapman Brothers in 1887, Bill's great-grandfather "was formerly one of the most successful farmers in Bloomington Township and ... owned a good farm of 500 acres. ... Mr. King was born in Somerset County, Pennsylvania, February 25, 1813, and was of pure German extraction." William King was "among the early residents of McLean County and favorably known as being numbered with its most valued and worthy citizens. In politics Mr. King was a member of the old Whig party, and served as Justice of the Peace for a number of years. The sons are all Democrats. Mr. King died October 28, 1854."

For the first years of his life, Bill lived on the farm — most likely on what was known as "the old King homestead" — and even went to a one-room schoolhouse for a time, but in February 1938 his father died at age forty-three. Bill never forgot what it was like to have his father laid out on the kitchen table for the two days from his death to his burial. Bill's mother, now a widow, had no choice but to move into town with Bill.

Geography helps form the allegiances — and mentality — of any young sports fan and Bill grew up right in the middle of Cubs and Cardinals country. He liked to listen to Harry Caray's calls of Cards games, but his biggest influence was Bob Elson, who broadcast the Cubs and White Sox from 1929 to 1942. Back then broadcasters rarely traveled with the teams they were covering, so Elson did the home games for both the Cubs and Sox. After the war he did both home and road games for the White Sox, and stayed with the Sox until 1970.

Living in Bloomington, Bill followed both the Cubs and Cards; his heart wasn't set on one team over the other. "Most of the time I rooted for the team that had a player I regarded with greater favor," Bill said later. For a time that player was the Cubs' third baseman Stan Hack, "Smilin' Stan," a product of Sacramento who finished his big-league career with a .301 batting average. Bill's allegiance shifted south when Stan Musial joined the Cardinals. "I was enamored of him," Bill would say later.

Bill was fourteen years old when he had the chance to meet his idol in 1942, Musial's first full year in the big leagues. Musial batted .315 that season for a Cards team that reached the World Series.

One of the charms of Wrigley Field is the proximity of the fans to the field, and Bill was there early that day with his autograph book to watch batting practice and hope for some luck. Musial finished his time in the cage and walked up the first-base line to pick up his glove before heading out to the outfield to shag flies.

"Hey, Stan! Hey, Stan!" Bill hollered out, as he recalled later in an interview for one of Marty Lurie's pregame shows.

"He looked over and I held up my autograph book and he walked right over to me and said, 'How you doing?'" Bill recalled. "He signed the autograph and then went out to the outfield. I was in seventh heaven, totally enthralled."

Sunday doubleheaders offered a feast of enjoyment for a young fan of baseball on the radio who listened so intently that he absorbed everything. If both teams were at home, Bill would switch back and forth and spend the entire afternoon monitoring the progress of two National League doubleheaders. "That was an absolute festival," as he put it.

In those days teams always double-dipped on the holidays and many of the Sundays. Bill would go out early and watch batting practice and take in the first game. "Then you had a hot dog and you talked about the first game and anticipated the second-game pitchers and what the lineup changes were going to be," he recalled. "That was the perfect day."

For Bill there was always something pleasurable and addictive about the act of talking. This went back to when teachers would call on him in class or later when he took part in school theater. "To not be able to verbalize is almost crippling to me," he told the *Examiner*. "And people would probably say, 'I know, you never stop.'"

Bill was a catcher, despite his relatively small stature, and always related to catchers, as people who have caught often do. (Bill was around five-nine and weighed no more than 165 pounds for most of his life.) He was also a good ballplayer. Bill Lawrence later recalled in an interview with the *Bloomington Pentagraph* what it was like having the bad luck to be Bill's backup at catcher when they both played for the Bloomington High team. "I didn't play that much," said Lawrence. "I only got in when the game was decided and there was some mopping up to do."

One of Bill's favorite players was the Cubs' catcher Gabby Hartnett, and in our years together I never got tired of hearing the story of the "Homer in the Gloamin'." Bill was ten years old in 1938 when Hartnett hit one of the most famous home runs of all time. The Cubs trailed the Pirates for most of that season. In fact, the Cubs' first-half struggles led to the firing of manager Charlie Grimm. Hartnett, at the age of thirty-seven, took over as player-manager and by the time the Pirates came to Wrigley for a late-September series the National League race was down to a game and a half.

An aging Dizzy Dean, so often the enemy during all those years he pitched for the Cardinals, won the first game of the series for the Cubs, 2–1, setting the stage for Hartnett's blast. As darkness descended upon Wrigley, the umpires informed the teams that the game would end after the ninth inning, no matter what happened. Bill listened to the beginning of that game at home and then went into town.

"I stopped at a couple of stores where they had radios and caught a half inning here and a half inning there," he said later.

He got home in time to hear Bob Elson call the ninth inning.

The game was tied 5–5. Then, in the bottom of the ninth, Hartnett hit an oh-two pitch off reliever Mace Brown into the left-field bleachers. Pandemonium broke out at Wrigley. The Cubs were in first place. Hartnett had to fight through a maze of humanity as he circled the bases and pushed his way through to home plate. Then he was carried off the field.

Bill was eager to read the next day's *Chicago Tribune*. "The *Tribune* ran a murky picture because it was dark," he said later. "Gabby was a big guy with a big, round face and he's kind of red. They used to call him Old Tomato Face. He was grinning from ear to ear like a slit watermelon."

One of Bill's most amazing experiences and something you wouldn't conjure in your wildest dreams came during the 1944 World Series between the Cardinals and St. Louis Browns. That was a rare series in which both teams shared the same park so all six games were played at Sportsman's Park, which later was renamed Busch Stadium after the brewery bought the Cardinals and the Browns moved to Baltimore.

"I was just a high school kid and through fortunate circumstances had the opportunity to sit in box seats for all six games," Bill later recalled in an interview with Marty Lurie.

This was during the war, when many players had been sent off to serve in Europe and the Pacific, leaving the rosters somewhat depleted. Still, there was great interest in the Series in St. Louis, with crowds at or near capacity for every game. Bill saw a lot of sportswriters and media people on the field before the games, but noticed there seemed to be very little if any security. So before either Game Three or Game Four, Bill brazenly suggested to his buddy that they try to go down on the field. Remember, these were two sixteen-year-old kids and this was the World Series.

"People were just milling around all over the place talking to players and lo and behold we got down on the field and I wandered over to the Cards' dugout," Bill remembered.

As an avid follower of the team, Bill recognized the bullpen catcher, a guy name Bob Keely, who would later become a coach for the Braves. Soon Bill was in the dugout carrying on a conversation with Keely. As a high school and semipro catcher, Bill knew enough to ask some questions and was soaking up all the information he could from Keely, who he said "was gracious and very accommodating."

Keely was playing catch with one of the Cardinals when Mort Cooper, the great pitcher, came up the steps of the dugout and out onto the field. Cooper, a four-time All-Star and former National League MVP, was a twenty-two-game winner that year. Keely started playing catch with Cooper, then asked Bill if *he* wanted to catch Cooper for a while.

"Are you serious?" Bill said.

"Sure," Cooper said.

So there was Bill King playing catch with the great Mort Cooper on the field at Sportsman's Park just before one of the games of the 1944 World Series. Finally Mort was finished playing catch, Bill tossed the glove to Bob Keely, and Bill and his buddy went to their seats to watch the game.

The next year, the Cardinals hired a new, young broadcaster by the name of Harry Caray, who grew up in a tough neighborhood of St. Louis and played a little semipro ball before getting into broadcasting. Starting the next season Harry was paired with a former manager and catcher named Gabby Street.

"Gabby was very voluble and really went into great detail discussing baseball," Bill recalled. "It was a great combination. He played off Harry and Harry played off him and they became legendary in the Midwest."

The Cardinals were a regional team with St. Louis the westernmost of any major-league team and the popularity of Harry and Gabby helped grow the Cardinals' radio network, which was sponsored by Griesedieck Brothers Beer. Harry was a natural salesman and sold a ton of beer for Griesedieck Brothers. By the time Anheuser-Busch bought the Cards in 1953, the network had swelled to more than one hundred stations in ten states.

Bill was in his car driving to a new job in Lincoln, Nebraska, on May 2, 1954, the day Musial hit five home runs in a doubleheader against the Giants in St. Louis. He had nine RBIs and added a single for twenty-one total bases. Harry was working with Jack Buck and Bill caught all the action on his car radio.

Bill, doing his best Harry impression: "Another home run for MU *SEE* UL!! HOE-ULLY COW!!"

My own experiences growing up in Southern California could not have been more different than Bill's, and yet there were similarities. I was a fan of the teams, but I became a student of the broadcasts. The Los Angeles Angels' first broadcast team featured Don Wells, Steve Bailey and Bob Kelley, who was a legend in those days in Los Angeles. He broadcast a nightly sports show on KMPC that was produced and written for a time in the 1950s by Bob Blum. KMPC was part of the broadcasting empire of "The Singin' Cowboy," Angels owner Gene Autry, the Golden West Radio Network that linked stations like KMPC in Southern California to KSFO in San Francisco.

Besides listening to Bill and the Warriors at night, I enjoyed having the games of the minor-league San Diego Padres boom into my bedroom over KOGO Radio. "KO-GO, Six Double O" had a great signal. I'm old enough to remember re-creations of Pacific Coast League games on KOGO that were broadcast by Al Coupee and Al Schuss. They had all the accouterments: the crowd noise that rolled on a continuous reel of tape and the sound effect that simulated the ball coming off the bat. The games were part reality and part was left to your own imagery.

The Padres played at charming little Westgate Park, which was nestled close to the hills that framed Mission Valley before shopping malls infiltrated the area. My dad and I went to a game there when we visited San Diego in 1967 and I remember being drawn to the intimacy of the place. It was a single-deck structure covered by a roof with seats that extended just beyond first and third base. Part of the allure of the minors is rooting for a veteran looking for one final shot in the majors. That day at Westgate Park, with about one thousand fans in the stands, we saw an aging former all-star from San Francisco named Jim Gentile limp around the bases after hitting a majestic home run to right field. But he never got back to the big leagues.

In the early and mid-'60s the Padres were an affiliate of the Reds, meaning a lot of future big-league stars cycled through. Tony Perez hit thirty-four homers there in 1964 and Lee May crushed thirty-four in '65 and hit .321. Tommy Harper, one of several stand-outs from the East Bay in Northern California, had a great year in '62, when he hit .333 with twenty-six homers and a .450 on-base percentage. His high school, Encinal High in Alameda, near where the A's play, produced the likes of Willie Stargell, Dontrelle Willis and Jimmy Rollins.

Al Coupee also broadcast San Diego State football on KOGO. The Aztecs had fantastic teams in the 1960s. Don Coryell was developing a passing attack that was ahead of its time, and from '63 to '66 one of his defensive assistants was a young up-and-comer named John Madden, who had been born in Minnesota, the son of an auto mechanic, but grew up near San Francisco and played football at Cal Poly San Luis Obispo.

I was fascinated by the magic of games coming in from faraway places. The minor-league Denver Bears on KOA. The New Mexico Lobos on KOB. When the SuperSonics were born in 1967, I listened to their games on KOMO as well. Dick Enberg joined the Angels' broadcasts in 1969, my senior year of high school. I listened to his first game, when he began the broadcast by talking about how he was a kid who grew up in the Midwest dreaming of broadcasting major-league baseball. Now here he was.

Bill enlisted in 1945 and served in Guam starting in 1948, shipping out from San Francisco. Back in those days trains traveled over the Bay Bridge connecting the East Bay to San Francisco and as his train rumbled across the Bay, toward The City, Bill was mesmerized. "He fell in love with San Francisco the moment he saw it," Bill's stepdaughter, Kathleen Lowenthal, recalled for this book. "Just think about this kid coming from the Midwest who was romantic already. He fell in love with San Francisco and never wanted to work anywhere else."

In his years serving on Guam, he had time to develop a deep love of the Pacific. Hank Greenwald says that's when Bill started reading books like *Mutiny on the Bounty*. Guam was also where Bill had his first taste of sitting behind a microphone. He worked for the Armed Forces station there, doing almost everything after requesting a transfer from his staff job driving a colonel around the island. This colonel, according to Bill, "lived in a militaristic ideology of around 1890. He was not pleasant to work for." I have to say that Bill and authority figures were like oil and water.

Back in Illinois, Bill wanted to play baseball. He considered trying to play minor-league ball or at the University of Illinois, but decided instead to pursue a radio career, and began at a small station in the central Illinois town of Pekin. He wasn't broadcasting sports — not yet, anyway.

"I got into sports by accident," Bill recalled in an interview included in a short Comcast Sportsnet biography.

The guy doing sports at the station, a "veteran of radio and a very good sportscaster," had fought a drinking problem, Bill said. "He had dried out, but suddenly one night about three months after I went to work there, he fell victim to the station vamp, fell off the wagon, disappeared. The next morning the boss walked in and said, 'Hey, anybody here know anything about sports?'"

"You're looking at him," Bill said.

By 1950, Bill was working in the Three I League in Quincy, Illinois, and those early days working in the low minors were building blocks for Bill.

"You were bound upwards in your own career and very wrapped up in it," Bill said. "And the players at that time were basically contemporaries age-wise, so we played together, ate together and did all of those things."

It sounds like a handicap to broadcast Western Union re-creations of road games from a studio, but like so many of his contemporaries, Bill found the experience invaluable.

"It was fascinating and made you concentrate and gave you an understanding and sense of feel and timing in the game," he said. "It was also a great test of your ingenuity and adaptability when a communications breakdown would occur and suddenly the line went dead."

Many of the play-by-play guys in Bill's day would use a tape delay, so to speak. Fearing the inevitable loss of communications, they would put an inning or two in the bank by starting the broadcast well after the actual first pitch. Bill didn't do this; he worked very close to real time, "and I didn't have part of a game built up."

The announcers took plenty of liberties and re-creations were legendary for long rain delays coming out of the clear blue sky or make-believe rhubarbs breaking out that would clear the benches and go on forever. It was a perfect opportunity for a young announcer to be creative and use his imagination. Nobody did it with quite the pizzazz of Harry Caray.

"I developed a helluva flair," Harry told *Sports Illustrated*. "When the ticker slowed up or broke down, I'd create an argument on the ball field. Or I'd have a sandstorm blowing up and the ballplayers calling time to wipe their eyes. Hell, all the ticker tape carried was the bare essentials — B1, S1, B2, B3. So I used the license of imagination, without destroying the basic facts, you understand. A foul ball was 'a high foul back to the rail, the catcher is racing back, he can't get it — a pretty blonde in a red dress, amply endowed, has herself a souvenir!'"

Bill worked in a studio with a Western Union operator with a telegraph key. The operator had a set of earphones and was in communication with someone at the ballpark. He would then type the information on a sheet of paper and hand it to Bill, who was sitting at the other end of the table. This system lasted a couple of years, and then Bill graduated to the use of a teleprinter, a machine that would provide a little more information on a long, thin sheet of a paper. "It was more information than before, but not a whole lot more," he said.

Bill spent nine years in the minors working for clubs in places like Lincoln, Nebraska, and the Illinois towns of Quincy and Peoria. When Bill was getting ready for his first pro season, he went down to Branson, Missouri, where the Yankees' minor leaguers were training. Bill was looking forward to a year of broadcasting in Class B ball. There were hundreds of minor-league teams back then, all the way down to Class D.

It was 1951 and Burleigh Grimes was a Yankee pitching supervisor. Grimes was one of the all-time greats, a Hall of Famer who won 270 games and completed 314. He threw twenty-eight complete games and went 25–14 in 1928.

"Just the thought of Burleigh Grimes was a little intimidating to me," Bill said. "I was just a young guy getting my feet wet in baseball."

The Branson camp was a kind of resort with cabins and a central dining area where all the teams would report in the morning. Bill had a little cabin of his own for the spring. He found Burleigh Grimes "immensely approachable and almost philosophical." Bill would wake up at 6:30 or so and there would usually be a knock on his door around 7 or 7:15. It was Grimes, smoking a pipe "with this huge, huge bowl. A very fragrant tobacco."

While Bill was shaving and getting dressed, Grimes would sit on Bill's bed and talk pitching and brief Bill on some of the young pitchers in camp. "That became almost a daily ritual." As for the position players, the most noted player in camp that year was a kid named Mickey Mantle.

As Bill's career took him around the Midwest doing minor-league games, Burleigh Grimes was traveling as a scout. Bill always invited the eventual Hall of Famer to spend a couple of innings on the air.

"He would usually come up in the second or third inning, and from that time on he would tell stories between pitches and between hitters," he said. "It was one of the most delightful experiences I had. It was an ongoing thing that lasted for several years."

I'm not sure there is any word to describe an experience with Casey Stengel. Just translating "Stengelese" was a major challenge. Once, while Bill was working in Quincy, he traveled on the same train as the Yankees to cover an exhibition game. Lugging a tape recorder that was the size of a suitcase, Bill was led up to Casey's compartment for an interview. He found Casey staring out the window at the countryside. Bill started the interview asking about Yankees outfielder Hank Bauer.

"Casey just sat there," Bill remembered. "He had that leathered face, big ears and he had huge hands. He sat there with his chin in one of those hands and just looked at the countryside."

It seemed to Bill like an eternity. Really, it was probably only about forty-five seconds. Finally, the Old Professor said, "Let me tell you about Hank Bauer." The monologue lasted for nearly fifteen minutes. "He went off on a dissertation about Hank Bauer in Stengelese which I can't replicate in any way, shape or form."

Bill had a few more questions, but time was running short and Casey invited Bill to meet him at the hotel after the train reached its destination. It was midmorning and the game was scheduled for around two o'clock. Bill and his engineer knocked on Casey's door and the great Bill Dickey answered. Bill, being a former catcher, immediately recognized Dickey. The retired Hall of Famer was one of Stengel's coaches.

"Sit down, kid, and have some food," Casey said.

He then ordered sandwiches from room service. Bill had a fifteen-minute show to fill and got to ask two questions.

"Casey was crazy like a fox," Bill said.

The Midwest was not going to hold Bill for long. He felt that to get established in sports broadcasting he would have to move to a major market, and as his stepdaughter Kathleen recalled, he had his eye on a return to San Francisco ever since he caught his first glimpse of the City by the Bay. He did not have a job lined up when he moved west in 1958, but he did have prospects and knew he was not taking a crazy risk with the move. Soon he had landed a gig doing color on the Channel 2 college basketball games with Bud Foster, one of the Bay Area's sportscasting pioneers. Bill's signature beard was not yet in evidence.

"When I first saw him he was kind of pudgy-faced, clean-shaven, wore horn-rimmed glasses and was in a suit and tie," said Scotty

Stirling, Bill's future broadcast partner with the Raiders. "It was typical of those early days."

Chick Hearn arrived in California one year before Bill, in 1957, but their friendship dated back to their days together in Peoria, when they broadcast Bradley basketball at the same time. This was in the days before "exclusivity" and back then three different stations carried the Bradley games, so there was plenty of opportunity for Peoria to nurture a cast of young broadcasters who cut their teeth calling Bradley games: Jack Brickhouse, Chick Hearn, Bill King, Bob Starr, Tom Kelly, Vince Lloyd and Charlie Steiner.

Bill's friendship with Chick proved important, because it led Bill to contact the sales manager at KSFO in San Francisco, Burt West, who had helped get Chick started in Los Angeles when he moved to California. Chick told Bill he needed to get in touch with West, a big proponent of sports on the radio, and soon Bill was playing understudy to Lon Simmons, sports director at KSFO, who had a recap show every day at 5:45 P.M.

"It was the only fifteen-minute sports show in town," Lon recalled for this book. "We had a pretty exclusive audience, but when I would go on the road with the baseball team, I needed someone to do the sports show and when I would go on the weekends to do football, I needed someone to work with Russ on the home games on baseball. So we instigated a nationwide search for someone and Bill came as the one who impressed us."

As sports director, Lon had a definite say in the hire and he said what made Bill stand out was "he sounded better than anyone else we heard in describing action."

Bill was a natural, Lon soon discovered, in more ways than one.

"He loved to be on the air," Lon said. "He loved to talk. On the day games there wouldn't be many scores. I'd say, 'Bill, there aren't many games, do you want to do the show?' So I'd leave the game and go to the market to get something for dinner and Bill would still be doing the show. He would recap it at the start and he would still be recapping it."

Bill was also the third man behind Russ Hodges and Lon, calling Giants games beginning in 1959. This was Bill's first major-league opportunity after all the years of traveling baseball's back roads in the minors, and it was fitting that the Cardinals were the Giants' opponent when Bill broadcast his first game. With Lon away doing football, Bill did play-by-play that day with Russ and was responsible for the pregame interview.

"I went down to the Cardinals' clubhouse and sought out Stan Musial and asked him if he would be my guest," Bill said later. "He was gracious, as always. To me, everything had come full circle with Stan Musial."

A big break for Bill came when KSFO acquired the rights to Cal football and basketball. Bob Fouts, Dan's father and a major presence in the Bay Area on radio and TV for decades, was doing the 49ers on radio and he moved to television. Lon became the voice of the 49ers on radio and Bill became the voice of Cal. His timing could hardly have been better. Cal's basketball coach then was Pete Newell, who had made a name for himself earlier at Michigan State and USF and took over at Cal starting in 1954, leading them to an NCAA championship over West Virginia in 1959, winning by one point over a team led by Jerry West. Every announcer sounds better when he's calling great games, and Bill helped make his name in the Bay Area with his work on Cal. Among those admiring his work was a young Cal fan named Wally Haas, son of the CEO of Levi Strauss & Co., who remembers hiding under the sheets when he was nine years old listening to Bill announce Cal games.

"Bill was doing play-by-play for Cal basketball and it just so happened that that was the last time Cal was really good," Haas recalled for this book. "Really good, to the point of here we are, Cal and West Virginia with Jerry West in the NCAA finals, and then the following year Cal was in the Final Four. It was at the Cow Palace and it was Cincinnati against California in the semis and the other semis was the NYU Violets and Ohio State, and this was how everyone got it wrong. Everyone figured the semis, the Cal-Cincinnati game, was really for the title. Whoever wins that is going to kill whomever they play in the finals. I was such a hardcore fan. I got to go to the semifinals and saw Cal beat Oscar Robertson and Cincinnati to get into the finals and then I watched the finals on TV from home and saw Ohio State just smash Cal, eviscerate them, with John Havlicek and Bobby Knight, a team that was just so loaded, and they just killed them.

"I was focusing on the Cal teams at the time, but what made it so interesting was Bill could paint a picture like nobody's business. This was before it was really on TV and so you really were at the mercy of the radio and however that announcer was going to do his thing. But listening to Bill you could see, it was in such detail. It was not just the play-by-play, it was the color he added at the same time and doing it all in sort of this machine-gun style, because you had to, because it was just a faster game. I loved it because it was Cal but I also loved it because it was Bill King. I listened to and watched any sport I could then and he stood out as being so much better than everybody else."

CHAPTER 2

JAZZ MAN

The pitch, there's a swing and a long drive — that might be the fireworks, it's deep into right field. It is foul by inches!

Full count with one out to Big Ed. Farrell into the motion, here it is. There's a swing, another drive way back into right field, that one is going, it is gone for a home run!

The San Francisco that Bill found when he arrived in 1958 was the perfect fit for him. Professionally, he was ready for the challenge of a new and larger market, and, off the field, he was hungry to take in everything and eager to enjoy the freshness and energy of the scene. *On the Road*, the Kerouac classic that was published one year before Bill moved to the Bay Area, evoked a world of Sausalito nights and jazz joints in San Francisco and a furious rush to experience it all, which Bill did with a voraciousness that, if Kerouac had known him, might have made him a character in the book.

There was a sense then of everyone focusing on San Francisco. The classic Alfred Hitchcock film *Vertigo*, starring Jimmy Stewart and Kim Novak and shot in the San Francisco Bay Area, opened in May 1958. The June 1958 issue of Hugh Hefner's *Playboy* featured a fifteen-page guide to nightlife in San Francisco. Herb Caen, the legendary columnist, wrapped up an eight-year stint writing for the *San Francisco Examiner* and returned to the *San Francisco Chronicle*, where he set the tone for The City for decades to come, coining the term "beatnik" in mockery of Kerouac and the Beats and later winning a Pulitzer Prize. It was a year of great beginnings in The City: Enrico Banducci, owner of the hungry i nightclub, which helped launch the careers of Bill Cosby, Mort Sahl, Barbra Streisand and Woody Allen, opened Enrico's in North Beach, a landmark for years to come, and former manager and baseball player Lefty O'Doul opened a saloon at 333 Geary.

That was also the year the Giants came to town. On April 14 a ticker-tape parade down Montgomery Street featuring such notables as Willie Mays and Shirley Temple Black attracted a crowd estimated at more than 200,000 and the next day 110 credentialed reporters — the most ever for a baseball game at that point — converged at Seals Stadium for history. As Bay Area sports expert Steve Bitker put it in his book *The Original San Francisco Giants: The Giants of '58*, "A standing-room sun-bathed crowd of 23,449 was on hand at Seals Stadium April 15 on a warm, breezy afternoon to witness the first major league game in West Coast history." The Giants beat the Dodgers that day, 8–0.

Two months later, Bill arrived in San Francisco to stay. He had been married previously and had a son, Mike King, but San Francisco really marked a new beginning to his life. By the next season he was working as the third man on the legendary Giants broadcast team of Russ Hodges and Lon Simmons. Hodges had been calling Giants games since the 1940s and he was in the booth for the most famous baseball call ever made, Bobby Thomson's "Shot Heard 'Round the World," which stunned the Dodgers and their fans and sent the Giants into the World Series as National League champs. Almost every fan has heard the call.

" *Branca throws. There's a long drive. It's gonna be, I believe — the Giants win the pennant! The Giants win the pennant! The Giants win the pennant! The Giants win the pennant! Bobby Thomson hits into the lower deck of the left-field stands! The Giants win the pennant! And they're going crazy! They're going crazy!"*

There were several broadcasts of the third game of that 1951 playoff between the Giants and Dodgers, but only one has lived forever: "The Giants win the pennant! The Giants win the pennant!" Hodges was on radio on the Giants' broadcast, while Red Barber described Thomson's home run on Dodgers radio. Ernie Harwell did the national telecast, in the infancy of national television.

The author David Halberstam wrote a fascinating *Los Angeles Times* piece in 1990 about Hodges' call and Barber's reaction, writing, "Barber, though, was openly critical of Hodges' famous call, labeling it 'unprofessional.' On National Public Radio, Barber lambasted Hodges, calling him an 'out and out rooter. He just started hollering, 'the Giants win the pennant!' I think he said it seven or eight times. I don't think that's reporting.'

"Years later, a tape circulated of Barber's account of Thomson's home run. Not unexpectedly, Red's description was emotionally guarded. He hardly raised his voice, treating the theatrical turn of events with laconic indifference. But his economy of emotional expression belied the frenzied crowd and the haunting and galvanizing impact it had on Dodger and Giant fans, respectively."

Talking about it all later, Bill took serious umbrage with Barber's comments. Hodges came close to crossing the line. But if you can move someone emotionally with a call — when it's genuine and you've taken it right to the edge, like Russ did — you've done your job. Plus, if ever there was an appropriate time for such a call, this was it. An epic Giants comeback against the arch-enemy Dodgers from thirteen and a half games down on August 11 was completed in one swift, outlandish moment. One thing about going crazy on the air, though: All that passion is great, but you have to be accurate, too. Hodges gave all of the pertinent information in the prelude to the call and also in the recap.

Within months of arriving in San Francisco in 1958 Bill had bought his first boat, *Kahuna*. Bill's stepdaughter, Kathleen — Kathy in those days — remembers it well as "a little wooden sloop about twenty-six feet." Bill had been reading about sailing for years and now he could take *Kahuna* out from the main yacht harbor in Sausalito, passing under the glorious red-orange expanse of the Golden Gate Bridge, and out into the Pacific. Bill was a man with many great passions, but he was never happier than when he was out on the sea. He never felt more himself.

"Bill certainly broadened my interests," Hank Greenwald told me for the book. "He got me involved in the South Pacific and he recommended books to me. I ended up going to Australia, and we went on trips that Bill used to talk about that he never got around to.

"He gave me a book from Fred Goerner, who used to work at KCBS Radio years ago, called *The Search for Amelia Earhart* that was a very captivating book. That was the first book he ever gave me. He used to talk about authors who had written about the South Pacific adventures, like Nordhoff and Hall and the *Mutiny on the Bounty* trilogy. I collected all these books because of Bill and because of him I ended up going to Samoa, Tahiti, Tonga and the Cook Islands. It all started because of him."

Those were days of easy camaraderie among all who loved the sea and Sausalito attracted all kinds, most of them colorful. Bill fit right in from the start. "Bill was part of a group of unique harbor characters who all gravitated towards the beautiful, sixty-eight-foot, old wooden gaff-rigged schooner, the *Valerie Queen*," Kathleen remembered.

Her mother, Nancy, was part of the *Valerie Queen* crew, and had been aboard when she sailed from Monterey to Sausalito. Bill got along well with Kathy and Johnny, Nancy's children from her marriage to Glenn Stephens, from the beginning. "I remember that Bill was working at KTVU-TV around 1960 — around the time he started dating Mom," Kathleen recalled for this book. "My brother and I thought Bill was very cool because he introduced us to Captain Satellite one night while we were having dinner at the old Bow and the Bell restaurant in Jack London Square."

Bill met Nancy in Sausalito within a year of arriving in San Francisco and was, by all accounts, immediately intrigued. In all the conversations I've had for this book, two topics have inspired the most widespread amazement and wonder from people. One was the way that Bill could sketch in all the details of a game for his radio audience, with passion and panache, and the other was what a figure he and Nancy cut, two bold personalities who spoke their mind and pulled intriguing people to them.

But in those early days, it's almost impossible to say what attracted Bill more, Nancy, beautiful and strong and free, or the *Valerie Queen*, also beautiful and strong and free. To go back now and read some of Bill's descriptions in the photo albums he painstakingly compiled of those days, with elaborate captions he typed out, is to feel almost a gust of salt air on your neck. Bill put together one album as a gift to Nancy, which Kathleen was generous enough to share for this project, and it's so beautiful, so full of love and passion for the sea and for Nancy, it feels like it deserves a film treatment.

The movie would be called *Sailing to Kingston* and the early scenes of the film would involve late-night conversations in Sausalito, fueled by cigarettes and jug wine, with the final exuberant rush of belief and the decision: Let's do it! Let's sail to the Caribbean! All of us must pitch in, must sacrifice, to make this dream come reality, but oh the times we will have! Everyone indeed pitched in. For Nancy that meant not only hours of work on the *Valerie Queen*, but also selling her beloved Steinway baby grand piano to raise money for her share of the expenses.

"Then came that decisive evening of January 8, 1961," Bill

typed out on a manual typewriter for a caption in his photo album for Nancy. "A cold, raw Sunday under gloomy skies that saw you bunked down ill, Stewart restlessly fidgeting about and a disgruntled Norman fuming over not making the FAIRWEATHER crew.

"There was the talk of the Caribbean ... subdued, idle talk on the surface. But this time it carried the overtones of reality. Capitan was deadly serious. As it became evident, the undercurrent of excitement, quiet but strong, took over.

"When the evening drew late and we scattered, few doubted then that the cruise was born. That it was indeed, and with it two months of bone-wearying but soul-satisfying preparations."

And in the album, a few pages later, a picture of the proud vessel, fully readied, and the Bill caption: "At last she's really 'Valerie Queen.'"

Nancy sailed off, and Bill had to wait for her. They did not really become a couple until after Nancy returned six months later, but the way they lived in those early days — the adventures they pursued, the great friends they gathered and above all the *Valerie Queen* and the romance and thrill of sailing out under the Golden Gate in pursuit of fresh harbors and fresh adventures — set a tone.

Sausalito, with its harbor and its beauty and its cozy shops and restaurants, was the perfect place for Bill and Nancy and their boats. It is somewhat of a myth that Bill lived most of his time on his boat. They lived on a boat in Sausalito for a time in the '60s after a fire gutted Bill's cottage. It was a thirty-two-foot sailboat, *Hurricane.* The next boat was a forty-four-foot ketch that Bill first spotted in New York and that he eventually had shipped out to Northern California. Most of the time, though, he lived just across the street from the harbor in Sausalito in a house that served as an unlikely but vibrant hangout for a cool crowd and a pit stop for weary sailors.

Bill and Nancy and the kids were in the upstairs apartment in the house. Not only was there no TV, they didn't even have a phone. When a call came in, downstairs neighbor Jerry Thompson, a radio engineer who doubled as a deep-sea diver with a company called Sausalito Underwater Search, would bang on the floor with a broom handle. Bill or Nancy would poke their head out the upstairs window, where they could hoist the phone up using a pulley system linked to Thompson's downstairs window.

"We were wonderfully disconnected," Kathleen remembered of those days.

Electronically, perhaps, but 319 Johnson Street, at the corner of Bridgeway, was a hive of activity. One day, Wilt Chamberlain might pull up in his lavender Bentley and come upstairs for the party. "He'd sit down and his legs would be just all over the place," Kathleen said. Another day — many days — sailors from around the world would sail into the Sausalito harbor and make their way to the yellow house where they knew they could get a welcome and a shower.

Despite what many people believed, Bill never had a houseboat. It was always a sailboat and Bill and Nancy were accomplished sailors. They sailed the Black Sea. They sailed to Hawaii and back. One of their most memorable trips was up to British Columbia and back. They were, according to Hank, "a formidable force together."

"Bill was a lot like Nancy, there was nothing halfway about anything with either one of them and their feelings about anything," Hank says. "They didn't like; they either loved or hated, and it was one end of the spectrum or the other — and boy did they feed off each other."

If there were opinions, they were sharp and intractable. If convention was expected, you did the unexpected. If you were supposed to conform, you didn't. If something was the norm, it wasn't. There wasn't a lot of giving in, although Bill relented once when it came to his addiction to golf in the early '60s.

"It's either golf or me," Nancy said.

Golf lost.

⚾   🏈   🏀

If you were to try to dream up your own cast of wild characters from that time and place, the Bay Area of the late 1950s, you'd do well to start with a real life cat by the name of Franklin Mieuli. He was born in San Jose, an hour south of San Francisco, at that time a wide swath of orchards referred to as the prune capital of the world, and his first-generation immigrant parents ran a nursery for years. Young Franklin was a sports nut and was "Boys Sports Editor" of the San Jose High School yearbook. Back in San Jose after studying advertising at the University of Oregon and doing a stint in the Navy, he took an advertising job with the San Francisco Brewing Company and, always a persuasive guy, soon convinced the company to sponsor San Francisco 49ers broadcasts as a way to promote its Burgermeister beer. Mieuli bought into the 49ers and soon had his own radio production company as well, which produced Giants broadcasts once they moved to San Francisco in 1958, which was how he met Bill.

They soon became friends, two utter originals who lived life on their own terms. "Convention was not a restriction for him," Bill once said of Franklin in an interview with the Bay Area Radio Hall of Fame and Museum. Bill might as well have been talking about himself.

"Franklin was a broadcasting guy," Hank Greenwald told me. "So he had a feel for and he could identify with Bill's outlook about things and to a lesser degree with me. It was in his blood. He was a producer when the Giants first came out here. He had the radio rights to the Giants and the 49ers."

Franklin took engineering and producing seriously. He was engineering the Giants broadcast on May 26, 1959, the day Harvey Haddix, the Pirates left-hander, pitched one of the more memorable games in baseball history. Haddix worked twelve innings of perfect baseball against the Braves in Milwaukee before he lost the perfecto and the game in the bottom of the thirteenth.

"In those days," Bill said, "communication was so much simpler and so word didn't spread as quickly. All we had was the old sport ticker which was a machine with a little glass bell on it and it spewed out very minimal information of each game on a little single strip."

Sometime in the late innings Franklin and the Giants' broadcasters became aware that something special was happening in Milwaukee. Franklin used his ingenuity. He called a friend in Milwaukee and had him hold the phone up to his radio so Franklin could hear the play-by-play of the game by Braves broadcasters Earl Gillespie, a legend in Milwaukee, and Blaine Walsh. Franklin relayed all the game details to Russ and Lon.

"In those days that was very innovative," Bill said.

Bill's duties were limited as the third man on Giants broadcasts starting with the 1959 season, but he had grown up with baseball as his favorite sport and he loved working with Russ and Lon. Those early baseball days in the Bay Area also gave him opportunities to come into his own, and one of those times was the final day of the 1962 season when he was behind the mic for one of the most memorable games ever played in San Francisco. "He worked with Russ on the final Sunday because I was over at Kezar Stadium doing a 49er game," Lon remembered.

If the Giants could defeat the Houston Colt .45's that day, they would go into a three-game playoff with the Dodgers to see who would win the National League pennant, a matchup of two California teams recently relocated from New York. Bill worked the game with Russ and the Giants won, sending them on to that three-game playoff, where they shelled the great Sandy Koufax and advanced to the World Series against the Yankees. Longtime Bay Area broadcaster Bruce Macgowan recalled: "When the Giants tied the Dodgers for first place on the last day of the 1962 season, it was Bill's great call of an Ed Bailey home run that I still remember."

Here's the call of that homer, which gave the Giants a 1–0 lead on their way to a 2–1 win, as transcribed from a recording housed at the Bay Area Radio Museum:

66 *Whitey Lockman, Wes Westrum pacing up and down in the third and first-base coaching lines respectively. Crowd sitting in anticipation waiting for some fireworks. The pitch, there's a swing and a*

long drive — that might be the fireworks, it's deep into right field. It is foul by inches!

"Full count with one out to Big Ed. Farrell into the motion, here it is. There's a swing, another drive way back into right field, that one is going, it is gone for a home run!"

The Lakers had moved from Minnesota to L.A. in 1960 and the NBA liked the idea of having another West Coast team. Franklin was a minority owner of the group, which included Diners Club and thirty other partners, that bought the Philadelphia Warriors for $850,000 and moved them to San Francisco, but he was the one calling the shots — and he knew he wanted Bill to broadcast the games.

That past summer Bill hadn't been needed much on Giants broadcasts, and wouldn't be busy until football season rolled around, so he took advantage of the free time and went on a sailing trip. Shaving wasn't a priority. Now, Bill was not unattractive, but he wasn't Cary Grant either. When he returned to the Bay Area from that sailing voyage with his new beard, Franklin took one look and decided it might be an improvement.

"I can't say I like it," he said, "but something had to be done!"

Channel 2 was not so amused. The station leadership made clear to Mieuli that they didn't want a bearded guy doing the Warriors on TV. Franklin intervened with a plan that called for someone else to open the broadcast on camera, throw to Bill for the game, and then the clean-shaven person would close the telecast on camera. Bill: "So this horrible vision of beardedness wouldn't appear on television and scare the daylights out of the Bay Area."

The beard was a big aspect of what Ron Fimrite would describe in *Sports Illustrated* as Bill's "satanic countenance," and Bill had some fun with it. Once, when Scotty Stirling was the Warriors' general manager, he went walking in Milwaukee with Bill before a game.

"In those days, Bill used to walk a lot no matter what the weather was," Scotty told me for this book. "This day it was dark and maybe threatening rain and we're out walking and about twenty-five yards in front of us, there's an old woman walking toward us with an umbrella in her hand in case it rains. And Bill says to me, 'This lady's gonna talk to me. I can always tell when they're gonna talk to me.'

"So this lady gets right up in front of us and she takes this umbrella and she holds it out and she's kind of like, jabbing him in his chest and she says, "You! I know who you are!" And King said, 'Yes. And you'll be with me soon.' Scared the shit out of her."

"Bill loved to tell that story," Kathleen said.

Bill admitted that he didn't know much about the NBA when the league expanded west, although the 1960 Olympic team helped bring credibility when so many of the stars of that team moved on to the pros. That team, coached by Cal's Pete Newell, featured the greatest array of talent ever assembled at the time, and maybe ever. Names like West and Robertson and Jerry Lucas and Darrall Imhoff, Walt Bellamy and Terry Dischinger.

The Warriors played their first game in their new home on October 23, 1962, one week after the end of the Giants-Yankees World Series. Wilt Chamberlain scored fifty-six points and the Warriors beat Detroit, 140–113. A crowd of 5,300 attended the game at the Cow Palace. Still, the college game was much more popular in that era. Even with Wilt in the lineup in the Warriors' first year in S.F., they were often relegated to the back pages of the sports section.

Hank Greenwald, having recently graduated from Syracuse University, was broadcasting the Syracuse Nats during the Warriors' first year in the Bay Area.

"When I started with the Nats there were eight teams in the league," Hank remembered for this book. "The rosters had eleven players and so there were eighty-eight players in the league. Everybody knew each other."

The starting guards on that first Warriors team in San Francisco were two holdovers from the Philadelphia days, Guy Rodgers and Al Attles. Rodgers, Attles and Chamberlain spent a lot of time hanging out together on the road and the group quickly accepted the team's play-by-play man. "I was born in New Jersey," Attles told me, "and grew up on the East Coast and so when we met Bill, he was kind of a different type of reporter. Bill, for a lack of a better word, was kind of a free spirit."

Bill taught the Bay Area about the NBA game. He would bring the games to life. You were in the arena with him. The early Warriors days, when it was only the players, the coach, a trainer and Bill, were some of Bill's favorite times on the road. This was in the time before teams flew on charter jets, so it was a traveling party of fifteen jumping into four taxis, in a league still relatively in its infancy, playing often before small crowds but with the kinds of bonds that develop when there are only nine teams and everyone had a stake in the league struggling to find solid ground. The Warriors drew only 100,000 fans for the entire home schedule in their first season and Wilt Chamberlain averaged forty-five points a game.

One of the other top scorers on that Warriors team was Tom Meschery, a six-foot-six forward. Meschery never had a brother until he met Bill King. Just the fact that they met was a long shot. Tom's parents were born in Russia, but fled their homeland after the Bolshevik Revolution, ending up in the city of Harbin in northern China, which was where Tomislav Nikolayevich Meshcheriakoff was born in 1938. Tom's dad came first to the United States and was hopeful the rest of the family would arrive shortly after him, but World War II put those plans on hold. In fact, Tom and his mother and sister were held in a Japanese concentration camp for the duration of the war.

The Red Cross brought the family to San Francisco when Tom was seven. He spoke no English, but had an aptitude for two things — writing and basketball — that would allow him to assimilate and also excel. He had a brilliant mind and serious interest in literature, which he traces back to his Russian heritage.

"Poetry is a true Russian tradition, so there was a lot of poetry in our house," Meschery wrote later in an article for the *Reno Gazette-Journal*. "A lot of American boys wouldn't hear poetry from their fathers because it's not considered manly."

The family felt that tradition strongly: Leo Tolstoy himself was a relative. Meschery's father would read poetry out loud to him, sometimes moved to tears, especially if he'd been drinking vodka; a strapping man at six-two and more than two hundred pounds, he was not someone who worried about what was considered "manly."

Young Tom's other avenue was basketball and it didn't take long for him to stand out in local games across San Francisco. Eventually, he starred at Lowell High and St. Mary's and in 1961 was drafted seventh overall by the Philadelphia Warriors, a team that had Chamberlain at center. Meschery would have to work to make a mark. On March 2, 1962, in Hershey, Pennsylvania, the Warriors beat the New York Knicks, 169–147. Meschery scored a respectable sixteen points. Wilt outscored him by eighty-four.

They both came west the next year when the San Francisco Warriors were born. Bill King and Chamberlain, according to Meschery, had a mutual respect. Wilt, of course, was a mythical, larger-than-life character. "Wilt hated phonies," Meschery told me. "I think Wilt admired Bill a great deal. One of the things about Wilt was he never bullshitted anybody and neither did Bill."

Meschery's first impression of Bill would be hard to say, because like everyone else on the Warriors, Meschery's eyes were fixed on the woman on Bill's arm.

"My most vivid memory," Tom told me over the phone early in 2013, "was that first year and Bill and Nancy walking into the arena and literally everybody stopped to look at Nancy because she was so beautiful and here was Bill and he had that goatee and he looked like Mephistopheles, with that black beard and mustache. Bill had this little smile and I think he was tickled to have this beautiful woman on his arm. I think we were all secretly in love with Nancy. I know I was. She looked like Dorothy Lamour."

Soon Bill and Tom and Nancy were inseparable. A foursome developed that first year with the Warriors, especially when the team had a night out on the road. It was Tom, Bill, George Lee, the forward from Michigan who later coached the team, and Gary Phillips, a guard from Quincy, Illinois, a town where Bill used to work. Sometimes Hank Greenwald would join the group along with his friend, Warriors coach Alex Hannum.

"After Gary retired, when we went out to dinners it was George, Bill and I and we went to some dandy restaurants," Tom recalled. "Bill knew restaurants and he knew food, and he knew more about the restaurants in every town than we did, so we followed his recommendations."

Tom got into it, too, and he studied some of the finer Russian and German places and loved the old London Chop House behind the Book Cadillac Hotel in Detroit. "That was fabulous," he said. Often the guys would eat together before games, but those dinners at 3:30 or 4 for a game at 7:30 or 8 were of necessity far more sedate, not the "serious restaurant hopping and bar hopping" when they had a night off in a city.

"We had these great conversations," Tom told me. "Talking with Bill was like talking with an encyclopedia. He had a memory that was fabulous. I'm not sure it was photographic, but it was close to it. If you wanted to talk sports, literature — when Bill talked you listened because he always had something interesting to talk about."

The Warriors struggled in the first year in San Francisco, finishing under .500. Meschery, living back in San Francisco again, soon established himself as a walking contradiction. Here was a guy writing poetry who was the most intellectual player around and yet his nickname was "The Mad Russian." He was known as one of the toughest players in the history of the NBA and led the league in fouls in the 1961–62 season. "I used to yell at the refs in Russian!"

Yet he made the All-Star team in 1963 when he averaged sixteen points a game and by the next year the Warriors had a very good club. They won the Western Division title in 1964 by beating the Hawks in seven games in the playoffs and then lost to the Celtics in five games in the first NBA final played in San Francisco. Meschery remembers a wild celebration in North Beach the night they clinched the West.

"That was a legendary night," Tom recalled. "Bill was there and Alex and (the big forward) Wayne Hightower. It was incredible. I think Wilt downed twenty-five milk and scotches, because that's what he drank. Milk and scotch."

Writing about the Warriors' come-from-behind victory over the Philadelphia 76ers in Game Five of the 1967 NBA finals, Dave Anderson of *The New York Times* counted him as the key to the comeback: "Tom Meschery, a twenty-eight-year-old jut-jawed cornerman who writes poetry, composed an eleven-point verse in slightly less than 5½ minutes. By that time, the Warriors had narrowed the 76ers lead to 101–90. Not long after that, Meschery incurred his sixth personal foul, but his spark lingered."

It's easy in looking back at an earlier era to think of these people merely as colorful characters, but Bill and Franklin and Tom were colorful because they were serious about their professions and didn't care about many of the trivial, cosmetic things that concerned other people. Franklin was an eccentric character, as everyone knew whether they'd ever met him or not, with his hunting cap and unpretentious style, but he understood broadcasting and he was loyal to his people. Like Bill, dressing the part was never a priority for Franklin, and it seemed at least once or twice a season an unkempt and bearded Franklin would find himself being stopped by an arena security guard who didn't believe he was the owner of the Warriors. Franklin was also the first of several great bosses who understood Bill and understood broadcasting. "He idealized the family concept," Bill used to say.

Al Attles grew up listening to the first legend of Big Apple basketball broadcasting, Marty Glickman, a former sprinter who had been unceremoniously dropped from the 1936 Olympic 400–

meter relay team amid charges of anti-Semitism. In the early '60s Howard Cosell started "telling it like it is," and nobody outside of the Bay Area knew that Bill was doing the same thing beginning with his first year with the Warriors.

"I think the first thing that you really appreciated was that he didn't sugarcoat it," Al told me. "Bill was a departure from the way it was; he told you exactly what was going on. If a player from the Warriors made a mistake, Bill told it like it was. You have to give Mr. Mieuli the credit for allowing Bill to do this because a lot of owners wouldn't."

Franklin was the kind of boss who trusted people to do their job. "He was an ideal guy to work for," Bill said. "He understood and he got it. If you did your job he left you alone."

Sometimes he would leave the whole team alone, literally. Once, in the '70s, Franklin took off on a sailing trip and didn't come home for two years.

Franklin and Bill shared a love of sailing and also a passionate interest in jazz. In fact, Franklin applied for and received a permit to establish a new FM radio station in San Francisco in January 1958, which went on the air on December 10, 1959, as KPUP (106.9) — and the following year changed its call letters to KHIP with, of course, an all-jazz format. The studios were at 505 Geary Street and Franklin was not only owner, but for a time also general manager. The musical selections were hipster back when that word meant something. The station, *Billboard Magazine* explained in early 1961, "caters to the jazz mores of a discerning yet critical FM audience."

All of Bill's other interests gave him separation from his job. His identity wasn't wrapped around his celebrity. It was Bill who turned Nancy on to jazz, and Nancy got Bill interested in ballet. They were aficionados of the opera and ballet and Bill ended up serving on the board of directors of the Smuin Ballet. They loved Impressionist art, theater, you name it. "When we met, he didn't know a thing about classical music," Nancy would say. "Now he knows more than me."

It wasn't unusual to find Bill and Nancy and Hank and his

wife, Carla, and others from the Warriors, like Alex Hannum, frequenting jazz clubs in North Beach in the '60s. Back then the jazz scene in North Beach was really happening. George Lee and Meschery would go too, and you could see big-time talents like Vince Guaraldi, who was from North Beach and went to Lincoln High and San Francisco State. Guaraldi won a Grammy for "Cast Your Fate to the Wind," and later scored many of the *Peanuts* television specials.

There was an acclaimed Brazilian guitarist named Bola Sete, who adopted the Bay Area as his home and would sit in with Guaraldi. Hank said he was comparable to guys like Herb Ellis and Barney Kessel. "These were serious jazz people."

They caught Miles Davis as much as possible in North Beach. Davis, by the way, recorded a legendary live album from the Blackhawk Club in San Francisco in 1961. There was a place they frequented called the Anxious Asp, at 528 Green Street.

"This offbeat bar was very beat," Bill Morgan wrote of the Asp in his book *The Beat Generation in San Francisco*. "It was run by a New Orleans creole, Bunny Simon. Kerouac read poetry there. Janis Joplin drank there and the bathroom walls were covered with pages from the Kinsey Report. Interracial couples felt at home and so did every free spirit. The place resonated with existential anxiety."

There was an Italian place on Broadway called La Casadoro, where the bartender sang opera. Bill and Nancy and Tom were in their element there. They loved it when the bartender, who also owned the place, would break into an aria while pouring a drink or two. Tom and Nancy and Bill went to the opera together a lot, and this continued for decades.

They gravitated toward people who shared their passions and their experiences, people like Treut Sperry, a San Francisco native who served in the Merchant Marine during World War II, then went to St. Mary's on a basketball scholarship. Treut was a big basketball fan and in the early '50s he opened a restaurant on Fillmore Street called the Mardi Gras that became a hangout for members of the Warriors and 49ers. Other notables from John F.

Kennedy to Prince Charles also dropped in from time to time, but Treut adopted Bill and his circle and often turned the restaurant into their own private salon.

"If they had a good group, a convivial group, they would lock the front door and they wouldn't care if anybody came in the rest of the night," Hank recalled. "It was like we had taken over the place. It was fine with Sperry and they would shut the door."

Tom Meschery departed the Warriors after the 1966–67 season, but he left an imprint on Bill, a love for all things Russian. "I'm not sure Bill would have been interested in Russia if he hadn't met me and we didn't start talking about it," Tom recalled. "Pretty soon he knew more Russian history than me!"

Bill was fascinated by Meschery's family history, which was complicated and intertwined with the Russian Revolution. The two men would spend hours researching Meschery's family tree, which included, on his grandfather's side, the over-procurator of the Holy Synod and lay head of the Orthodox Church who was a senator in the Russian Duma. Bill got connected with a guy named Boris who taught Russian history at the College of Marin and began studying under him.

He learned to speak Russian, although, according to Meschery, not real well. "It is a tough language," he said. "I helped him and he learned a whole lot about the language and we spoke some Russian together. He really became a Russophile."

Their conversations also influenced Tom. They talked for hours about Russian literature and how Tom was interested in people like Dostoyevsky and his relative Leo Tolstoy and how much Tom enjoyed reading and writing poetry.

"I started dabbling in it while I was playing," he said. "I wasn't very good, but I was reading a lot of poetry, particularly the Russian poets."

Meschery remembers going over to Bill and Nancy's place and Nancy would always have a big bottle of rum waiting for him. She was a tough cookie. They argued like brother and sister, and for Nancy arguing was like sport. The topics ran the gamut.

"She was just so beautiful and a tough gal," Meschery recalled.

"Nancy and I were both so stubborn that we didn't know we were being stubborn."

Sometimes Bill would get so pissed off listening to the two of them go at it that he would head downstairs to his office and work, or just take refuge under the living room table. "Nancy and I were the only people who would have each other," Bill once told me.

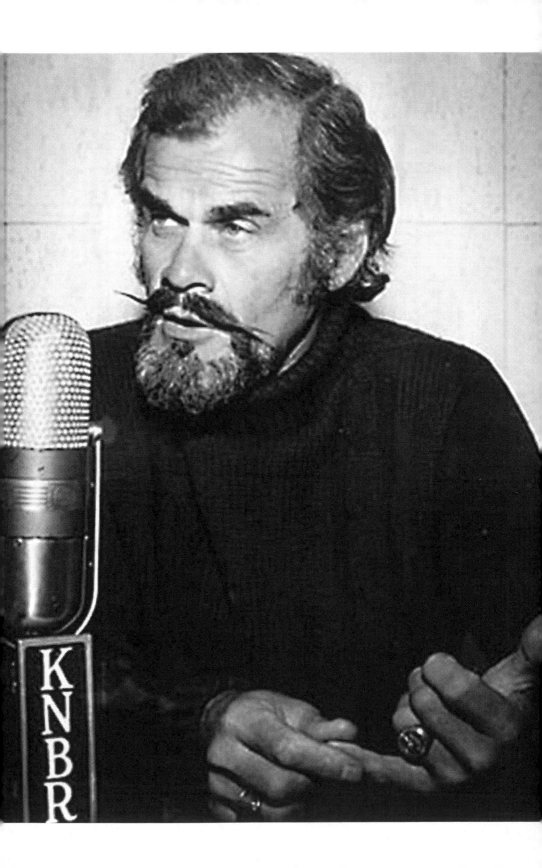

CHAPTER 3

MOTHER'S DAY

You m-----f-----!

nyone who lived through 1968 will always talk about how it was a year unlike any other. I turned sixteen that year, played on the basketball "B" team as a junior in high school and went to my first Temptations and Four Tops concert, so I'm not going to say I didn't have fun. But it all took place against a backdrop of dramatic events and I was pretty tuned in to politics. So many dreams were shattered by the bullets of Sirhan Sirhan in Los Angeles the night Robert F. Kennedy won the California Democratic primary on June 5. This was just two months after the assassination of Martin Luther King, and completed a trilogy of horror: JFK in '63, and MLK and RFK in '68. Students at San Francisco State, led by a coalition calling itself the Third World Liberation Front, began a strike action protesting the Vietnam War and pushing for an ethnic studies program, a strike that would make national news. That summer things boiled over in Chicago at the Democratic National Convention. These events left me numb and cynical and for sure it was "The End of the Innocence," as Don Henley would later sing. The Beatles released the *White Album* in '68, five years to the day after the assassination of JFK. We used to have debates at school: Beatles or Stones? Truth is I was much more of a Motown fan back then, but that began to change when I saw the Stones live for the first time the next year.

It's usually crazy to compare real-life events to basketball, but 1968 was such a tumultuous year, it seems somehow fitting that the all-time Bill King story with basketball officials took place that year. By this point in his career Bill was already well known for lashing out at officials when he felt they deserved it. He was honest and, as I've said, Bill and authority figures were like oil and water. Almost every night there would be an explosion or two. They were colorful and often incisive, so much so that Bob Rose, who would go on to a career in sports PR, remembers a morning ritual when he and his friends at Placer High School in the Sierra Foothills town of Auburn would gather to share tales of what Bill had said the night before.

One story stands out and will always be known as Mother's Day. Twenty-five games into the season the Warriors, coached by George Lee, set out on a quick road trip to Phoenix and Seattle that started off with a lopsided 126–97 loss to the Suns of Gail Goodrich and Dick Van Arsdale. The next day, the winner of the Heisman Trophy for that year was announced: USC running back O.J. Simpson. Mother's Day came on December 6 that year. The Warriors were playing the SuperSonics in Seattle that night. Bill was on radio and Hank Greenwald worked the game on television. It was the night Bill boiled over at referee Ed T. Rush.

The Mother's Day game was close all the way. The Warriors led by two at the end of three quarters. One of the oddities of the game was that Bill's great friend Tom Meschery, who played six seasons with the Warriors, led the Sonics in scoring with twenty-nine points. Tom remembered how a sentimental Franklin Mieuli had retired his number and had a small "14" stitched onto the Warriors' jerseys while Tom was playing in Seattle and "I was beating the hell out of his team." It was such an intense game, especially down the stretch, that Steve Bitker remembers that he was watching the game on television but emotions were running so high, he switched to the radio because he just had to listen to Bill call the action.

What pushed Bill over the top? Shortly before the game went into overtime, Rush called Rudy LaRusso of the Warriors for travelling. Bill was of one mind with the entire Warriors bench in being certain that one of the Sonics players, probably center Bob Rule, in jump-switching out on LaRusso, had low-bridged him across the neck.

"When the incident occurred that invoked the ire of Bill," Hank Greenwald recalled, "he got out of his chair, ripped off his mic harness and said to his engineer, 'Cut my mic' — and then he yelled, 'You motherfucker!' thinking his mic was cut. But the one that was two seats over was still open. There was a scorekeeper, there was an empty seat and I was where the TV spot was, maybe two seats farther down, and I couldn't hear him because the crowd noise was pretty loud. But I could see him ready to take on the world and it was only later that I think somebody said something to George Lee."

The assumption was made that Lee, the coach, was the one who screamed the X-rated barrage at Rush. In fact, after the game when Lee talked to Bay Area reporters by phone — they didn't travel in those days — somebody asked Lee if he had really said that and, given the way he'd been screaming at Rush all game, he figured maybe he had.

Franklin Mieuli knew better. He was not in Seattle. He was, however, listening to the game, driving his car through the Santa Cruz Mountains, and he knew Bill King when he heard him. "As he was driving he was already formulating his response, that it must have been some crazed Warrior fan up in Seattle who came down behind the press table and yelled, 'You motherfucker,'" Hank recalled. "He was going to protect Bill. But in the final analysis, it was Bill."

Mike Marquardt was Franklin's partner in Mieuli and Associates, a relationship that dated back to the Warriors' first year in San Francisco. He engineered most of the home games for Bill and some of the road games, especially on days on which there was no television, because he also spent several years directing the Warriors' telecasts. He wasn't working on Mother's Day and spent the evening watching the game on television.

"We had set up a tape recorder at the (Mieuli and Associates) office that was timed and recorded the game," he said. "Franklin wanted to hear everything Bill was saying and he had a tape machine in his car so he could listen while he was driving."

Mike would set up the timer and then go home if it was a game he wasn't working. He heard "The Magic Words," immediately knew it was Bill and the next day he went to the office and "Watergated" it.

"I cut it out, just in case," Mike told me. "The original is on a CD I have called 'Bill King's Greatest Hits.'"

In our years as partners, Bill and I talked about the incident quite a bit. It was always fun to hear him share the story, especially when it was over dinner with folks who had never heard it before. I didn't take notes, of course, so here's Bill's recollection of that night as delivered in an interview with Steve Bitker: "Hank was on TV on the opposite side of the floor," Bill said, offering a recollection of events different than that of Hank, who thought he was seated on the same side of the court as Bill.

"My engineer was running a 103 temperature that night," Bill told Steve. "He was pretty woozy. I knew exactly what I was going to do and I had a chest mic that used to hook on to a clamp and I took it off and used it like a hammer on the table so I knew it would pound into his earpiece and he would immediately cut my mic, which he did, but what I failed to notice — and he was too woozy — was that the crowd mic was lying on a towel on the table just about two feet from me and as I stood up and cupped my hands like a megaphone and shouted 'The Magic Words,' it crossed right into the crowd mic. I still have that tape."

It has been widely reported and long accepted as fact that Bill received a technical foul and the Warriors were fined over the Mother's Day outburst. Not true, according to both Hank and Bill.

Sitting courtside to Bill's right that night in Seattle was a man named George Gochnour, an accountant who had parlayed a friendship with Sonics PR man Hal Childs into meeting Bill at the arena in Seattle before a Warriors game. George lived in Sunnyside, Washington, and for the next sixteen years, whenever the Warriors were in Seattle or Portland, George kept stats for Bill. On December 6, 1968, he was seated between Bill and his engineer, John Cameron, later the chief engineer at KNBR. John wasn't the only one with the flu that night. Both George and Mike Marquardt remembered several members of the Warriors' traveling party being stricken with the Asian flu.

"Because Bill was short he used to sit on his briefcase," George told me. "He had a regular folding chair and he put the briefcase on the chair. The Warriors probably should have won the game but they got some really bad calls. I'm not sure Bill ever saw a call against the Warriors that was a good call.

"He grabbed his mic out of the harness and must have hit the button to kill it, but they had the crowd mic on a towel on the table in front of me. When Bill jumped up he tipped his chair over and I reached to catch his chair and briefcase. That's when he started beating on the scorer's table with the handheld mic and swearing at Ed Rush."

Just to set the record straight, Hank's recollection of where he was that night runs like this: "I was sitting a couple of spots down from Bill. I was doing TV that night and what happened was on the nights I didn't work with Bill, our engineer would put out a microphone, in front of the spot where I would usually sit, as a crowd mic." One can debate where the mic was actually positioned, but it is clear that it was the crowd mic that captured Bill's words that night.

The use of a harness mic, another Bill trademark, only added to his mystique. Fans would come into the arena and they would be fixated on Bill, amazed to be seeing in person the fascinating guy they had been hearing on the radio. Bill sat courtside with the harness draped around his neck, sitting on a briefcase, long hair flowing along with his beard and handlebar mustache. His feet were in constant motion, tapping the floor as frenetically as he was talking.

"The harness mic came from his college days, a metal kind of a triangular-shaped thing with a mic on it and a loop that went around his neck," Marquardt explained. "And somebody made the leather harness and riveted the metal part to the harness so that he could strap it on there so it would stay steady and wouldn't flop around. It was a leather harness with a strap in the back and he could clip it and wear that. Bill didn't like anything on his head — didn't want to muss that hair at all. You put something on his head, he didn't like that at all."

I can confirm that. One of the things that anguished Bill was his receding hairline and the inexorable onset of gray. He took great pride in the long, thick, wavy black hair of his younger days, and often told me that if he had kept his hair, he surely would have dyed it black. The legend of the harness mic is another of the Bill King stories that has various permutations. John Trinidad, for twenty-five years a producer/engineer of our A's games and a fixture courtside at the Arena for NBA games during his time working for Mieuli and Associates, said Marquardt found an old harness that was used in the Navy by sonar operators, so they could talk into a mouthpiece that was on a leather patch that sat on their chest. Bill wasn't much interested in hearing himself in loud, earmuff-style headphones — he really liked hearing the crowd — so Marquardt got him lightweight earpieces that hung like a stethoscope and served a purpose if Bill wanted to listen to something like an interview on tape.

Bill looked back on that night in Seattle with a notable lack of contrition, but did let a tinge of delight creep into his recollections. Bill was in a way at his best in those moments of high anger and outrage, or at least those were moments that fans — and players and coaches and his fellow broadcasters — often remembered the most vividly.

As to the fallout of the incident at the time, NBA commissioner J. Walter Kennedy — dubbed "J. Walter Calamity" by Hank — did not take immediate action, but later handed down a fine for, as Bill put it, "far less egregious remarks." That led to a lively meeting between Mieuli, Greenwald and King.

"Franklin called us in and said, 'I'll pay this because I believe in having a strong commissioner, but if he ever tries it again he'll never get another cent out of me,'" Hank recalled. "Franklin sensed that the reason for the fine was to maybe plant it in Franklin's head that he might not be able to afford to keep these guys because it was going to cost him."

That was barking up the wrong tree. Mieuli, with his broadcasting background, knew just what he had in Bill and Hank and he was not about to muzzle them.

"Franklin never tried to get Bill to stop," longtime *San Francisco Chronicle* columnist Glenn Dickey told me for this book. "Probably knew he couldn't. The odd thing was the officials weren't bothered.

They'd often chat amiably with Bill during timeouts. The NBA at that time had a limited audience, more like a club than a sport, and those involved felt a kinship that was not part of baseball or the NFL."

Ed Rush survived Mother's Day just fine. One reason is that he has been honest with himself. He looks back on those days in the NBA with fondness, but with an introspection that allowed him, back then, the realization that he wasn't very good and he would have to work like heck if he wanted a long career as a basketball official.

A long career would be an understatement: Ed Rush worked thirty-two years as a pro basketball official, more than two thousand regular season games and, in the postseason, 247 playoff and thirty-two NBA Finals games. He was also the NBA's director of officiating for several years. He is in his early seventies now, but the passion and dedication to basketball and officiating is still there. He was driving from an NBA Developmental League showcase in Reno down to the Bay Area when I called him and mentioned December 6, 1968. He chuckled, knowing exactly what I was referring to. He was also happy to tell me about his days starting out in the league as a green twenty-four-year-old, offering some context for that night's events.

"I started in the league in '66 and we didn't have any training," Ed told me. "And my competency level at that time, I would say in a self-assessment, on a good night was 50 percent. You came into the league and you learned on the job and they said it took four to six years before you really learned your way around the floor and understood the game and the personalities. I was a work in progress."

Ed was blunt in assessing the reputation Bill had among officials: "We thought he wore the Warriors' shorts and that he was the home team announcer," he told me.

But Ed was also remarkably candid in assessing his own performance the night of the Mother's Day game. "The game was emotional and a lot of stuff was going on," Ed told me. "There was more than the normal amount of emotional pushback. Basically, without having video to look at, I probably missed a lot of plays. It was probably not a Hall of Fame performance, to say the least."

Ed Rush never heard "The Magic Words." Everything was happening so fast on such a fervent night of action, especially in the wild final minutes of regulation when the big moment came. It wasn't until the next day, or maybe two days later, when he talked on the phone with a friend in San Francisco, that Ed learned the incident was beginning to take on a life of its own. Word was spreading that Bill was going to get fined or suspended and that Franklin and the radio station were in trouble.

"I knew in my gut that I wasn't very good that night and at the same time all of these other things were going on on the periphery and I was oblivious to it," Ed recalled, forty-four years after Mother's Day. "It was one of those stories that became bigger than life. Mother's Day and what he said that night."

Ed Rush was, and still is, a good sport about the whole thing:

"I found it to be humorous and I thought, 'We are going to have a new holiday in the Bay Area!'" he told me.

Ed Rush is a Pennsylvania native and has spent most of his life living in the East. For a time in the '70s, though, he lived in Fountain Valley, California, near Los Angeles. He got the idea for a Mother's Day card for Bill when the Warriors were scheduled to play the Clippers in San Diego. He searched everywhere, but it was tricky that time of year finding a card for a May holiday. So Ed settled on a generic, all-purpose card and wrote "Happy Mother's Day" inside and hand-delivered it to Bill.

On the inside of the card Rush wrote, "You don't know how hard it is to find a Mother's Day card in December."

"From that point on it became our thing," Ed told me. "I always thoroughly enjoyed visiting with him pregame or in the press room and finding out how he was doing. We had great dialogue and it was our connection, and we would agree to disagree on officiating matters and he knew how much I respected the quality of his work and what he meant to our sport. Ultimately he got to know Ed Rush beyond just the referee and we developed a mutual respect."

That was true, but it didn't mean that Bill was going to let up. Ed remembers games at the Oakland Coliseum Arena when he would glance over as he ran down the floor and Bill would be jumping out of his seat and Al Attles would be yelling at him, and Ed would think, "Who do we deal with first here, Bill or Attles? Well, we had no control over Bill."

Ed Rush knows that he will always be linked to that game in Seattle, and he's fine with it. "It was one of those things when I would show up and work a Warriors game it was my label. It was like, 'Here's Ed Rush, the guy who was with us for Mother's Day.' I still hear that from people from back in those days."

Ed Rush cares deeply about the NBA game and officiating. He takes great pride in knowing that he dedicated much of his life to the league. When he looks back on December 6, 1968, it's not with bitterness that some biographer of Bill King was going to dredge up an uncomfortable night in Seattle when all hell broke loose and that people might remember Mother's Day more than they would his remarkable career and contributions. What he remembers is how crazy and fraternal those early days in the '60s were.

"We'd fly on the same planes, stay at the same hotels and eat at the same places as everybody else," Ed recalled. "Heck, one time I was on a flight after a game and I sat down right next to a guy I had ejected a couple of hours earlier."

He also remembers the man with the harness mic who was there, like Ed was, in the nascent days of a league that was like a teenager looking to spread its wings but not really knowing where it was headed. Even after Mother's Day, Ed was a big Bill King fan because he recognized the greatness and how much Bill helped grow the game they both loved. Like most anyone working in pro sports, Ed lived half his life in hotel rooms. On his off nights he would turn on the radio, place it up near the window, and if he positioned it just right he might be able to hear Bill or Chick Hearn. "They were the voices of basketball," Ed told me. He marveled at how Bill connected with the game in a way that delivered the action like you were there.

"Bill was the most unique guy that I have ever run across because of his diversity and understanding of so many topics, and being so good at what he did," he told me. "I'd put the radio out the window and keep turning it to certain angles and it would go in and go out. I'd listen to the Warriors and the Raiders. To do all three sports like he did, he was phenomenal. He was out of this world."

CHAPTER 4

'GET YOUR BIG BUTT OUT OF HERE!'

There's nothing real in the world anymore!
The Raiders have won the football game!
This one will be relived forever!

I f you were to use two words to sum up the American Football League, they would have to be "Al" and "Davis." Davis personified the qualities that defined the league — upstart, renegade and of course maverick. Davis was called "maverick" so often that you'd be excused for thinking it was part of his name. To put it in baseball terms, Davis was a home-run hitter — he wasn't interested in singles and didn't much mind striking out — and his personal style mirrored an offensive philosophy gleaned from the future Hall of Fame coach Sid Gillman that had at its core stretching the field vertically. Davis had the guts of a thief and didn't care what anybody thought, especially those who ran the established NFL. It was "Just win, baby," and Davis, the Raiders and the AFL did a lot of exactly that as the leagues' tug-of-war for players escalated into a no-holds-barred affair.

I was attracted to the AFL from the minute I watched my first game on television. Seeing an underdog in action has always brought the fan in me to the surface. (That's probably why as a boy, despite my affinity for Vin Scully, I was much more emotionally invested in the Angels than the Dodgers.) The AFL was a league full of mavericks — that word again — that got its start in 1959 when eight businessmen hatched the idea of taking on the NFL. It was a roll of the dice, a long shot at best, but the timing was good: The AFL kicked off just as television was starting to transform the American sporting scene. The most important game in NFL history was played in December of '58, the Giants-Colts championship game at Yankee Stadium dubbed the "Greatest Game Ever Played," which did as much to put the tube on the map as it did the NFL.

The networks were ripe for something new to fill Sunday afternoon programming and the AFL got an early boost from a deal with ABC. Not that it guaranteed success for the new league. Far from it. The AFL teetered on the brink of extinction almost from the day it was born, thanks in part to small crowds and poor facilities and a widespread view among fans that it was minor league compared to the staid and established NFL. The fortunes of the league's team in Los Angeles, the Chargers, epitomized the problem: Despite reaching the first AFL championship game, attendance for the Chargers' opening season was so small at the L.A. Coliseum — only 9,000 fans saw them clinch the Western Conference title — that they became the first team to relocate, settling on Balboa Stadium in San Diego for the 1961 season.

San Diego became the epicenter of a revolution in the game. I may have been in the minority, but it was hard not to be smitten by the style of play. The AFL was wide open, anything goes and the renegade image that was part of the public perception of the league matched what was happening on the field. It wouldn't be an overstatement to say that the modern passing game was born there in those years.

Don Coryell was weaving his magic at San Diego State while Sid Gillman was orchestrating a breathtaking passing attack with the Chargers. Gillman was an aerial savant who looked like a college professor with his bow tie and sports coat. Even for decades after his head coaching days his wisdom was sought by coaches all over the country. It was pure fun to watch that team play, especially when the Chargers rolled out an array of exciting offensive talent led by quarterback John Hadl, running back Paul Lowe and Lance

Alworth, an acrobatic receiver nicknamed "Bambi." The Chargers reached the title game again in '62, but up in Oakland things were as bad as they were good in San Diego.

The Raiders' inaugural season was also the first for the league, 1960, and they won all of six games under a coach named Eddie Erdelatz, who grew up in the Bay Area, played football at St. Mary's and went on to coach at the Naval Academy for nine years. Under Erdelatz the Raiders were outscored 99–0 in their first two games and he was fired before the 1961 season. The next coach, Marty Feldman, had been a football and rugby star in his college days at Stanford and, as it happened, was a distant cousin of mine. Poor Marty didn't have much to work with and the Raiders went 2–12 that year. When they started the '62 season 0–5, Marty was fired, too.

The Raiders' early struggles to gain acceptance in Oakland changed when Al Davis took over in 1963 and led them to a 10–4 season that had the fans starting to pay attention. Before that Davis had been down in San Diego cutting his teeth as a young assistant coach under Sid Gillman. One of Davis' most significant moves after leaving his job as an assistant at USC for the Chargers was to woo Alworth, who had been drafted out of Arkansas by the 49ers, to the Chargers. Davis was a New Yorker and was actually as much of a hoopster as a football player as a kid. He wanted badly to play basketball at Syracuse, but he never got further than the junior varsity team. He was at Madison Square Garden in 1950 when Syracuse played in the same NIT tournament that Bill broadcast back to Peoria for Bradley University. His lack of success on the gridiron may have been a blessing in disguise, because he became a regular at Syracuse practices and studied the game as if he was preparing for a master's thesis.

When Davis became head coach of the Raiders, the team's radio broadcaster was a Notre Dame graduate named Bob Blum, whose life up to that point had been marked by a Forrest-Gump-like knack for crossing paths with the famous. Bob was born in 1920 and grew up in South Bend on the same street as Knute Rockne and often played catch with the legendary coach after Rockne returned from practice. One of his English teachers at South Bend

Central High was a future basketball coach named John Wooden, whom Bob would eventually recommend for a job at UCLA. Upon enrolling at Notre Dame Bob figured he would give football a try until he got his head smashed in during the first day of practice. Dazed, he looked up at the Irish coach Elmer Layden, one of the "Four Horsemen" from the Rockne days, and immediately decided it would be safer to cover sports than running backs.

Bob started broadcasting in Indiana in 1940, served in the Air Force during World War II and then returned to Notre Dame to finish his studies. I kidded Bob over the years about how he invented radio, and he liked to say he was the first Jew to graduate from Notre Dame. Both stories were exaggerations, but that's how it seemed. Eventually, like Bill, Bob migrated west. He spent twenty-three years working in various locales in California, finally settling in the Bay Area around the time Bill got there, and they got acquainted when Bob was helping Franklin Mieuli produce San Francisco Giants broadcasts. Bob spotted talent in Bill and in fact could see himself objectively enough to know that Bill was more talented than he was.

One of the problems with broadcasting Raiders games in that era was that until Davis arrived in town, no one was listening. He tried to change that and put Bob to work on the problem. The crowds swelled at the Raiders' temporary home, Frank Youell Field, in part because Davis was a savvy coach and businessman and realized the potential of radio at a time when you could barely hear the Raiders in the Bay Area. Davis was smart enough to trust Bob's ability to move forward with the building of a radio network by offering the games for free, covering all the production costs, and getting the stations to agree to let the Raiders have half the ad time for their network sponsors.

Steve Vucinich, an original Oakland A's employee and current equipment manager, was a Raiders fan from the day the team was born. His dad had season tickets beginning with the first season at Candlestick Park. He remembers Frank Youell Field as a funky place that had stands so close to the press box that it was hard to hear Blum over all the crowd noise.

"He was a good announcer," Vuc told me, "but part of the problem was that at Youell Field the fans were right there — and I mean literally two feet away from him. If they were yelling, he had a hard time talking over them. He didn't have the deep baritone voice that could carry over that and so he blended in more than anything. But I thought he did a wonderful job. I actually heard him a little bit while the team was on the road coming from a better press box and he was outstanding, very well enunciated and he could keep track of what was going on in a football game."

By the middle of Davis' first year the Raiders were a major force. Frank Youell Field was rocking. "You wondered if it was going to fall down because it really shook and rattled and stuff, but it was just girders and a bleacher system," Vuc told me. "They added seats after the first or second year. They actually had a back entrance where you came up through the seats instead of just from the ground. There was an end-zone section which was only about twelve to fourteen rows and they had a makeshift press box. The locker rooms were behind the stadium underneath the Nimitz Freeway, the same overpass as now. There were Quonset huts underneath there and a lot of the players didn't have lockers — they had a couple of nails on the wall and that's where they hung their pants and helmets pregame."

Blum had the rights to the pregame and postgame shows while he was doing the games. Then, according to Blum, when a new flagship station ownership came in after the 1965 season, they wanted to change announcers. Blum would no longer do the games but was retained to produce the broadcasts.

"Bill King is your guy," he told Davis.

Scotty Stirling was on the Raiders beat for the *Oakland Tribune* when Davis began as coach and general manager. Davis hired him in 1964 as public relations director, and eventually Scotty became assistant GM and then the club's general manager, when Davis left for New York in April 1966 for what turned out to be a four-month stint as commissioner of the AFL.

Scotty met Bill for lunch at the Seafood Grotto in Oakland's Jack London Square to talk about Bill calling Raiders games starting with the 1966 season. No agents, just two guys talking over lunch. They discussed money and it didn't take long to agree on a figure. But as Scotty told me, Bill knew some of the owners were "establishment guys" and he had some concerns about how he looked.

"What about the beard?" Bill asked Scotty.

"I don't give a shit about your beard," Scotty told him.

That was a relief to Bill.

"He really appreciated that," Scotty said. "Later on when I worked with him, he would bring that up."

Yes, Bill had to miss a few Warriors games when there was a conflict with the Raiders, but he flourished despite the demands of the schedule. One reason for this was Bill's disdain of sleep, which to him was a necessary evil and an impediment to him enjoying life twenty-four hours a day instead of nineteen or twenty. He had so much energy, he used to boast that he was perfectly fine on three or four hours of sleep.

He never wanted to miss anything and in those days, keeping tabs on the wild and woolly AFL was a challenge. Stirling, in his pre-Raiders days as a sportswriter for the *Oakland Tribune*, also moonlighted for Davis as a recruiter. He flew to Memphis at one point on a mission to procure the services of an immensely talented Memphis State offensive lineman named Harry Schuh. Davis gave Stirling $5,000 in $100 bills to take with him, which of course made him a nervous wreck. "I'm scared as hell," Scotty remembered. "I'm walking around Memphis and I'm on airplanes and I've got this five grand in an attaché case."

Schuh had been drafted by the Rams, but as Scotty recalled, it was a war for players and "you did whatever you had to do." Scotty went to the Admiral Benbow Inn in Memphis to meet Schuh and give him the sales pitch on the Raiders, which was not going over that well. Schuh was interested, but wary.

"That's when I opened the attaché case," Scotty said. "I spread the bills on the bed — they covered the bed. He gets on the phone and he calls his wife and he says: 'Honey, you can't believe what this man just put on the bed here.' So I signed him that day. There was no control over us, nobody to police what we were doing."

Davis and Bill would eventually become close friends who often went out to dinner on the road, and Davis the Syracuse grad felt a connection to Bill because of his time announcing Bradley teams. But their first meeting was less than auspicious. Davis was roaming the grounds of training camp before the 1966 season along with Stirling when he spotted a bronzed man with no shirt and no shoes taking notes on the sideline during practice. "It was the middle of summer," Scotty recalled. "He was really tan."

"Who is this scrawny little guy and what can he possibly know about football?" Davis asked.

"That's your new announcer," Scotty told him.

It didn't take long for the Raiders' brass and fans to realize how brilliant Bill was on football.

"One of the things that has always stuck in my mind was how prepared he was," Scotty said. "He knew the Raiders cold. He knew the opponents, he had them down cold. He spent hours the day before a game getting ready."

Glenn Dickey of the *Chronicle* didn't really get to know Bill until he joined the Raiders beat in 1967. That's when Glenn learned about Bill's attention to detail. Dickey told me how he remembered Bill poring over transcriptions of plays from exhibition games.

"One time I remember in particular: The Raiders were playing the Denver Broncos and at one point, the Broncos were in punt formation," Glenn recalled for this book. "Bill told listeners the Broncos had faked a punt in this situation during the exhibition season and they might try it again. Sure enough, they did. Of course, it failed."

Bill used to talk about how he made very little money, especially in the early days with the Warriors and Raiders, and that he really didn't start making good money until he was hired by the A's.

Bob Blum, in his autobiography, *Started Talking at 11 Months ... Still Talking*, told one of his favorite Bill stories.

"We hired Bill to broadcast the Raiders games for $3,000 for the first season," he wrote. "One day while in Las Vegas for an exhibition game, Bill, Ken Korach and I went out to dinner after an afternoon game. 'Tell me,' Bill questioned during dinner, 'I made $3,000 that first year with the Raiders, how much did you make for producing?'

"I knew when I blurted out the answer, '$6,000,' it was probably a mistake. Without missing a beat, Bill ordered another bottle of $150 wine and indicated to me, 'You're getting the tab for dinner, you know.'"

Bill's first broadcast partner was Van Amburg, who many in the Bay Area will remember as a legendary news anchor on Channel 7 in the '70s and '80s. The Raiders moved into the Oakland Coliseum in Bill's first year, but they had to play all of their exhibition games and the first two regular season games on the road because the Coliseum wasn't ready.

Many of Bill's Raiders calls are burned into the collective memory, thanks to NFL Films and the success of the Silver and Black. The most famous of all would have to be the Holy Roller, in San Diego, in 1978:

" *Stabler back. Here comes the rush, he sidesteps. Can he throw? He can't! The ball, flipped forward, is loose! A wild scramble, two seconds on the clock. Casper grabbing the ball. It is ruled a fumble. Casper has recovered in the end zone! The Oakland Raiders have scored on the most zany, unbelievable, absolutely impossible dream of a play! Madden is on the field. He wants to know if it's real. They said yes, get your big butt out* *of here! He does! There's nothing real in the world anymore! The Raiders have won the football game! The Chargers are standing, looking at each other, they don't believe it. Nobody believes it! I don't know if the Raiders believe it. It's not real. Fifty-two thousand people minus a few lonely Raider fans are stunned! ... This one will be relived forever."*

The Holy Roller works on so many levels and is a perfect example of the many dimensions Bill brought to a call. First, the call itself is brilliant in its detail. Listening, you knew exactly what was happening. Bill had a showman's flair and an accomplished actor's sense of the dramatic. He used his voice to accent a sense of wonder at the improbable nature of the play in a way made possible by his ability to match his words and his inflection to what was unfolding. He knew good theater when he captured it. He also didn't care what anybody thought, least of all the coach of the team whose rear end he made famous in the call. The "get your big butt out of here" part of the call is what people remember most, and it is a little subplot after the description of the touchdown. Bill delivers the punch line with perfect timing when he says, "He does!"

I asked John Madden what he thought the first time he heard the Holy Roller.

"Yeah, get your big butt off the field," he told me. "It was just part of it, just his excitement and people really associated. In those days, it was more a family thing, people were closer to the team, the fans were part of the team, the players were part of the fans and part of the local thing, and Bill was part of that too. It kind of all melded together. We were kind of all in it — the players, the coaches, the broadcasters, the fans — it was kind of one big thing that we all did. You obviously didn't listen to the radio broadcast, you didn't know what he said, but you did hear highlights and all those things."

Another of Bill's most memorable moments, the Sea of Hands, came on December 21, 1974, in Oakland. It was the Raiders against the Dolphins, who were at the height of their powers, in an AFC divisional playoff game.

Bill:

" *Fifty-four thousand and twenty are here and I don't think anybody has left today. The ball on the thirteen and a half yard line. It is third and about a foot. So Frank Pitts has come out. Stabler asks for quiet. He's got to get the first down, that's of primary importance, Hubbard is in. They give to Davis, Davis drives to the eight yard line heading off the left side and the Raiders expend their last time out. They are on the eight yard line, it's first and goal to go and now thirty-five seconds are left....*

"Stabler is talking to Madden at the sideline now. They've got pivotal words and opinions being exchanged here. The crowd peaking itself for it hopes an explosion, but the Miami Dolphins, they try, looking to be the first team ever to play in four straight Super Bowls and win three straight. They are a team that has been through it all and they know that they can come up with one big play."

Scotty Stirling:

" *This crowd, not one soul has left, and they are letting the Raiders know just how they feel. This is really, I don't believe I've seen anything as intense and as tight and to use your word, as tingly as it's been at this park in its nine year history."*

Bill:

66 *Thirty-five seconds left first and goal for Oakland, they
trail 26–21, the Promised Land is eight yards away.
Branch to the left against Stuckey, Biletnikoff to the
right against Foley. Back to pass goes Stabler, looking,
looking, looking, he runs, he's at the fifteen he throws
— it is a* TOUCHDOWN RAIDERS! *TOUCHDOWN RAIDERS! I
can't even see the receiver. Clarence Davis! It looks like
Clarence Davis! He's being mobbed. Stabler was hit as
he threw, he was falling down, Stabler threw the ball
in a loop. I still can't tell if it's Davis. I thought it was.
It is a touchdown. Everybody in the booth — yes, here
it is, Davis got it! Everybody in the booth believed with
me it was Davis, but he went down in a heap of tacklers
and then was mobbed by fans. The Raiders have taken
the lead, 27–26.*

*"When Stabler had to loop the ball up because he
was hit as he threw and looked like he might have been
lobbing it into the Promised Land for Miami but no,
Mike Kolen couldn't get there, Davis got there first and
it was the Raiders' Promised Land. Blanda kicks the
conversion is good, but now there are twenty-six seconds
are left and you and I know what twenty-six seconds
mean in a National Football League playoff game!"*

Then, after the Raiders kicked off: *"The Miami Dolphins dy-
nasty is hanging by a thread of twenty seconds."*

The Raiders won the game, 28–26, and thirty-eight years later,
Scotty Stirling reflected on what it was like to be in the booth that
day with Bill King:

"Late in the game, Kenny Stabler's rolling out, he gets hit
and he throws the ball into the end zone as he's falling," Scotty
recalled. "There are three Dolphins players there and a Raider
player, and they all go up, so there's like eight hands going up in
the air. And I swear to you, King was the only one in the whole

stadium who knew it was Clarence Davis catching the ball for the Raiders.

"That's how good he was. There were 54,000 people there and he picked it out. You still see that when you see highlights of the Raiders in the old days. They still use that call. They show that play and you can hear King's call above it. He was just fantastic. I mean, it was an unbelievable call. I'm sitting next to him and I'm watching the game, and I kind of knew who was going to be in the corner. He spotted it and it was just incredible to me. It's one of the great calls I've ever heard. You've seen it. It's almost impossible to tell who's in that pack.

"Anyway, his perfection went to the extent that he knew who was going to be in the corner. He watched the Raiders, he paid attention to the plays, but he never talked about his own expertise in watching it. But he figured who was going to be in the corner when that catch was made and he had it cold."

Bill was on the other side of the play many people believe to be the most historic in NFL annals. Or at least the most controversial. The Raiders played the Steelers on December 23, 1972, for the AFC Championship at Three Rivers Stadium in Pittsburgh. Kenny Stabler's touchdown gave the Raiders a 7–6 lead with 1:17 left. Then the Steelers, desperate, had a fourth and 10 with :22 left on their own 40. Terry Bradshaw went back to pass.

❝ *All right, here it is. Back he goes, they've got one man out, four-man pattern, he looks deep, he's in trouble. He's run to the right by Jones, he reverses, throws way up field — batted down by Tatum! And it's taken, caught in the air by Fucqua, Fucqua at the forty; no, it's Franco Harris! Harris goes all the way for a touchdown. I don't believe it! Franco Harris goes forty yards. The place has exploded! The place has exploded!"*

It took forever for the officials to sort out what had happened. The NFL had a rule back then that nullified a reception if the ball was deflected from one offensive player to another without a defender touching the ball in between. It was hard to tell if Jack Tatum hit the ball first, or if the carom came directly from Fuqua to Harris.

Bill recalled John Madden "feeling it was the most hopeless feeling in his life, because there was no time to respond."

The call I like the best from the Super Bowls came from the game with the Vikings, Super Bowl XI in January 1977:

> **"** *And he looks and throws. Intercepted by the Oakland Raiders. Willie Brown at the thirty, forty, fifty, he's going all the way.* OLD MAN WILLIE!! TOUCHDOWN RAIDERS!!***"***

I moved to Santa Rosa in 1979 to take a job as an assistant to my friend Kelly Wolfe, who was the head professional at Bennett Valley Golf Course. By the late '70s Santa Rosa had grown into a decent-sized city and now, with all the sprawl, it's not unusual for a commuter to live up there and drive over an hour down to San Francisco. But in 1963 when the Raiders first began a twenty-two-year training camp run in Santa Rosa, it was a big deal having the team in town, and as you can imagine there was ample nightlife. Author Peter Richmond, in *Badasses*, his book on the '70s Raiders, called it "the perfect frontier town for the perfect outlaw team."

The weather was conducive, too. You'd get some of the marine layer in the morning but things would usually heat up in the afternoon. It wasn't unusual for the temperature to reach 100 maybe about one week or so every month. Players got in shape up there with two-a-day practices. It was good Bill King weather. He would show up at training camp typically dressed in very little.

Santa Rosa was where Bill first got to know John Madden back in his days as Raiders coach. Madden has had one of the most amazingly layered careers in the history of American sports. Our daughter Emilee — and a lot of younger readers — know him from his video games. I go back to listening to San Diego State games in the early '60s when Madden was an assistant under Don Coryell. He would coach the Raiders for ten years, after spending two seasons as an assistant. Few have had more success. He never had a losing season and he was the youngest coach to reach one hundred wins. In January 1977 he led the Raiders to a win over the Vikings in the Super Bowl — the Raiders' first Super Bowl victory. He was inducted into the Pro Football Hall of Fame in 2006.

Madden went on to become the most popular and decorated NFL analyst ever. He was the perfect match for Pat Summerall's play-by-play. Summerall set him up and Madden took the ball and ran with it. One of Madden's biggest broadcasting influences? Bill King.

"You know what I got from Bill, and it probably helped me when I went into broadcasting too, is that he didn't make preparation (into) work," Madden told me for this book. "You never saw Bill King sweat in getting ready. He just hung around. You knew it was getting close to the start of football when Bill King would come to training camp. He would just come up to training camp in a T-shirt and a pair of shorts and flip-flops, and he'd just kind of stand around there and absorb what was going on. He wasn't one of those guys who was taking a lot of notes. I don't know if he ever took notes or had a tape recorder or anything like that. He was just there, and he'd be out there at practice and then he'd be sitting out by the swimming pool, and eating. He'd bring his own bread or some doggone thing."

Al Davis was ahead of his time in many areas, and one of them was how he arranged for the Raiders to train in Santa Rosa. In those years, teams would often train at small college campuses and live in dorms. Davis, beginning in 1963 and for the next twenty-one years, took the Raiders to the El Rancho Tropicana. Eventually the hotel grew from a handful of rooms to almost 300. Davis built two practice fields and a locker room on the grounds.

Seeing Bill at training camp was a common sight for Madden. We can learn a lot by observing, and that is what Madden did. He watched Bill King watch him and the Raiders. He absorbed the way Bill absorbed. Bill always did plenty of reading and writing away from the field, compiling notes and data that he'd pore over at home, in hotels and on airplanes. But Madden learned, by watching Bill, that it was also possible to be yourself and enjoy what you were doing; if you were good, and did the work to prepare, you could be relaxed enough on the air to be both precise and likable. That was why that kind of preparation was so important.

"He just did it in a different way and when I started in broadcasting, that's what I did," Madden said. "You don't have to do a lot of reading and writing and all that stuff — although he probably did that — but you just kind of hang out and observe, and then it'll come out and that's the way you learn. That's kind of what Bill did. In those days, when I was coaching and he was broadcasting for the Raiders, they were really part of our team. They would go to practice, they would be on the airplane, they would stay in the same hotel, you know, so there was a lot of opportunity for that, and I always thought Bill was a master of that."

I asked Madden if Bill was an influence on the way he went about his business during his own great broadcasting career.

"Yeah, a big influence because that's what Bill did," he said. "Bill just hung out and absorbed, and didn't have to ask a lot of questions even though he was a great conversationalist. A lot of times, you'd get into conversation and pretty soon it would be, 'What's that book you're reading?' And it would be a Russian book or something like that. And you'd have no idea what he was talking about." But the lesson Madden took from Bill was that it all started with preparation — a quality that Bill also praised in Madden's work. He would go to high school games on Friday nights, Bill told me, "and he would put himself into game situations while watching. He was always prepared for every situation."

CHAPTER 5

BILL'S FAVORITE TEAM EVER: THE '75 WARRIORS

Barry's got it, the ball game is over, the ball game is over and Al Attles' Golden State Warriors are champions of the world, they are the unbelievable champions of the world, the Cinderellas of the sports world!

Talking to his club in the locker room at the dingy Cap Center in Landover, Maryland, before Game Four of the 1975 NBA Finals, Al Attles never mentioned winning a championship. He *did* tell his team that if they won one more game they would do something no one thought they could do.

The game was heated from the start and before long Bill King became a boxing announcer for one of the most bizarre and intense situations in NBA history. As Bill recalled in an interview with Tom Spencer, the Bullets' Mike Riordan was "goading Rick Barry from the start." Riordan threw a punch at Barry. Attles, decked out that day in a white suit, came off the Warriors' bench to try to separate the two.

"The guy was trying to take Rick's head off out there and I wasn't going to let that happen," Al told me. "I didn't care what the situation was."

Bullets center Wes Unseld was attempting to restrain Al, who had a reputation as a fierce competitor who didn't back down from anyone. All of a sudden, it was like Don Dunphy was at the mic and it was the Friday Night Fights, sponsored by Gillette, that Bill used to listen to on his radio back in Bloomington in the '40s:

> " *Attles now is in a wild slugging match with 245–pound Westly Unseld, started to trade punches with Attles. Attles was out purely as a peacemaker. And Attles is being dragged away by his assistant coach Joe Roberts. Barry is still trying to keep Attles away. Attles has gotten a technical now. You had to know this was a violent and flagrant act by Mike Riordan to draw that kind of attention from Al Attles. Barry is telling Manny Sokol that he has handled it very badly. Richie Powers takes Al Attles over to talk to him now. Attles, one of the great gentlemen of the game, he has been given a technical. Riordan has not been thrown out.*
>
> *"He's thrown Attles out of the game! This is disgraceful, this is disgraceful! Al Attles has been ejected.... The Warriors are going crazy. Cliff Ray started after Powers. Richie Powers has just committed I think the most disgraceful decision of a very distinguished officiating career. I cannot believe this!"*

"Riordan was paying absolutely no attention to the rest of the game and he was manhandling Barry as he was driving to the hoop," Bill said later. "Al raced out there and he was enraged. I've never seen Al go on the floor as coach to be in combat. He always went out to break it up. People in the league said, 'Don't ever get in a tangle with Al,' as he'd proven a few times over the years. He was really hot; he was raging. It was obvious that whether K.C. Jones urged Riordan to be physical or to go farther than that, Riordan decided the only way to do it was to be blatant."

Attles spent the rest of the game in the locker room. Barry felt that Attles getting ejected might have won the game for the Warriors. Forced to watch on television as the Warriors fell behind by as much as fourteen points, Al noticed things he might not have noticed. Rick remembers his halftime breakdown being spectacular.

"Sometimes you get so caught up in it," Al told me. "There is nothing like seeing it differently."

The Bay Area was a magnet for colorful characters like Franklin Mieuli and Bill King. You can add Dick Vertlieb to that list. Like me, Dick grew up in the Los Angeles area. His father was a bookmaker who did time in jail and reportedly had clients connected to the mob. Dick, a former stockbroker who knew how to add, was in for some bad news when Mieuli hired him as general manager of the Warriors in 1974. As Vertlieb later told the *Seattle Post-Intelligencer*, Franklin "jumped on his catamaran and sailed to Australia. He handed me the keys and a checkbook that showed the team was $44,000 overdrawn and there was a payroll to meet."

Vertlieb was the West Coast version of the great showman Bill Veeck, Hall of Fame owner of the White Sox and other clubs, and he had Veeck's eccentricities and promotional flare. When Vertlieb was the general manager of the Seattle Mariners, he tried to get the team to wear all-black uniforms. "I wanted us to be the toughest sons of bitches in the world," he told the *P.I.* "I wanted a uniform where it looked like, when you slid into second base, you'd break the other guy's leg. "

Mariners vice president Randy Adamack recalled that Vertlieb wanted the team to be known as the Pros instead of the Mariners. "He wanted to be upfront that we wanted to win baseball games and be profitable," Adamack told me.

As GM of the Sonics Vertlieb tried to get the team to wear the blue and gold colors of Olympia Beer so he could land the brewery's sponsorship dollars. Visitors to his office were asked to sit in a barber's chair. "He was a combination free-thinking, free-flowing and optimistic," Adamack said. "And he loved life!"

Like Bill King, he was a man governed by his passions. Like A's general manager Billy Beane, he was so emotionally invested in his team that he turned peripatetic during games, often wandering the halls of the Coliseum Arena unable to watch. Sometimes if the game was close near the end he would jump into his car and just drive around, going no place in particular, while listening to Bill on the radio. Once, as his former PR man Hal Childs told the *Chronicle*, he was so wrapped up in the action that he ran out of gas.

When Vertlieb traded future Hall of Famer Nate Thurmond, a beloved figure in the Bay Area, it served to cement Vertlieb's reputation for not quite playing with a full deck. People scratched their heads over the decision to deal Nate to the Bulls for a journeyman named Clifford Ray just five weeks before the start of the 1974–75 season. But the move wasn't a basketball trade in the traditional sense. Trying to balance the books, Vertlieb saved $500,000 on the deal. (The Warriors also received a future first-round pick in the trade that they ended up using to select a forward named Joe "Jellybean" Bryant, the father of a kid named Kobe.) Three days after the Thurmond trade, the Warriors lost their second-leading scorer, forward Cazzie Russell, who signed with the Lakers as a free agent.

The Warriors had been 44–38 and second in the Pacific Division in 1973–74, but missed the playoffs after losing six of their last seven games. They averaged only 6,500 fans that season and were the furthest thing from a hot ticket you could imagine. "You couldn't give tickets away," remembers Art Spander, who was on the Warriors beat for the *Chronicle* back then. He warned Vertlieb that the Bay Area just wasn't pro basketball country.

"You watch," Vertlieb replied.

The Warriors went into the 1974–75 season with a decent assemblage of talent, but there was nothing about them that suggested a championship run was in the cards. They featured a cadre of good guards: a veteran leader in Jeff Mullins; a sharpshooter from Louisville named Butch Beard; and two kids with Bay Area ties, Phil Smith from USF and Charles Johnson from Cal. Clifford Ray shared the pivot with George Johnson — the "two-headed center," as Bill called them. Jamaal Wilkes, a smooth rookie from UCLA, started at one forward and Rick Barry started at the other. At this point in his career Barry had by his own admission lost a step, but he was still one of the best players in the game.

Barry joined the Warriors in 1965 out of the University of Miami, a skinny six-seven kid who could run the floor and had great quickness. It was fitting that Bill soon dubbed him "The Miami Greyhound." In baseball, they talk about "five-tool players." Barry was a five-tool basketball player. He could run, shoot, pass, rebound and play defense. And he had a sixth sense as well — an intuitive feel for the game that made everyone around him better. Barry, only twenty-one at the time, was immediately intrigued by the team's broadcaster.

"My first impression was, who the hell is this guy with that crazy mustache?" Rick told me for this book. "It was such a bizarre look, which I think actually kept him from ever getting network stuff. Plus he was always smoking those damn cigars when you were in a taxi or in a car with him. But certainly it became very evident when you had a chance to spend any time at all with him that he was a very cerebral guy. Not too many people I know were self-teaching themselves how to speak Russian back in those days. He was very well read, a very bright guy and a very interesting guy to sit down and have a conversation with."

As he did with John Madden, Bill was able to pull Rick away from the one-dimensional existence that can too often define life with a professional sports team. The NBA was a much smaller league back then and teams went to the various cities more than just once or twice during the season, which gave Rick the chance to get out and explore. He had the perfect tour guide in Bill.

"He was going to the art galleries and the museums and the various other things," Rick recalled. "He was not your typical sports guy in that everything in his life was wrapped around sports. It's not that we didn't have conversations about basketball, but the beauty of it was that we had intellectual conversations about other things. I think this helped to broaden my perspective because I was just a young kid."

By the time Rick was twenty-five he had bolted the Warriors for the insurgent American Basketball Association, but because of a legal squabble he had to sit out his first season with the Oakland Oaks. Over the next five years his résumé included stops with the Washington Caps, Virginia Squires and New York Nets. He landed back with the Warriors in 1972, which was Al Attles' second full season coaching the team.

Attles, who played at North Carolina A&T, took over from George Lee in 1970 as Warriors player/coach and did not trade his jersey for a coat and tie until two years later. By 1975 Attles was an experienced coach despite being only thirty-eight, and confident enough to make the unconventional decision before training camp to bring in Menlo Junior College coach Bud Presley to work with the Warriors on defense. Presley was well known in the Bay Area, but still he was a junior college coach. Al didn't care about that. He had known Presley for a long time and he knew Presley could teach defense.

"Sometimes you need someone with a different perspective just to change something that you are hearing," Al told me. "If you hear the same thing all the time you unintentionally tune it out. He helped lay the groundwork and the guys bought into it."

Bill compared the Warriors' defensive play that year to what he witnessed when he was broadcasting Cal basketball, where the legendary coach Pete Newell had been known for his deliberate approach to offense and his mastery of defensive fundamentals.

"I'm sure Bill probably talked about watching Bud Presley show up at training camp to put a defensive mindset in us that I think, without question, was probably the best coaching move that Al Attles ever made," Barry told me.

The fact that Barry, especially, bought into the approach reflected his understanding of how defense could win a championship. Just talking about it wasn't enough. Like Newell, Presley stressed a commitment to defense and, according to Attles, it took a week at training camp for the lessons to sink in. Guys began taking charges and flying all over the floor. Al realized that his team's success would depend in large part on rotating in a lot of players in short spurts so they could dig in with great intensity on the defensive end.

Dick Vertlieb had a theory about the NBA. "If you have a star, you should go no worse than .500," he said. The Warriors had that star in Barry, and the young players on the team quickly discovered that the best path to success was to rally around him. "He took over the team and the young players sort of followed him," Spander said. "Rick gave me the old line: 'Out of the mud you make a lotus grow.'"

The Warriors came out of the gates fast and by December 3 they were 16–6. They reached fifteen games over .500 with a win over Seattle on January 10 and from then on they knew the playoffs were a lock, giving them a chance to exorcise past demons. The Warriors had reached the postseason seven times after the move to the Bay Area from Philly. Their best chance at a title came in Barry's second year, 1966–67, when they took down the St. Louis Hawks in six games in the Western Conference Finals to advance to face Philadelphia for the NBA title.

It was in that raucous, intense St. Louis series that Barry found himself in the middle of a bizarre incident having to do with his endorsement of Snickers candy bars. Franklin Mieuli's contentious relationship with Hawks owner Ben Kerner helped give the series an undercurrent of added tension. Franklin hired security guards from the Burns Detective Agency because the fans were right on top of the benches at Kiel Auditorium in St. Louis, edging so close they were almost inside the Warriors' huddle during timeouts. Things got out of hand near the end of the sixth game when fans began pelting the court with Snickers bars and eggs.

There used to be an NBA rule that gave a team two shots after the second foul in the last two minutes of a quarter. Hank Greenwald, working with Bill on Warriors radio, joked, "That's the first egg in the last two minutes."

The finals against Philadelphia brought together Nate Thurmond and Wilt Chamberlain, who already had a very involved history together. Thurmond joined the Warriors in 1963 after a stellar college career at Bowling Green, and his addition to the team created a bit of an awkward situation, because now the Warriors had two centers and one of them was the living legend Chamberlain. For a while Nate served as Wilt's backup, but they eventually spent time in the lineup together, well before anyone had conjured the term "Twin Towers." Nate took over the job full time when Wilt was traded to the 76ers during the 1965 All-Star break.

Nate and Wilt were at the center of a bitter Warriors overtime loss in Game One of the finals. The game was tied in the waning seconds of regulation and the Warriors had the ball, looking for a chance to win. But they never got it, thanks to a no-call that Rick Barry has never forgotten on a play where Wilt hammered Nate going for a block.

"It would have changed the whole complexion of the series," he told me. "It would have had a huge psychological impact. Nate went in and to this day, I remember — I wish I had some film to validate this — what happened was I hit Nate on the pick-and-roll and Wilt came from behind him and went right across his arms as Nate went up to make the shot. He fouled him. There was no question in anybody's mind because I remember everybody stopped. It was like everybody was waiting for the whistle, but the whistle never blew."

In an interview more than thirty years later, Bill recalled: "When they came out to start the overtime, Wilt and Nate shook hands and Wilt said, 'I fouled the hell out of you, baby.'"

In sports you're taught to roll with the punches and move on after a big disappointment. It's hard to do that when you are as emotional and competitive as Rick Barry. You would think time would have peeled away some of the frustration from that game and the no-call on Wilt. It hasn't. There was no guarantee, of course, that the Warriors would have taken the series if they had won Game One, instead of falling to the Sixers in six games. But don't tell Rick Barry that. Even with his legacy as one of the game's all-time greats secure, the play at the end of Game One of the '67 finals will gnaw at Barry forever.

"That series was one of the most memorable I was ever around," said Bill.

Even in defeat, Barry's reputation was enhanced by his brilliance in the postseason. He scored forty-four points in the riveting Game Six, which the Warriors lost 125–122, and he averaged forty-one points a game in the finals.

Eight years later, Barry had another opportunity to make a run for the title. Attles coached the Warriors to a 48–34 record and the Pacific Division title, then the team handled the Supersonics in six games in their first playoff series and braced for a bruising battle against the Chicago Bulls, a team with a grinding style personified by players like Norm Van Lier, Jerry Sloan, Bob "Butterbean" Love, Chet Walker, Tom Boerwinkle and the Warriors' old center Thurmond. To handle the Bulls, they had to match the Bulls' toughness. Bill talked often about the Warriors' gritty play, especially the way an ancient Bill Bridges, who had been induced out of retirement late in the season, "was pounding on Bob Love."

Game Four of the Bulls series was huge because the Warriors were staring at a three-to-one series deficit for much of the game. Their stirring comeback had Bill and his listeners on the edges of their seats:

> 66 *Here's cj, top of the key, works the dribble to the left, backs into the left corner, causes a switch. Over to Barry. Barry guarded by Van Lier, the smaller man. Barry, dribbling to the baseline, thirteen-footer. He had a good look. Good! 94–90. Barry now is on a runaway tear!"*

Then with the win secure:

> **❝** *The Warriors have come from nineteen behind to even the series, one of the great comebacks in the thirteen-year annals of the Warriors in the Bay Area!"*

After losing Game Five the Warriors summoned a resolve that would carry them the rest of the playoffs. They won Game Six, 86–72, and then held the Bulls to thirty-two points in the second half in the deciding seventh game, showing once again how crucial the defensive mind-set instilled in training camp proved to be. Attles recalled those last two games and the five- to ten-minute stretches of maniacal defense his players gave him and how he felt it was one of the best and grittiest efforts he had ever been part of. With a trip to the finals secure, Bill looked around from his seat at courtside and saw a Coliseum Arena ready to explode: *"The ballgame is over, 83–79, and the crowd pours onto the floor!"*

Despite their great run through the playoffs, the Warriors became orphans during the NBA Finals because the Coliseum was booked for the Ice Follies, leading to an unusual itinerary for the teams. The Washington Bullets had tied the Celtics for the NBA's best record during the regular season at 60–22 and they were even more of a juggernaut at home with a 36–5 record. They had home-court advantage for the finals, where they were heavily favored. So lightly regarded were the Warriors that Spander remembered a story in one of the local Washington papers calling the Warriors "the worst team ever to play in the finals."

The Bullets featured an all-star cast coached by K.C. Jones, a star at USF in the Bill Russell era, and led by Elvin Hayes, Wes Unseld and Phil Chenier, who played at Berkeley High and then in the same backcourt at Cal with Charles Johnson. The NBA gave the Bullets their choice and they chose a 1–2–2–1–1 format, which meant they would play the first game at home and then travel to San Francisco for games two and three and the teams would then return to D.C. for the fourth game. Little was made of it at the time, but Jones and Attles were the first African-American coaches to face off for a championship in any major-league American sport.

Fresh off a grueling series with the methodical Bulls, the Warriors shocked the Bullets by handling them in Game One, 101–95. As the Warriors were leaving the court after the game, Butch Beard yelled out, "It's destiny, man!"

It may have been, because this is where the quirky schedule worked in the Warriors' favor. Up a game already, they were going home to the Bay Area for the next two games at their old arena, the Cow Palace. "Here was the 'worst team ever' winning the first game," Spander said. "It was like the Fates were with them. Now they have the big edge playing the next two games at home and everything bounced right for them."

The '75 Warriors' run to the title was an ensemble performance. Barry made the point of saying that Al understood that he only had a few guys who needed to play a lot of minutes but that he had a whole bench full of players who could help. Bill also noted that the trade of the iconic Thurmond to the Bulls had actually made the team better, because "they found out how good the rest of the cast was."

"Attles went deeper than any team ever goes," Rick told me. "He played a lot of people and gave everybody a chance. If a guy went in for two minutes or twenty minutes, he was going to play as hard as he could play and do the best that he could do."

The Warriors, back to their Bay Area roots playing at the Cow Palace, fell behind early in Game Two and trailed 27–17 after one quarter. They exploded for sixty-one points in the second half, compared to only thirty-eight in the first half, and clung to a one-point lead in the closing seconds.

Here was Bill's call on the Bullets' final possession:

66 *Nineteen seconds. Porter reverse pivot, feed Unseld high. George out to challenge him. Unseld double-teamed for the moment, now he has twelve seconds, a lot of time for it. To Chenier on top. Chenier reverses, double-teamed, triple-teamed, over to Riordan on the right, shoots over Barry hurriedly — in and out! Heartbreak! Hayes rebounds and shoots, misses, rebound to George Johnson, and the Warriors have it, the game is over!"*

Led by Barry's thirty-eight points and Wilkes' stifling defense on Elvin Hayes, the Warriors took Game Three with relative ease, 109–101. It was back in Maryland for Game Four that all hell broke loose with Al Attles entering the fray and getting ejected. Coach Joe Roberts took the reins, filling in admirably, and the Warriors won the game 96–95 to claim the title, coming back from eight points down with five minutes to play. Barry, named MVP of the finals, averaged 25.1 points per game in the playoffs. I've always thought one of the keys was the job Wilkes did defensively on the great Elvin Hayes, who was held to only fifteen points in the last game. Unseld's tip-in made it a one-point game with one second left, and as the Warriors inbounded the ball from midcourt, Bill spoke the words that pronounced the Warriors as champions:

" Barry's got it, the ball game is over, the ball game is over and Al Attles' Golden State Warriors are champions of the world, they are the unbelievable champions of the world, the Cinderellas of the sports world!"

While the team was rejoicing on the floor after the final buzzer, it was a little surreal for Attles because he was in the locker room and had to wait until the team came in to join the celebration. In typical classy, modest Attles fashion, he said he's never regretted not being with his team on the floor because those moments were for the players. "That was the furthest thing from my mind and we had a great scene in the locker room," he said.

Rick Barry called it the greatest year of his life. I asked Rick why he thought Bill — who broadcast four Super Bowls, three World Series and three NBA Finals — felt the 1975 Warriors were his all-time favorite team.

"It was the way the game was designed to be played and the way a team was designed to conduct itself," he said. "We didn't have any great ego problems. Everybody rooted for one another. We hung out together. We went to the movies together. We went to go eat together. It was really more like a family than a team. It was a very close-knit group of guys, which made it that much more rewarding for us to be able to accomplish what we accomplished. It was without question the biggest upset in the history of the NBA."

Rick has always stressed that his teammates never got the credit they deserved for that championship. "I mean, we weren't even on the cover of *Sports Illustrated*," he said. "And I really feel badly for my teammates because it wouldn't have happened if it weren't for the group of guys that we had and the commitment that we all had made. And I think Bill really enjoyed it."

This was echoed by Attles, whose thoughts on why it was Bill's favorite team mirrored his own: "It was a group of people coming together for one common goal. There was no jealousy and we just believed in each other. That was our mantra. And Bill was outstanding announcing those games because everybody was uplifted by that group of guys."

Al became emotional when I talked with him about the owner of the Warriors, and how much it meant to Al to help deliver a championship to Franklin Mieuli. Franklin, of course, welcomed everyone in the organization as a member of the family, but the family had endured many tough times over the years.

"I think it is very important and we very seldom talk about it," Al told me, his bass voice getting soft, almost to a whisper. "The person we were most happy for was Mr. Mieuli, to a man, and me more than anybody. I was probably closer to him than anybody over a period of time. What he had to go through to keep this team here. It wasn't until later on after he sold the team that he was able to collect some money because he was going through some financial things. The big struggle was coming into a college area with a professional team. When you play forty-one home games versus ten college home games it was a culture shock for people here. He really stuck with it and I was really, really happiest for him."

The Warriors had galvanized the Bay Area like they had never done before. "The fans were just going crazy," Spander told me.

"I think I wrote they set an NBA record for standing ovations. Everything caught on and it was so much fun and I think Bill got caught up into it — we all did."

The flight home from Washington was one of the most joyous of Bill's life. But Bill and the rest of the team had no idea what lay in store for them at San Francisco Airport, where elated fans had gathered to welcome their team home.

As the team plane was making its descent into SFO, the pilot came over the loud speaker to announce that they couldn't land because the gathered fans were so delirious in their excitement, they had spilled out onto the runway. The Warriors were diverted to Oakland, which was fine with Al Attles because he lived in the city and was ready to hit the sack after a five-hour flight. But another call came in saying there were people on the runway at SFO and the authorities were worried about what might be developing.

"They said if we don't get over here there are going to be riots," Attles recalled. So even though it was the middle of the night, the Warriors boarded a couple of buses and headed over to the airport in San Francisco.

"There was basically hysteria," Bill recalled. "This team captured some sort of imagination partly because, aside from Rick, it was an ensemble. People really enjoyed the tenacity on defense. I was not prepared for the huge volume of humanity that engulfed SFO. We were in a school bus and the fans started pouring over it and the bus was rocking back and forth. Bill Bridges was shouting, 'Get us out of here!' He was really scared."

"We get there and they are shaking the buses and a couple of guys started to panic," Al recalled. "They were a little frightened. People were just trying to show their appreciation and the crowd was very nice, but there was so many of them."

Rick Barry was a tough competitor. He wore his emotions on his sleeve and he was outspoken, which meant he didn't endear himself to everyone. In a 1983 story in *Sports Illustrated,* Rick said the way he looked and the faces he made while he was playing alienated some people. But Bill talked with me often about his respect for the way Barry played the game and his forthrightness.

"He still doesn't smile much," Bill was quoted saying in the same article. "It gives people the impression he's closing them off and sets up an immediate barrier that is very hard to break down."

Those barriers were no problem for Bill. He was drawn to great competitors like Barry who could put teams of lesser talent on their back and elevate everyone else's play. This is how much Bill King meant to Rick Barry: When we talked for the first time for this book, Rick mentioned a notebook that Bill updated after every game that contained notes and stories from the '75 championship year. Rick told me how badly he wanted to have that book to remember a season and a friendship he cherished.

Bill had read from the book in a retrospective he hosted for SportsChannel Bay Area on the twentieth anniversary of that championship season. Sitting on a chair in a television studio, Bill interviewed Barry and other guests and led viewers on a tour of the season.

"I actually have that video," Rick told me. "One of the things that was so cool was we sat down and we had a talk reminiscing about what took place, and Bill had the book and he pulled it out and said, 'OK, on this date here.' I mean, he was so into that season and he had that ledger. I can remember it was like a grayish little color, red corners on it or something, hardbound little thing that he kept every single game in. He had notes and highlights of what was there. That would just be such a cool thing to have. He was awesome in that show because he had such a handle on what took place because he had it all documented."

Rick Barry let Bill know how much it would mean to him to have the book, to be able to turn the pages of a story that ended with the word "togetherness" being written on the Warriors' NBA championship rings. Bill was one of those people who never threw anything away. Kathy and Johnny sifted through stacks upon stacks of scorebooks and media guides and all the ledgers that contained Bill's notes and bookkeeping dating back to his first year with the Warriors and continuing until his last game with the A's in 2005. I was thrilled when Kathy and Johnny told me that they had sent a copy off to Rick.

CHAPTER 6

LON AND BILL

*Rickey goes, the pitch taken, he's going
to have it, he does! Rickey Henderson, no
contest, steals third base, jerks the bag from
its moorings and holds it aloft, representing
Number 939. Rickey pounds it with his left
fist, hands it to equipment manager Frank
Ciensczyk, who gives him a big hug.*

Pick any minor-league club, from Walla Walla to Winter Haven or Lodi to Little Falls, they would have been embarrassed to have just 653 fans show up to their ballpark for a game. But on April 17, 1979, that was the sad reality for the Oakland Athletics, a major-league franchise driven into the ground by the brilliant but capricious and penurious Charlie Finley. Rumored to be on the way to Denver one minute and then New Orleans the next, the A's lured just 306,000 paying customers to the Coliseum that entire season. That was fine with me: I actually enjoyed the sparse crowds. I'd head out to the Coliseum with my tape recorder, spread out with plenty of room and — in virtual privacy — practice broadcasting baseball and try to put together an audition tape.

With the team at its nadir, a group of Oakland businessmen approached the Levi Strauss magnate Walter Haas to gauge his interest in buying the A's. Haas sent his son-in-law, Roy Eisenhardt, on a fact-finding mission that eventually led him to Chicago and the contentious and colorful Charlie O.

"That meant many cans of Budweiser beer," Roy remembered.

When all was said and drunk, Eisenhardt had negotiated a deal for Haas to buy the franchise, at which point he assumed his little project with the A's was done and that the A's would bring on a baseball man. Wrong. It soon became clear that no one "married to traditional concepts and old school thinking," as Roy put it, was going to pull the A's out of the abyss they had spiraled into during the late Finley years. So Roy, ready to take a different approach, stayed on, setting the stage for the revitalization of the A's, a new phase in Bill King's career and one of the most remarkable pairings in baseball broadcasting history.

Back in his law student days at Cal in the early '60s, Roy Eisenhardt began listening to broadcasts of the San Francisco Warriors, new in town after their move west from Philly. He savored Bill's unflinching and precise descriptions of the action. Roy can still recall being tuned in when the Warriors met the Philadelphia 76ers in Game One of the NBA Finals in 1967, and remembers vividly how Bill was "on fire" at the end of the game, when that last-second no-call on an apparent foul by Wilt Chamberlain on Nate Thurmond denied the Warriors a chance to win the game in regulation. Roy came to believe deeply in the power of sports on the radio, but when he began running the A's, the team's broadcasts often had limited reach.

"There was a time when the radio station had a range of forty-two juice cans and twelve miles of strip," former A's marketing guru Andy Dolich recalled.

The A's had begun the 1978 season with the Cal student station, KALX, carrying the games after Larry Baer —the same Larry Baer who is now the president of the Giants — negotiated a deal with Charlie. Baer, then a junior at the university, also did some play-by-play on the broadcasts, although few likely heard him, given that the KALX signal was all of ten watts.

Still, Roy thought that radio done right could be the preeminent tool for the A's to connect with fans. Television wasn't nearly the omnipotent force it is today. With just thirty A's games televised, it "played a minor role," Roy recalled, while "radio was huge." Fortunately for Roy and the A's, KSFO was eager to get back into baseball after losing the Giants to KNBR three years earlier, and in 1981 the A's struck a deal to have KSFO carry their games. That gave the team a jolt of credibility, along with a strong signal. And with a solid station lined up, Roy knew exactly who he wanted in the booth: Bill King, who was flattered to be sought after and more than willing to dive into baseball full time.

"In terms of fan recognition across an entire spectrum, Bill's voice was Number 1," Roy said. Bill had the chief quality Roy was looking for: credibility. "He didn't touch up the x-rays," Roy said. "Radio was major distribution for the team. As we were trying to create a feeling around the team, a lot of what we had to do was restore equity with the fans so they would believe that this was a serious organization."

Getting Bill on board was easy, but Roy also had to convince Bill's better half. A meeting was set up at the Sausalito harbor with Roy, Nancy and Bill's attorney, Hugh Lawrence, on Hugh's houseboat. Nancy had questions: What was working full time in baseball going to mean for Bill's life away from the game? How much of a disruption was it going to be? And just who were these people he would be working for? Roy knew, of course, that Bill wouldn't be available for every game since he wasn't going to give up his work with the Warriors and the Raiders. He also knew how much Bill and Nancy loved New York. So in the negotiations he assured Nancy that Bill would be granted a series off, either before or after an A's trip to the Big Apple, giving the two of them the chance to enjoy a brief vacation in the city, unencumbered by baseball.

"That sealed the deal," Roy told me. "Bill called me and said, 'We're all set to go.'"

Bringing the legendary Raiders and Warriors announcer over

to the A's was a coup, but Roy wasn't finished. It took a team to do a broadcast, and Roy had an inspired idea in mind: Team Bill up with Lon Simmons, who was out of baseball after KNBR hired new announcers in 1979.

Of the new Giants announcers, Lindsey Nelson and Hank Greenwald, Hank proved to be a popular choice but Lindsey was not. Lindsey was a legendary figure in broadcasting but Giants fans never felt he was one of theirs, viewing him as a guy past his prime, his radio skills dulled by years doing TV. Lindsey actually saw the handwriting on the wall before his first broadcast. In a book he wrote, he recalled pulling into the parking lot at Candlestick Park and telling the security guard he was one of the team broadcasters. The security guard responded by saying, "You don't look like Lon Simmons."

He didn't sound like Lon, either. But who did? Lon sounded like baseball, and it wasn't just the richness of his voice. Lon's rhythm gave you time to contemplate the next pitch or let your mind drift toward images of hot dogs and beer or a great catch or the sound of the ball popping the catcher's mitt. Along with Russ Hodges, he was there for the birth of major-league baseball in the Bay Area. Thousands of kids grew up with Lon and now hoped someday he would be back in the game. But would Bill be open to pairing up with another Bay Area heavyweight? Roy broached the possibility.

"Oh my God, that would be terrific," Bill told Roy.

Roy was relieved to rule out any concern that Bill would "have a competitive thing with Lon," as he put it. When they sat down to decide who would call which innings, it was clear Lon didn't have a competitive thing with Bill either — he never did. Lon recalled to me one season back in the '60s when, because the Warriors TV broadcasts didn't want Bill and his beard onscreen, Lon was asked to come in and do the play-by-play of telecasts.

"I did it," Lon told me, "but about halfway through the year I said, 'You know, if I was watching this game on TV, I'd turn down the sound and listen to Bill King.' That was the last year I did *that*. The TV station decided they didn't want someone plugging someone else on the air. But I was just saying what I felt."

When the two were signed up to do the A's, Bill, Lon and Roy went into a room at the Coliseum and Roy drew nine boxes on a piece of paper. Of course Bill was going to open and close the broadcast. "Bill, you do one and two," Roy said. "Lon, you do three and four." When they finished the meeting it was agreed that Bill would do innings one, two, five, six and nine and that Lon would do three, four, seven and eight. "That was fine with Lon," Roy told me. "We all have an ego, but he wasn't hung up on it."

Suddenly, the A's were relevant, with Berkeley High product Billy Martin orchestrating "Billyball" on the field and with two legends in the booth, although unless you were an ardent fan of the Giants from two decades earlier, you probably had no idea that Bill had ever broadcast baseball.

"Everyone in our neighborhood would listen to Bill on the radio and turn down the sound on the TV during Raiders games," said Bay Area television producer David Feldman. "But we were astonished when he was hired by the A's. The other sports, football and basketball, were so fast and baseball was slower. And nobody knew he had done baseball before. So we were shocked and thrilled when he got hired by the A's."

It wasn't just the fans who were thrilled. Oakland has always been fertile ground for producing athletes, and going back to the '60s you could have built a great club around an outfield of Oakland guys like Frank Robinson, Curt Flood and Vada Pinson, who played together in the 1950s at McClymonds High, the same school where future NBA Hall of Famer Bill Russell was making a name for himself. The list of future A's born in Oakland in the '50s includes Dave Stewart ('59), Dennis Eckersley ('54) and Shooty Babitt ('59). Rickey Henderson was born in Chicago on Christmas Day 1958, but his family moved to Oakland when he was seven and he starred in all three sports at Oakland Tech and played with Babitt at Bushrod Park, where the Raiders also used to practice in the early '60s. For all of them, growing up in Oakland, listening to games on the radio was a constant. For all of them, Bill was the voice of sports.

"I played ball most of the time during whatever season it was, and I would come home and my parents, especially my mom, would be listening to a game," Babitt, a teammate of Rickey's on the '81 A's, told me. "Whether it was football or basketball, Bill King was always the commentator. His voice was synonymous with sports for me."

Attendance spiked to 1.3 million in Shooty's only year in the big leagues, despite a work stoppage that cost one-quarter of the season. It didn't hurt that the A's season got off to a rollicking start. They opened on the road, sweeping Minnesota and the Angels, and came home 8–0. Fifty thousand fans packed every nook and cranny of a refurbished Coliseum for the home opener, and the A's crushed the Mariners, 16–1, behind right-hander Steve McCatty. After the game, Bill sat in the broadcast booth of an empty Coliseum with Roy Eisenhardt. "Roy's eyes were just glistening as he looked out at the field and reflected on a ninth consecutive victory," Bill remembered with Marty Lurie. "The sprinklers had been turned on, the grass was green and it appeared the sky was the limit for that A's ballclub."

The mood was much more somber down in the Mariners clubhouse, where a twenty-two-year-old outfielder named Dave Henderson was quietly hiding his feeling of satisfaction. He had done something in the game you dream about, but you don't celebrate a personal accomplishment after your team has just been drubbed by fifteen runs in front fifty thousand fans.

Dave was from the small Central Valley town of Dos Palos, a two-hour drive from the Coliseum, and he felt like all of Dos Palos was in the stands for his first game in Oakland. Dave didn't listen to a lot of sports when he was a kid — he was too busy playing — but he certainly knew of Bill's prominence in the Bay Area. Now he had just played in his seventh major-league game and up in the broadcast booth Bill had called Dave's first home run, a shot over the left-field wall in the top of the second inning. It was a dream come true, but none of Dave's family members or friends, all in attendance that night, had heard Bill's call.

But the next time the Mariners played the A's, Dave was in for a surprise: Bill approached him before one of the games and presented him with a cassette of the home run call. When Dave gave it a listen, he was shocked by how much Bill knew about him. Dave was a great football star in high school, but Dos Palos is a town of only around two thousand and not the kind of place that gets a lot of media attention.

"He called me the 'local hero' in the area, the football player and the baseball player. So he knew my whole background. Not the stuff you read in the media guide — he knew things about me and I never found out how he came about that, but he must have seen me play football in high school."

That wasn't the last Dave would hear of that call. Back in Dos Palos in the off-season a banquet was held to honor some local athletes. Dave was feted as the baseball player of the year and when his name was announced, there it was, Bill's call of that memorable first home run, booming out of the speakers, filling the room.

The A's, as first-half West winners in the strike-divided 1981 season, reached the playoffs. They swept Kansas City in the first round before losing three straight to the Yankees in the ALCS, and in the span of one year the organization was light years ahead of where it was before the new ownership came in. Winning was a big factor, but the men behind the radio mics had a lot to do with it, too. It seemed inconceivable to many, including me, that two broadcasting giants like Bill and Lon could be paired. It went against the grain. Normally, a broadcast is constructed with a Number 1 announcer and a Number 2, or a play-by-play man and an analyst. The A's had two Number 1s!

"They were like gods to me," said A's equipment manager and team historian Steve Vucinich. "I remember my friends in the Bay Area were just amazed you could put these two guys together. It was like merging NBC and CBS." Dolich, for one, counts the pairing of Bill and Lon as the single most important move ownership made to establish credibility in the market and the best tool they could find to bring fans back to the Coliseum.

I was working in Petaluma but living a little farther north in Santa Rosa when Bill and Lon started together. The radio broadcasts were my link to the team, especially because I lived in a remote area without cable TV. Those broadcasts were the soundtrack of my summers and Bill and Lon sounded like summer should sound. Wintertime is cold and can be harsh and when the sun sets you barely notice it, but in the summer the days are long and the twilight is soothing, just like listening to Bill and Lon broadcast baseball. They were different. Bill, much more intense and studious and Lon, the dry wit, the laconic tempo and the richest baseball voice ever. The contrast in styles meant "I didn't have two machine guns," Roy said.

"Bill was incredible about the amount of detail he was able to provide without making it just totally confusing," former A's general manager Sandy Alderson recalled for this book. "Lon was more of a generalist. If you ever heard Lon Simmons broadcast 49er football, on a one-hundred-yard run he'd miss about sixty yards, but you'd enjoy it because there was so much excitement. Bill was more into detail."

Andy Dolich referred to them as "A and L" for amphetamine and Librium. Growing up in New York, he'd listened to announcers like Marty Glickman and Marv Albert who were "triple threats" and worked baseball, basketball and football. "I had heard about this triple threat in the Bay Area," Andy told me. "I didn't know Lon and I think it takes longer for people to appreciate Lon's incredible sense of humor. Bill King, he was a triple threat of Biblical proportions."

The pairing of Lon and Bill was typical of the A's fearless approach to doing things in the '80s. They respected baseball smarts, but they weren't lashed to all the old ways of doing business. It was that attitude that led them to hire Jay Alves, a recent University of Arizona graduate in radio and television who had grown up in Half Moon Bay, California, listening to Bill and Lon.

Jay joined the A's in August 1981 for a series at Comiskey Park in Chicago and carried with him a newfangled device that one might have expected the tradition-bound Bill King to scoff at — a primitive Apple computer with a green screen. Jay lugged it around in a large case that is still used today by the A's athletic trainers to transport some of their gear from town to town. He sat upstairs in the booth with the engineer, Chuck Suggs, and installed monitors for Bill and Lon down below. Using a system developed by Richard Cramer, Jay would put things up on the screen he thought were interesting. Like, if a pitcher was warming up in the bullpen, Jay would research the next five hitters and their lifetime averages against the pitcher warming up. Or he'd look for possible pinch-hitters and their numbers. At the bottom of the screen Jay would list current statistics and lifetime averages.

Nobody was doing this stuff back then. The funny thing was, these first baby steps in what would become a revolution in baseball were often misinterpreted at the time. Billy Martin assumed Alves was a spy for management who came armed with fancy equipment. Others thought if he had a computer he must be running the show.

"I was in every magazine you could think of," Jay said. "Computer magazines, science magazines. CBS News came out and did a story on me. The story spread that I was telling the manager what to do and there were going to be computers in the dugout. It got out of control." That was the better story, but in reality, Jay told me, "ninety-five percent of what I did was for the broadcasters."

Bill King, an analog man in a burgeoning digital age, was naturally reticent at first. His routine up to then was to prepare two or three weeks ahead of a series, updating his box scores and getting an idea of who was hot and who wasn't. Jay's machine saved Bill some work by putting the last ten to twenty-five games on the computer with trends and matchups. Lon's style was more conversational, so for him Jay would put information on the computer he thought Lon could use in a story he told on the air. But it was Bill, who was much more into the statistical side of things back then, who found the computer information the perfect adjunct to his big yellow binder, where he kept all his bios and clippings.

"Bill King was the most prepared, most organized broadcaster I've ever been around," Jay told me. "He was amazing."

The way the game is now, by the time I finish our A's postgame show, half the team is already in the parking lot heading home. Bill, Lon and Jay used to sit in the booth after games and Jay got a baseball education as they rehashed the games. "It would have been great radio to have a mic up there," Jay said. Although Bill was known by most fans then as the Warriors and Raiders announcer who had recently joined the A's, Jay said Bill's true allegiance came out in those sessions. "You could tell baseball was Bill's first love," he said. "It was amazing the passion and love of the game that came out of those guys."

When Bill returned to baseball with the A's in '81 it was the rekindling of a romance that began when he was as kid in the Midwest. "Baseball was the sport that had a hold on America," Hank Greenwald said, "and so we grew up with it and we grew up with it on the radio and were very strongly influenced by radio."

In the first half or so of the twentieth century, radio was where history was captured, and that sense of the medium's role was deeply engrained in Hank and Bill's generation. The A's presented Bill with plenty of big moments to deliver to fans, and he rose to the occasion. When Dave Stewart was etching his name into the record book in 1990 — not once but twice — Bill was there to make the calls:

> **"** *The Blue Jays, one out left here, five-nothing A's. Swung on, high drive center field, Dave Henderson signaling, 'It's mine, it's mine.' It is!! And it's a no-hitter for Dave Stewart in the Skydome, this June 29, 1990. The fifth no-hitter in the history of the Oakland Athletics, and it comes six years and nine months to the day since the last one, pitched by Mike Warren in 1983."*

> **"** *Here it is. Ground ball right of second, Gallego's over, has it, throws in time. Stewart with a triumphant gesture! Dave Stewart's twentieth victory, a signal moment in a career of signal moments!"*

The next season Bill got a chance to be part of an even bigger historical moment, but only thanks to Lon's generosity. On May 1, 1991, Rickey Henderson was on the verge of breaking Lou Brock's career stolen base record, just one behind, and it was Lon's inning. Rickey stole second but Lon and Bill had the sense that he wasn't done. Seamlessly, Lon turned the play-by-play over to Bill, recognizing with characteristic generosity that Bill had calls in the football and basketball halls of fame, and it was time for one to make it to Cooperstown.

Bill didn't miss a beat:

> 66 *Rickey goes, the pitch taken, he's going to have it, he does! Rickey Henderson, no contest, steals third base, jerks the bag from its moorings and holds it aloft, representing Number 939. Rickey pounds it with his left fist, hands it to equipment manager Frank Ciensczyk, who gives him a big hug."*

Ray Fosse was sitting between them that day. "Nobody knew it was going to happen, Bill didn't know, I didn't know," he recalled of Lon's handoff. "But Bill never left the booth during a game. He never wanted to miss anything and even though Lon surprised him, he was so into the game that he was very quick to take over."

Thirty-one years earlier, Lon Simmons was in his third year as a big-league broadcaster. His partner, Russ Hodges, had seen it all, including the Shot Heard Round the World. It was Lon's birthday and it was Juan Marichal's major-league debut. Lon did the third, fourth and seventh innings and Marichal, pitching against the Phillies, had a no-hitter through seven. At that point, Russ told Lon to continue with the play-by-play, since Lon had never broadcast a no-hitter and this might be his shot. Marichal lost the no-hitter but Lon never forgot the birthday present from his partner.

"You could have gone through the entire list of announcers in major-league baseball," Lon recalled in Steve Bitker's *The Original San Francisco Giants,* which chronicled the early days of the Giants in San Francisco, "and never found anybody else who would have done that."

It was clear to anyone who listened or spent time around Bill and Lon that these were two men of great character. Mickey Morabito joined the A's when Billy Martin brought him from New York to do

PR for the A's in 1980. He's still with the team and his fondness for both men and his memories of Lon and Bill are right at the top of his personal list when he reflects on his time in the game. He said of Lon giving that call of Rickey's steal to Bill: "That's the way Lon was as a human being and a broadcast partner. He didn't have an ego in stuff like that and that's one reason the pair worked so well together. This guy was the personification of class."

That didn't mean they always understood everything about each other. One of Bill's many quirks was that he never felt a car was worth more than $500, and for Lon that made for some hair-raising moments. "Bill wouldn't have a car if he couldn't see the pavement through the floorboards," Lon said for this book. "He always had an old car. The chrome would fall off and he'd pick it up and put it in the backseat."

After a game at Candlestick, the lot had cleared out and Lon's gleaming new Ford convertible was parked next to Bill's old clunker in the media parking lot.

"I can't start the car," Bill told Lon. "I need a push."

Lon saw no way to decline.

"Our bumpers got hooked up," Lon recalled. "Bill took off and my bumper went with him. I never heard, 'Thanks for the push' or, 'What happened to the bumper?' I guess it fell off and he never knew."

On New Year's Day 1978, veteran Bay Area broadcaster Bruce Macgowan was on the Raiders' team flight back from a bitter loss to the Broncos in the AFC championship game when he realized he might be stuck at the airport since he didn't know anyone who could give him a ride home to Marin to pick up his car — no one but Bill.

"So I went over to his aisle on the plane and asked if there was any way I could hitch a ride with him over to Marin," Bruce recalled for this book. "Bill told me it would be no problem. When we picked up our bags at the airport and got out to Bill's car, I was stunned when I saw the condition of his old jalopy. It was faded, had dents, a crack in the windshield and a coat hanger was functioning as the antenna for the radio!

"'Hop in,' he happily told me after we put our suitcases in the back. 'As you can see, I'm not big on cars. For me, they're strictly for transportation and if I can get from point A to point B, that's all I need them for,' he explained.

"I nodded in agreement, as cars had never been high on my list of priorities either, although I wondered if this old 'flivver' was going to be adequate enough to get us home.

"Even with the windows up, it was cool in the car driving up the freeway, but as soon as we got on to the Richmond Bridge heading over to San Rafael I really began to notice a lot of cold air rushing in. It seemed to be coming from below my feet and when I looked down, much to my surprise there was a hole in the floorboard the size of a human fist, through which much of that cool air was whooshing in.

"'Bill, do you realize you've got a hole in the floor of this car?' I asked incredulously.

"'Oh that, don't worry about it, Bruce. That's just natural air-conditioning!' he chuckled."

The A's playoff appearance in 1981 was their last until the Bash Brothers were in full flower in 1988. In the interim, the A's featured managers like Steve Boros and Jackie Moore and the results on the field were pedestrian at best. That changed in 1986 when a decision was made in Chicago that would be felt in Oakland for the next nine years. Tony La Russa was fired by the White Sox after a slow start that year but he was only out of baseball for three weeks. Sandy Alderson hired the brilliant and savvy La Russa to manage the A's and the move proved to be seminal.

That was also the year in which Ray Fosse joined the A's radio team and I can still hear Bill's words and the delight in his voice on days when Ray was with us in the booth. "Ah, a Fosse day!" he would exclaim.

Ray Fosse, at just twenty-three, had been on his way to becoming one of the greatest catchers of all-time, the American League's answer to Johnny Bench, when Pete Rose barreled into him during the 1970 All-Star Game in Cincinnati. He wasn't quite the same player after the collision, although he was an All-Star once again and won his second Gold Glove the next year — but when he got traded to the A's just before the start of the 1973 season he quickly became a great teammate and a reliable backstop and clutch hitter on two world championship teams.

It was Andy Dolich who approached Ray about working with Bill and Lon on radio in 1986, five years after Ray had retired from the game. He had gotten a taste of doing color when he joined Monte Moore in the A's booth while he was on the disabled list in 1974 with an injury that was the result of breaking up a fight between Reggie Jackson and Billy North in the visiting clubhouse in Detroit.

Lon orchestrated Ray's next radio appearance. Ray's duties on the broadcast were supposed to be confined to doing the pregame and postgame shows ("Bill and Lon didn't do windows," Ray said) and sitting in the booth and observing the legends. Bill had finished the first two innings of a game at the Metrodome in Minneapolis when Lon asked the engineer if Ray's mic was working. The engineer responded in the affirmative.

"Well I'm sure he has a few things to say," Lon said, and that's how Ray Fosse's career as an analyst began.

"Ray was the perfect personality to go with Bill and Lon," Andy said. "He is also a good man and when you are going through a baseball season, he was another person that you didn't have to create another room to get their ego into." But despite Ray's success on the field, he was a rookie in the booth and he felt like it, especially when he sat down next to someone with the stature of Bill King.

"It was very intimidating to me, because here was the broadcaster who had done the Warriors and the Raiders and all three at one time," Ray recalled. "I knew that Bill always wanted to set the stage the first inning and I wouldn't say anything unless he asked me something. Over time there was the matter of comfort of knowing when I could step in and say something. When Bill would say, 'It was a Ray day, there is no TV and Ray is going to be with us,' that really made me feel great."

Along the way, he was getting a broadcasting lesson from Bill. "He didn't know it, but the things I do now are a result of learning from him," Ray said. What he learned more than anything was how to prepare. When he did those games with Monte while back in '74 he figured broadcasting was easy, that all he had to do was show up in the booth and talk. Watching Bill and his diligence and attention to detail, Ray realized he had to bring something insightful to each broadcast and had to be concise.

"On radio, when the pitcher raised his arm I knew when to shut up." He also learned from Bill's ability to paint a picture. The wordsmith in Bill encouraged Ray to develop his vocabulary. "He would say, 'You know, Ray, if you learn one word a day you'll be fine.'"

Even as he grew as a broadcaster himself, Ray continued to be amazed by Bill. Bill's intros, seemingly scripted but actually never written out, would amaze him. "It was remarkable," Ray told me. "It just flowed out of his mouth."

The A's had an assortment of broadcasters in the '80s besides Bill and Lon, including the great slugger and Hall of Famer Harmon Killebrew. Bill always felt that Harmon, as modest and unassuming a gentleman as you could find, had potential on the air that never came to fruition. Once on a cab ride back to the team hotel Harmon began to tell Bill a great story from his playing days. Bill was enthralled. "Harmon," he said at the end of the tale, "it would be great if you could tell some of those stories on the air."

The decision to give up television after the 1987 season was easy for Bill, and Lon was more than happy to follow suit. No doubt radio played much more into Bill's strength, which was calling the action and being descriptive. He got no enjoyment out of TV, but he was a team player and did it for six years because he knew it helped build the A's brand in the Bay Area. On TV he felt like he was the caption for the pictures, nothing but an instrument of the director. This certainly wasn't personal with Bill, who was friendly with the A's TV production crew, one of the finest in baseball.

"Radio is the way that people learn baseball," Roy Eisenhardt told me. "Television is training people to watch baseball as though they're watching '24.' If there's a low point now, they get bored.

And radio doesn't do that — radio sustains it. Usually when you're listening to the radio, you're doing something else."

Bill's move to radio full time coincided with the development of a great team on the field. With shrewd drafting the A's developed a slew of great young players, and Sandy Alderson orchestrated the acquisition of veterans and reclamation projects that became the final parts that fit perfectly with the sturdy foundation of home-grown talent. One of those players was the kid who had hit his first major-league home run at the Coliseum in 1981. Dave Henderson had moved from the Mariners to the Red Sox (where he hit one of the game's most famous homers in the 1986 playoffs against the Angels) and then to the Giants before he joined the A's in 1988 as a free agent. He quickly established a unique rapport with Bill.

"We just joked around a lot," Hendu told me, "I called him 'the Devil' because of the mustache and stuff, and as you know I have a pretty good sense of humor. Somebody called me the 'Gap-Toothed Center Fielder' and he jumped onto that moniker. We just had that funny relationship of razzing each other a little bit. Some friendly humor when we'd meet before games or after games."

The Bash Brothers were the poster boys for those teams, but the anchor of any club is its starting rotation. Bob Welch had some success with the Dodgers but he flourished with the A's. He had great respect for Bill and this went beyond Bill's ability to broadcast.

"If I had a hitter I had trouble with, I'd ask Bill how I should pitch him," Bob told me during spring training in 2013. "He always had a good answer. There was never a time when I didn't think he was totally in the game."

Another of those veterans was Dennis Eckersley, who became the best closer in the game starting in 1988. "Bill and I became close," Eck told me, "and one reason was because we both liked to bronze and so we spent a lot of time together at the pool on the road."

Eck had many moments of vindication after Kirk Gibson's home run in a career that would earn him first-ballot enshrinement in Cooperstown, but he'll always be tied to Gibson for what happened in the ninth inning of Game One of the 1988 World Series. As a crippled Gibson was limping around the bases, Vin Scully was telling his NBC audience, "In a year that has been so improbable, the impossible has happened."

Vinny's call was spot-on and so was Jack Buck's exclamation on CBS Radio: "I don't believe what I just saw!" Those two highlights have been played over and over again and it's hard to separate the moment from the calls, and, thus, Gibson and Scully and Buck have become confluent in a sort of baseball immortality. Bill should have joined them on that summit, but nobody ever remembers Bill's call because you never hear it. I was listening when Scully called Sandy Koufax's perfect game against the Cubs in 1965, and his ninth inning was so brilliant that it has been included in anthologies of the greatest baseball writing. Only, of course, it wasn't written. Nor was Bill's call of one of the most memorable at-bats in the continuous and suspenseful epic that is baseball, Eckersley vs. Gibson, circa 1988:

66 *Eckersley has lost Mike Davis and walked him, ball four. And now the tying run is on and here comes Gibson and a high moment of drama approaching, the crowd rising as one here at Dodger Stadium! This is the man who fired the engine all year long.*

"Mike Davis, capable of the steal, now at first base. Eckersley, who has a relatively slow leg kick; Lasorda will be looking for the possibility of a steal. Two out, but the Dodgers still alive. In twenty postseason games, Gibson has six homers and nineteen RBIs. Two big homers against the Mets in the Championship

Series. *The ability to rise to the occasion and overcome physical maladies.*

"Gibson stands to the side and takes a few practice swings. Eckersley giving up that base on balls on a rare moment. Now he sets, Davis doesn't go and here's a swing and a foul coming back upstairs and it's strike one.

"Eckersley walked only eleven batters in the regular season and two of those were intentional. He walked two in the American League playoffs over six innings and now he's walked Davis. Gibson waiting, now a throw to first, just a lob toss, a token. Davis a swift runner at first base, Gibson up there left-handed waiting. Swing and another pop-up foul out of play to the left and the count now to strike two, oh and two.

"Davis stole only seven bases this year but he stole twenty-seven in one of his best years with the A's, thirty-three in another. He has the lead and Eckersley throws over there and Davis is back standing. The Dodgers took a quick two-run lead on Hatcher's first-inning homer, Canseco grand slammed in the A's second, the Dodgers picked up one in the sixth and here we are, ninth inning.

"Eckersley with a two-strike count to Gibson. Now he sets and throws over to first again and now Davis is forced to dive back into the bag, indicating he might have had running on his mind. When he's healthy he's one of the fastest runners in baseball. That time he was going at a very controlled jog halfway down the first-base line. Even has a slightly noticeable off-gait when he walks. That problem is a strain of the medial collateral ligament and tissue in his right knee. Game Seven of the National League series when he sustained that. That knee has since been injected with cortisone and xylocaine. They'll examine him tomorrow. Right now here's the exam: Outside with a fastball on the next pitch.

"Here's a snap throw to first base and Davis has strayed away but he's back diving in. Ron Hassey rifling one down there. The outfield is straight-away and deep. Eckersley taking the sign, Gibson up there battling. The pitch, Davis goes, fly ball foul down the left side out of play. Count remains at one ball and two strikes.

"In his earlier years in the American League the A's were able to pitch

Gibson up and in with hard fastballs successfully off the plate. But in this kind of a ballgame that's a risky proposition because if you don't get it in the right place, a guy such as Gibson can pull it deep on you. Eckersley continues to stay outside and here's the next pitch, ball two it's wide and the battle goes on. Two balls and two strikes and Steve Sax, one of the better contact hitters, on deck.

"Four to three A's! This is the out Eckersley needs. Davis at first moves out to the lead and again draws a throw and he's back diving. The base on balls to Davis rekindled life after Eckersley retired the first two batters. This is where he wants to get a decision, he doesn't want to go to a full count and then get Davis, a fast man, running.

"Here it is, Davis running anyway, ball three no throw as Davis steals second base! The pitch was away and Hassey is acting as if it were ball four and he's talking to plate umpire Doug Harvey now. He looked around at Harvey, perhaps he thought Gibson was nicked by that pitch.

"Let's see the replay. Oh Gibson was across the plate! Gibson was leaning out over the plate blocking any avenue for Hassey to really get off a good throw. So rather than risk an errant heave he didn't throw it and Hassey is telling Harvey he thought he was interfered with. Now it's three-two as Gibson has battled back from two strikes. Oh, the moment is reaching excruciatingly dramatic proportions! The tying run is now at second and it will not take much to get Davis in.

"Eck has not thrown that backdoor slider to Gibson. Here's the pitch, swung on drive right field deep! Way back!! Gone! Gibson has won it on a home run into the right-field pavilion and the Dodgers have won the first game of the World Series! Gibson greeted by the entire roster at home plate! The hobbled hero battling Eckersley to three and two and then launching a shot into the right-field pavilion between the three-sixty and three-seventy marks! A devastating blow with the A's just one strike from victory!

"And the Dodgers now continue what Lasorda has been labeling, "The Miracle Performance." Gibson is mobbed and gets a big kiss from Lasorda and the A's have been thrown a challenge here tonight, one that they have to come back to tomorrow *and try to answer when they encounter Orel Hershiser. What an incredible finish at Dodger Stadium!*

"And so all of Lasorda's preaching and the Dodgers obviously have to believe now. A walk to ex-A's outfielder Mike Davis and a three-two home run by Gibson. Here in the ninth: two runs, one hit, no errors and nobody left on base. Final score: Los Angeles five, Oakland four."

It was only nine words, but Bill's immediate prelude to the home run, when he said, "Eck has not thrown that backdoor slider to Gibson," was brilliant. It was a nuanced example of grasping the situation and having a feel for the actors in the drama. Sure enough, it was a backdoor slider that Gibson hit. Bill had an intrinsic feel for that moment, as did Gibson who remembered, just before the pitch, a suggestion from Dodgers scout Mel Didier: Look for the backdoor slider when Eckersley gets to three-and-two on a left-handed hitter.

It seemed like hours to Bill before the crowd quieted down, but it only took a few seconds for him to understand how much Gibson's shot would shape the rest of the Series. During the commercial break, Bill whispered to Lon, "We just lost the World Series." Bill was right, even though it was just the first game, but there would be redemption for the A's and it came the next year against the team on the other side of San Francisco Bay.

Bill King had a complicated relationship with the Giants and much of it came with some associated good fun. He didn't like the Giants, let's be clear about that. I think most of it came from his competitiveness and that went back to when he was playing ball as a kid. When he joined the A's the team was fighting for acceptance in a two-team market and he was also the most anti-establishment person of all time (Tom Meschery told me that Bill could have run for president of the Libertarian Party; that is if Bill had any respect for the political process), and he certainly considered the Giants the establishment. This was a little ironic, because three of his closest friends and favorite announcers — Lon, Hank and Jon Miller — have been the voices of the team. But as I've written, Bill never saw anything or did anything halfway. There were times, I swear, he liked it more when the Giants lost than when the A's won. If our engineer Mike Baird sent word through Bill's headset that the Giants had been beaten, Bill's face would light up. "My night has been made!"

But on the air it was a different story. At his core, Bill was a professional broadcaster and he was a professional about the thing with the Giants. He would often show me how he listed the teams on the "out of town" scoreboard that Baird kept on two sides of a piece of paper. This was always done in pencil, by the way — Bill never understood my preference for ink. The Giants were always at the top of the National League side.

"We're in the same market, and I'm sure some of their fans are listening, so I am always going to give the Giants' score first in the National League," Bill said.

One of the players on the A's 1989 juggernaut was a talented but underachieving reserve outfielder named Billy Beane. Billy had eschewed a scholarship offer from Stanford to sign with the Mets after they drafted him Number 1 in 1980, but by the time he joined the A's he had drifted from the Mets to the Twins and Tigers and had played in only 101 major-league games. Billy and Bill King shared an appetite for knowledge away from baseball. On the A's plane, Billy often sat in the row in front of Bill.

"I would have a lot of conversations with him and it was fascinating because it was very rarely about baseball," Beane told me. "He was a man from my own heart because he would go on the plane with flip-flops on, which I thought was perfectly fine and still do. The best part about Bill wasn't just that he was so good at his job but that he was so interesting outside of his job. His mustache epitomized that. He looked eccentric and he *was* eccentric, in a good way."

In October 1989, the Bay Area was buzzing about the first-ever World Series matchup between the A's and the Giants. There was all the hoopla surrounding the Series that you might expect, but the A's were focused squarely on wiping away the memories of that Kirk Gibson home run and the loss to the Dodgers.

"We said we would never let this happen again," Henderson told me. "We were on a mission in '89 and we pounded people and we never took the foot off the neck. We thought we were the better team in '88 and things just didn't go our way. We didn't want that to happen again, especially Dave Stewart, Carney Lansford and me."

They won the first two games in Oakland but then at 5:04 P.M. on Oct. 17, 1989, the Bay Area landscape would be changed forever. Literally. It was Game Three of the World Series and Candlestick Park started shaking. Steve Vucinich was in the visiting clubhouse and heard a roar but the clubhouse was too far back from the stands for the roar to sound like the normal pregame activity. When dust began coming out of the air vents, Steve knew it was a quake. He quickly ran outside — it was only about twenty yards from the back door of the clubhouse to a parking lot — and saw a guy up on a light standard trying to free a flag "and he was holding on for dear life."

Ken Pries, who was a producer of the A's broadcasts back then, was in the third deck with his wife, Karen, and Bill's wife, Nancy. The power went out in the visiting radio booth where the late Mike Schweizer was engineering, so Schweizer used battery power to stay on the air. In the KSFO studios, producer John Trinidad had no power and the place was shaking so badly that JT was under a table taking cover but the slatted wooden floor was rolling up and down and his fingers got caught under one of the boards; he extricated himself and focused on keeping the broadcast from going dark, which he and Schweitzer did by figuring out a way to bypass the station and send the broadcast directly from Candlestick to the KSFO transmitter.

As Candlestick cleared out, Bill stayed on the air, "in his element," Pries recalled. He had Schweizer find him a phone book and, becoming a newsman, a guiding voice for thousands of listeners, he read out emergency numbers and delivered other information for three hours while tragedy and chaos was engulfing much of Northern California. With all of the bridges closed, the team bus headed down the 101 freeway and didn't head north on 17 until they reached San Jose, forty miles away. The drive up to the East Bay took hours.

Life didn't really return to normal for months in the Bay Area, but the World Series was resumed after a ten-day break. The A's eventual sweep of the Giants delighted Bill no end, but, ironically, he was muzzled by laryngitis for the last two games. With the A's on the verge of winning the Series, Bill was unable to broadcast but he made himself useful by passing notes to Lon during the broadcast.

Hank Greenwald was the voice of the Giants back then, and so he was in the Giants booth when the Series resumed and Bill was in the A's booth writing notes for Lon. When we spoke for this book, Hank recalled a similar experience with Bill "back in '69 or '70." Bill came down with laryngitis on a Warriors road trip. Hank remembers doing three or four games for Bill, including one at the old Boston Garden. Bill was passing notes to Hank. "Stuff like, 'So and so set a good screen,'" Hank said. Then late in the game Bill was really getting into it. He passed one note that said: "THAT WAS A TERRIBLE CALL!"

CHAPTER 7

L.A., BABY

Skins deep in their own territory, on their own twelve yard line, twelve seconds left in the half: Theismann back, looks off to the left, he fires it out there. Intercepted! Jack Squirek! Touchdown Raiders! I don't believe it!! Holy Toledo!!!

ill King had to have been the most set-in-his ways man I ever met, so I figured that the disruption in his schedule when the Raiders moved to Los Angeles for the 1982 season would be a major hurdle for him to overcome. After all, up until then Bill had been doing the impossible — he was the voice of three major-league teams and loving every minute of it. He may have disdained driving, but since Warriors, Raiders and A's home games were all played in the same complex in Oakland, he'd had only a thirty-five minute commute from his home in Sausalito on days when traffic was light. Now he would have to fly to every Raiders game, home or away. But what did I know? Bill not only took the move to L.A. in stride, he loved every minute of calling L.A. Raiders games just as he had loved every minute of calling Oakland Raiders games, and also did some of his best work in Southern California. Bill the consummate San Franciscan, at home in Los Angeles! Who would have thought?

For many people, it was incomprehensible to think that Al Davis might move the Raiders away from Oakland, where the team enjoyed as passionate a following as any in the NFL. The issue came to a head during a Raiders home game against Denver on December 2, 1980. That day, "a demonstration by almost everyone in a crowd of 51,583 upstaged the football game," as William N. Wallace reported in the *New York Times*. Al Davis, the article continued, "was the target of the demonstration because of his intention to move the franchise to the Los Angeles Coliseum. Almost all the spectators in the stadium, acting with precision and intensity, twice displayed placards reading 'Save Our Raiders.' — once two minutes before halftime, once again two minutes before the end of the game."

I asked Bill many times about the Raiders' move to L.A. and he told me he welcomed the opportunity to work in a new market. For Bill, the joy of calling games, of being *in* those moments, was not something he wanted to give up. Bill was hugely loyal to Al Davis and so he was inclined to endorse the move south, but more than anything he wanted to keep doing the games. The Raiders could have moved to Omaha, and Bill would have felt a powerful tug to follow them there. L.A. was enticing, not for the sun or the food, but for the chance to work and be tested professionally in the nation's second largest market.

There might have been fans out there who wished Bill had spurned the Raiders and Davis, who was viewed by some as nothing less than a traitor, but the ones I've talked to were overjoyed to have Bill stay on. As painful as it was to cheer for a team that was now four hundred miles away, breaking up is hard to do when the emotional commitment is so deep. Having Bill in L.A. with the team made it easier for the fans to hang on to a share of what for many was a lifelong investment.

Bay Area columnist Monte Poole grew up in Oakland and became a huge Raiders fan because of Bill, just like another Oakland kid of that era, the great A's pitcher Dave Stewart. Monte was so in love with the team and found Bill's broadcasts so spellbinding that he and his friends couldn't wait to go out and play if the Raiders won that day. But if the Raiders lost they were so bummed that they often didn't want to do anything except stay in their rooms. Monte went to high school at Castlemont, less than five miles from the Coliseum. The Raiders were *his* team and he felt Bill belonged to Oakland.

"We were kids playing football in the street," Monte remembered. "And when the Raiders were on TV we would literally listen to the radio broadcast while the game was on. ... What I remember most were the fantastic calls. The George Blanda year, when every Sunday Blanda was doing something to win a football game and Bill became synonymous with those miracles. The thing that captured me most is that when the Raiders lost, it ruined the day. It made Sunday suck."

The Raiders were incredibly popular in those days and the games were always sold out so it was hard for Monte to get a ticket, but he had Bill to listen to and that made it all OK. "He was the connection," he said. "He was the link between me and many other fans and the football team. I know I felt energized and a lot of it had to come from him, from listening to him describe the game."

"I was a big, big Raiders fan," Stewart told the *San Francisco Chronicle*. "Man, with football, he was the Raiders to me. Listening to his broadcasts, it was like you were on the field and you could see the guys cut. 'He's at the five, the fifteen, the twenty!' I didn't even want to watch the games on TV — because I could see it and feel it in Bill's voice."

The Raiders, born in 1960, gave Oakland an identity. Those were different times. Players had off-season jobs and started local businesses and hung out and were recognizable figures around town. Art Spander worked in the Bay Area for the *Chronicle* starting in 1966 and was on the Raiders beat from 1977 to 1979. "The Raiders were the social event of the East Bay," he told me. "Women came to the game and were all dressed up almost like a movie premiere. It was a huge thing for them. The Raiders gave the area cachet. The A's didn't come until '68. People didn't know where Oakland was. You said, 'I lived in San Francisco' or, 'I'm from the San Francisco area.' The Raiders then started winning and people knew where Oakland was."

Losing the Raiders was a tough pill for their Bay Area fans to swallow. The thing that struck Monte Poole was the sense that even if someday they might return, things could never be the same.

"Since they moved to L.A. there has been no team so ingrained in the community," Monte told me.

For the players and coaches, the move was anything but easy. Since the team practiced in Northern California that first year, they were either flying to L.A. or another city, making every game a road game.

"It wasn't an easy thing to do," Tom Flores, the head coach at the time, told me. "People don't realize how tough that was, and plus it wasn't very glamorous. You're living in a hotel and you go back after wins and your family all goes home, and you look at the walls in a hotel."

When word had started to filter out that the Raiders were seriously considering Los Angeles, George Nicholaw, the general manager of KNX Radio in L.A., had the foresight to roll the dice and acquire the Raiders' radio rights as a network. Nicholaw's prescience paid off when the move became official and he was able to work out a deal to become the flagship station of the Raiders network.

This was huge for KNX and also for the Raiders, because — like KCBS in San Francisco — KNX had a big signal, was a CBS-owned-and-operated station and had plenty of prestige as the Number 1 all-news station in the market. It was a given that Bill would come south with the team and remain the play-by-play man. The bigger question was what to do about an analyst.

Monty Stickles, the old NFL tight end, had done the color at the end of the Raiders' run in Oakland. Monty was a popular figure in the Bay Area — besides working with Bill, he had spent many years doing sports reports on local radio and television and his tastes were almost as eclectic as Bill's. He collected art, loved to cook and was into jazz. So when Monte was fully engaged, he and Bill made for a good team. I really enjoyed listening to those guys, but I learned later that Bill had his moments of frustration. Bill never accepted anything less than total dedication from everyone else in the booth, and he told me that there were a few times when

Monty's focus would wane and he would have to reel the big guy back in, once even threatening to do the broadcast himself.

Rich Marotta was an established broadcaster at the time of the Raiders' move, having done color for the L.A. Kings and before that Air Force football. He was in the right place at the right time, as the KNX sports director, when the Raiders announced their move. Nicholaw, wanting to "bridge the old and the new," felt that having an L.A. person on the broadcasts would help make the transition more seamless. So KNX went to bat with Al Davis for Marotta to do color with Bill.

It was also a matter of convincing Bill. Marotta's recollection of his first meeting with Bill had a familiar ring to it, as if Scotty Stirling were telling the story of Davis' first encounter with Bill at training camp in Santa Rosa. Marotta had a pretty good idea what Bill looked like. Still, he showed up at training camp while the Raiders were practicing, spotted this scrawny guy on the sidelines wearing nothing but Speedos and flip-flops and said to himself, "This can't possibly be the great Bill King."

Once they got acquainted over lunch, Bill signed off on Rich, telling Al Davis, "You have nothing to worry about. This is going to work out just fine."

Rich decided at his first Raiders training camp that the best way to mesh with Bill was to immerse himself in his homework and also figure out creative ways to augment Bill's play-by-play in a manner that enlightened the listener rather than just regurgitating what Bill had already said. So many analysts just recap the action. Bill had that handled and then some.

"I went crazy preparing," Rich said. "Every night, I would go back to my room at training camp and I would just cut out articles and read every magazine, every single thing I could get my hands on. I felt that the bar was very high. I wanted to at least be able to do my part and do a good job and be accepted by Bill."

They talk about point guards having great court vision in basketball. Bill was like a point guard in the booth, which actually made it a little difficult for Rich because Bill saw everything on the field and would work so much into the play-by-play.

"If you listen to his calls, they are so different from the current crop, which just ticks off the number of yard lines, for example — fifty, forty-five, forty, thirty-five, thirty, twenty-five, twenty," Rich told me. "Bill fills in every single little thing and would top it off with some terrific phrase like, 'He tiptoed through the tulips into the end zone,' or, 'He did a little dipsy-do to get out of there.'

"Bill would say, 'He dodges a man at the fifty, steps out of a tackle at the forty, he now cuts over to his right down at the thirty, he's being chased by two men.' He got it all into that play-by-play and it was incredible. It forced me to really approach it in a different fashion. I mean, I really had to listen to everything he was saying."

Rich eventually came up with a good formula that allowed him to look for different things that were happening during a play. He would look away from the ball for a key block or a late hit on the quarterback and his homework on the Raiders proved valuable if there was historical context to what was unfolding on the field.

A work stoppage expunged part of the Raiders' inaugural season playing in L.A., so they didn't play their first game at the L.A. Coliseum until late in November. They finished with an 8–1 record and lost in the playoffs to the Jets, but the success of the regular season presaged what came next.

"We had a lot of excitement even though it was a strike-shortened season," Rich told me. "I don't think it was much of an adjustment. I don't think he adjusted his play-by-play or the way that he did it, but I think he really appreciated the fact that he was being heard by this whole new audience for the first time and that people were taking to him."

The Raiders went 12–4 in 1983, sending them into the playoffs, and after wins against the Steelers and Seahawks, Bill and Rich found themselves in Tampa for Super Bowl XVIII on January 22, 1984. The defending champion Redskins were favored, and for good reason — they finished the regular season 14–2. They hammered the Rams in their playoff opener and then prevailed in a tight, tense struggle against the 49ers to reach the big game.

This was Tom Flores' second Super Bowl as Raiders head coach, and besides Al Davis, it is hard to imagine anyone whose ties to the team run any deeper. He had joined the Raiders as a quarterback in the Raiders' first season of 1960 and spent six years as a player with the team before he was traded to Buffalo. After retiring as a player he served stints as an assistant with the Bills and Raiders, and it was Flores who replaced John Madden on the Raiders' sideline in 1979. Flores coached the Raiders to their second Super Bowl win in 1980, when they clobbered the Eagles in New Orleans in a game that featured an eighty-yard pass and run from Jim Plunkett to Kenny King. Bill's call:

66 *The Raiders come up third and, oh, just about four. The ball is on their own 20, Branch is to the left against Edwards, Chandler to the right against Young. Plunkett on a straight drop back, here comes the rush, steps up, can't find anybody yet, takes off running to the left, throws on the move. It's caught by King at the forty. He'll get down to the fifty. He'll go all the way! Nobody there! To the twenty, to the ten, to the five. Touchdown Raiders!!"*

That New Orleans Super Bowl was a rematch since the Raiders had lost to the Eagles in a defensive struggle, 10–7, in the regular season. Super Bowl XVIII in Tampa also matched two teams familiar with each other, and the fact that the Raiders had pretty good book on the Redskins would serve as a template that Flores and his staff used to great advantage in their preparation for the game.

Rich Marotta got to the stadium early on Super Bowl Sunday to do his prep and take part in an expanded pregame show and Bill did a double-take the first time he saw his partner. Rich was used to dressing up for his broadcasts since he has been one of the preeminent boxing commentators for years. For the Super Bowl he featured a tuxedo, thinking it might be his only chance to call the NFL's ultimate game.

"It was really funny because Bill used to take his pants off and he'd broadcast in shorts for most of the game," he said. "So there's Bill in shorts and me in a tuxedo, so it was a truly odd couple. And

Bill saw me and he goes, 'Now I know you are truly a Raider. Anybody that has the balls to do that is truly a Raider.'"

The game was no contest. It was really Marcus Allen's day. He ran for 191 yards and the crowning moment was his seventy-four-yard run, a Super Bowl record at the time. But the play that turned the momentum came with the Raiders on defense at the end of the first half. For some reason, rather than running out the clock deep in their own territory with twelve seconds remaining, the Redskins tried a screen pass. Jack Squirek disrupted the play, intercepted the pass (Marotta: "Bill's voice had in it an expression of shock.") and raced into the end zone for the Raiders:

❝ *Theismann back, looks off to the left, he fires it out there. Intercepted! Jack Squirek! Touchdown Raiders! I don't believe it!! Holy Toledo!!!"*

When the Raiders played the Redskins in the regular season they had run a similar play from their own territory, with the only difference that back in October the screen pass went to the right side. When Washington lined up with twelve seconds left in the half in the Super Bowl, the Raiders had made a change at linebacker on the suggestion of assistant coach Charlie Sumner. Sumner smelled another screen and so Squirek, who was a better cover man, was in the game instead of Matt Millen.

The fact that Bill was so quick on his calls was no accident. He had an instinctive sense of anticipation and was so interested in football strategy — and was so trusted by Flores — that he went into a broadcast well versed on the game plans.

"Usually it was Saturday, he'd come in and after a very light practice he'd ask some questions like, 'Is there anything special you're gonna do?' or, 'Is there anything that I need to know?'" Flores recalled. "I would tell him what we were trying to do. I trusted him like he was one of the team, which he was, so there was never any fear of, 'Why am I telling this guy? He might tell someone else.' I used to show him in preseason how the depth chart was going to end up. So you gave him an idea of that and a timetable, and during the regular season just a heads-up about, 'We might be doing this, or we might be doing that.'"

The second half was a canvas for Bill's artistry. Everybody remembers Allen's run, but earlier in the third quarter Bill, like his idol Monet, painted a detailed little masterpiece of a five-yard run:

" *Plunkett, giving the ball here to Allen, cuts back over the middle, three, two, one, touchdown Raiders! A marvelous piece of zigzag dancing! 28–9."*

The Raiders had a play called 17 Bob Tray O. Most everything in that game went exactly as planned for Flores and the Raiders, but Allen's seventy-four-yard run on 17 Bob Tray O was a piece of improvisation: "It was designed to be an off-tackle to the left side," Flores told me. "They blew it up so there was nothing. It was all Marcus."

" *Plunkett giving to Allen, sending him wide left. He has to reverse his field and he gets away for a moment. Comes back up the middle to the thirty, thirty-five, forty, runs past two men at the fifty, down to the forty picking up a blocker. Holy Toledo! Touchdown Raiders! Seventy-four yards!!"*

Marotta, sitting next to Bill in the booth at Tampa Stadium, craned his neck and was hanging halfway out of the booth to get a better look at the play and noticed it was the wide receiver Cliff Branch who secured the touchdown with his downfield block.

"The call on Marcus' run was just an example of perfect description, just painted the radio picture," Rich recalled twenty-nine years later. "He said Marcus was running left, he has to reverse his field, he's being chased and as soon as the play was over, he said, 'You know who gave him the block at the end? Cliff Branch.' And then he said, if I remember, 'Marcus Allen is being mobbed by his teammates!'

"It was always that ability to utilize the language. He was the greatest wordsmith I've ever been around. To be able to apply it, to snatch that perfect phrase out of the air, no matter how old he got — I don't know that he ever failed in that."

The final score of Super Bowl XVIII was 38–9. It was an out-of-this-world performance by the Raiders and their voice, who summed it all up:

> 66 *The Raiders are champions of the world in this or any other universe!"*

Jimmy Buffett sang that he "Spent four lonely days in a brown L.A. haze." Bill's time in L.A. really came in shorter spurts that were limited to flying in on Saturday, doing the game on Sunday and then flying home, unless, of course, he had Warriors or A's games to broadcast, which made for several red-eye flights and quick transitions from one sport to the other. It didn't bother him. The man had unbelievable stamina, and I think this came in part because he was in love with every aspect of his life.

He couldn't wait to get up in the morning. In fact, Ray Fosse said Bill usually slept with the blinds open so the rising sun would wake him up. He had so much energy that he could exist for days, flying all over the country doing the different sports, getting only his three or four hours of sleep a night. The secret was his ability to nap. Any place, any time. Bill could rest at the drop of a dime, on planes, the team bus, in the booth before a game. I'd get on the A's bus after a game and turn around to say something to Bill and he'd be gone. It took a split second. I resented the crap out of him for this. I think I've spent much of every baseball season wishing for just one or two more hours of sleep a night, never feeling quite rested.

Bill was ready to go for each broadcast, no matter the sport and no matter how arduous the travel. Not that he needed validation, but the success of the Raiders in their first two years in L.A. cemented Bill's acceptance in a market he had never worked in before. One thing that is axiomatic in our business: When the team is playing well the broadcasters are pretty good too. I've never heard anyone say "good broadcast" after a loss.

Working on this book I kept hearing from veteran broadcasters that Bill was more of an influence on them than I'd ever known. I was at Yankee Stadium for an A's-Yankees series in May 2013 when I sat down for breakfast with my old friend Paul Olden, who is the public address voice of Yankee Stadium. Paul did Rams play-by-play for three years on KMPC Radio in Los Angeles while Bill was doing the Raiders. As we talked he showed me an old picture of himself with Bill, circa 1990, before a Rams-Raiders game at Anaheim Stadium, Paul in coat and tie and Bill looking like he had just gotten off the boat, casual shirt unbuttoned with his sunglasses hanging from the open shirt about halfway down. Paul looks at the picture now and wishes he could have been like Bill back then, on the air and off — at ease, not caring what anyone thought about how he dressed and how he acted.

"Here I am tight and all locked up and he's nice and relaxed," Paul said. "Had I been more loose and free-flowing with just my life I probably would have had a bigger career than I had."

Paul has done play-by-play for the Indians, Angels, Yankees and Rays. Even now he isn't shy about admitting that Bill was much better than he was. He would tape Bill's games and try to learn from them: how Bill was a master of the language, speaking in complete, articulate sentences and how he could see things other play-by-play guys couldn't, like if the right tackle had moved over slightly it meant a running play was coming.

"It's that ability to analyze right on the scene quickly, and absorb and then relate it to the audience, that not many broadcasters have or had the ability to do," Paul told me. "The other thing I learned from him was to have a summation line if a big play happens. He would have these great summation lines that were part poetry, part humor, part drama and color all put together in one line. He didn't have to sit there for a few hours and think, 'What am I going to say if something big happens.' It all came out of Bill because that was his education; that's how he observed things."

I've said many times, and it is a thread that runs through this book, that I owe so much to Bill for the way he welcomed me into the booth and went out of his way to try to make me look good. It was the same for Rich Marotta and that eased his transition to working with Bill.

"I can still remember: we were up in San Francisco, it was an exhibition game and he was asking me, when we'd go to a spot, 'Do you feel comfortable? Are you getting in everything you need to say? Do you need any more time?' I couldn't believe the way he was leaning over backward to make sure that I was comfortable. And let's face it: A guy like Bill, with his reputation, he could have screwed me, he could've been a real jerk, but he was just the opposite. He did everything possible to make me comfortable."

That's also what Bill did for Ted Robinson, even though the circumstances were different. Just twenty-six, Ted was the first person to follow Bill as the voice of the Warriors. At that age, I was still two years away from deciding I had the dedication and energy to pursue a career in broadcasting. Robinson wasn't just embarking on his first season in the NBA, he was hoping not to be smothered by the huge and long shadow of Bill. (Later, when Ted joined the A's television team, Ron Bergman of the *Oakland Tribune* wrote that Bill and Ted together were like "the choirboy and the devil.")

"Bill's passing of the torch was on the front page of the *Chronicle* — not the Sporting Green, but on Page One," Ted told me. "Within all the coverage, Bill was clear in endorsing me as his successor. Amidst the deserved praise, he used his stature and respect to anoint me as worthy of a chance." Ted said that Bill fully understood what Ted called the John Wooden-Bear Bryant syndrome, which he used to illustrate that following a legend often swallowed up the successor. "So he told the Bay Area to give the kid a listen. No gesture has ever meant more in my career."

Feeling anxious about working with or following Bill is a common thread that ran through so many of my interviews for this book. Actually, a better word would be intimidating, kind of like the Silver and Black themselves. It wasn't anything Bill did. It was just that he was so damn brilliant and so accomplished that unless you were oozing with self-confidence, working with Bill would bring any self-doubt to the surface.

This applied to announcers like Robinson and Greg Papa, who became the voice of the Raiders in 1997, and it certainly affected Rich Marotta. "I was a little bit intimidated," Rich told me. "Not by Bill on a personal level, because he was so nice and funny and everything, but by his reputation and his excellence."

Papa could relate. He began broadcasting for the Warriors in 1986, so he didn't replace Bill — that daunting assignment went to Robinson (who confessed to me, "I wasn't prepared for the magnitude of it"). Greg also never worked in the same booth as Bill, but started traveling with him in 1990 when he was named to the A's television team. He would look to his left during the games and see Bill in the radio booth and ask himself how he possibly could stack up, his feeling of inadequacy manifesting itself any time he compared his vocabulary to Bill's. He felt that if listeners or viewers had a choice of Bill or him, he would have no chance.

"How could I ever have his choice of words?" Greg asked himself. "The most difficult job in sports broadcasting would have been to be Bill's partner."

By the time the 1992 season rolled around Bill and Rich were grooving like a couple of musicians who knew exactly where the other one was going from riff to riff. They also saw the writing on the wall as that season began. There was a good chance that the ownership of the radio rights would shift from Bob Speck Productions to Nederlander Sports Marketing, a company run by a guy named Roger Blaemire.

"We had been hearing rumors that Bob Speck, who had produced the broadcast for a number of years, would not be back," Marotta told me. "With that being the case, we kind of felt like we may not get renewed, which eventually turned out to be correct."

Certainly Bill would have continued with the Raiders had Nederlander not low-balled him with an offer that Bill's attorney Hugh Lawrence said was forty-seven percent of what he had been making. (Bill told me that Al Davis tried to intervene after it came to light that the Nederlander offer was unacceptable. At that point Bill, who never saw the world in any shades other than black and white, had moved on. He wasn't coming back.)

When I spoke to Bill about the end of his legendary run with the Raiders, he always talked about his warm feelings for his last Raiders broadcast. Aware of what was unfolding, he wanted to make his final game memorable. The Raiders were finishing a mediocre season but fittingly, the last game — on the day after Christmas in 1992 — was a nail-biter that the Raiders won 21–20 at RFK Stadium. Late in the game, off mic, Bill turned to Rich and said, "Partner, if this is our last game then this is as good as it gets."

"It helped that it was one of those Raider comeback wins, down to the wire," Marotta recalled of that day in D.C. "If I remember right, Vince Evans threw a touchdown pass near the end of the game to win it for the Raiders. It was a great game, they barely won. It was a throwback game for us to what we considered the best days we had had broadcasting the Raiders in '82, '83, '84, '85, the kind of win that they used to get. So there was an element of poignancy to what we were doing that day. We were on. We were doing our thing and the Raiders did their thing. As it turned out, that was it for Bill and me."

I listened a lot to Bill and Rich during the course of their eleven years together. They were tremendous. I don't think I've ever heard two broadcasters on football who complemented each other any better, and as a result I had a ritual near the end of a Raiders game if I was watching on television. I was living in the Bay Area for most of the time the Raiders were in L.A., but network broadcasts were easy to get, and so if the game was close in the fourth quarter I always turned the sound down on the set to listen to Bill. The way he could bring a close game so clearly into focus was one of his trademarks; no one could deliver the denouement like Bill.

"My great regret ever since then is that I never felt there was any reason for us not to continue," Marotta told me. "I don't think we ever got a bad review from anybody. We were extremely popular with the fans and everyone. New producers come in and they pick their people. That's kind of the way that went. I thought they insulted Bill with the offers they were making to him. I kind of thought I was going to be back on the broadcast and picked up the newspaper one day and read there was a new team, and it wasn't us."

Of course if you are an NFL aficionado today there are times when it almost feels like Bill never left. With all of the sports networks on television and the NFL's own network, it is hard to miss the old highlight shows produced by NFL Films. Bill's voice still makes those Raiders memories come alive, and even Greg Papa will tell you that Bill will always be the "Voice of the Raiders." How do you measure what a broadcaster meant to a franchise?

"What's left after the performers and the game is what people write and what people remember and most of the time people forget what they read, but they don't forget what they heard or what they saw and heard," Tom Flores told me. "Bill was the epitome of planting that in the legacy of the Raiders."

Flores has quite a legacy himself. He was an all-star player and coached two Super Bowl champions. He was one of the trailblazers in the early days of the AFL and when he took over for Madden he became the first Hispanic head coach in NFL history.

"Bill made some of the great plays in the history of the Raiders even greater with his description," Flores went on. "They were vivid. Those moments were kept alive in his voice."

By the time Bill and I started working together in 1996 he said he didn't miss doing football and basketball. Well, maybe if they had airlifted him in for the games and there were no other responsibilities. When he did the Raiders, Warriors and the A's at the same time for those three years, he involved himself so deeply in each moment you'd forget that he had an overflowing portfolio of work. There have been many instances where an employer has felt that someone trying to do multiple sports was spread too thin to be identified with their team. That was never the case for Bill. No one ever said that about Bill.

In 2012, Tom Hoffarth, the veteran radio/television columnist for the *Los Angeles Daily News*, tried to quantify the nearly impossible. Looking back over eight decades of sports on the air, Hoffarth attempted to list the ten most influential sportscasters in the L.A. market. He had to leave several great ones off the list, but he also was compelled to expand his list by one to include someone who only spent eleven years working in Southern California: Bill King.

"OK, so he turns the dial up on this to 11," Hoffarth wrote. "A Bay Area legend for doing all the big events in Oakland with his handlebar mustache, pointed gray beard and calling out the phrase 'Holy Toledo!' at just the right time. But he was one of our all-time favorites for his brief time doing the Los Angeles Raiders games, swooping in with Al Davis' NFL franchise for that run between 1982 and 1994."

CHAPTER 8

BILL AND KEN, PARTNERS

It will go as a single, but it's a long drive plating Rodriguez and the Rangers have come from an eight-run deficit to defeat the Athletics on a night that you wouldn't conjure in your wildest alcoholic dreams!

knew Bill was quirky long before we ever worked together. I found out just how quirky a few minutes into our time as partners on A's radio broadcasts. It was a Friday night in early March 1996, and I met Bill outside the A's team hotel in Phoenix. I got off on the right foot with him because I was driving, and driving of course topped the list of things Bill did with great reluctance. I needed some money and stopped at an ATM, only to see a look of incredulity on Bill's face.

"You mean you can get money out of that little machine?" he asked me.

Well, yes, Bill, I explained. You put a card in there and it was all pretty easy. He didn't trust the machines and since banks were considered institutions — you know, a "banking institution" — they had two strikes against them already.

We were headed to meet Ray Fosse for a dinner that would serve to kick off our new pairing in the A's radio booth. I had a good feeling this was all going to work out because although Bill wasn't part of the interview process for the job, we had spent several hours on the phone once I got the position. Those calls were surreal. I'd get off the phone and my wife, Denise, would ask me if I knew how long we had talked, but I never did because the time just flew by. There was an element of magic to it. The voice that had been coming out of my radio for thirty years was now coming out of my phone.

At dinner, Bill did most of the talking. Things were moving along smoothly until near the end of our main course, when he turned serious and announced there were some things he had to tell me that I could never do.

"Oh, shit," I thought. "Now he is going to lay down the law."

I had a flash of fear that my freedom in the booth might slip away before the season had even begun. I was more than prepared to assist Bill however I could as the Number 2 man, but it would create a little uneasiness if this morphed into more of a sycophantic relationship. So when Bill turned my way to deliver his talk on "the three things I couldn't do," I cringed.

Number 1: "Don't ever thank me when I throw it to you for your innings." He felt this little ritual was trite and sounded phony. "If they don't know who we are, well then there's not much we can do about that," he said.

Number 2: Never say "grand slam home run." It was redundant — a grand slam *is* a home run — and a major Bill King pet peeve. When Bill heard another announcer say it, it was like the sound of fingernails dragging down a chalkboard.

Number 3: Never use the term "early on." This also drove him nuts, since he felt the "on" was superfluous.

I exhaled. OK, I thought, I can handle that.

Most of us who have worked in the minors have had times when a legend from our youth comes to life, and for me in 1981 that moment was embarrassing. I was doing play-by-play that year for home games of the Redwood Pioneers, a Single A affiliate of the Angels. Preparing for the season, I went down to Arizona for spring training. When I arrived at the Angels' minor-league facility in Casa Grande, south of Phoenix on the way to Tucson, I asked where the Class A players were working out and was directed to a dusty field in a far corner of the complex. I sat down behind the screen and took up a conversation with an older man who was watching batting practice. He had a two-day beard, wasn't wearing a uniform and his shirt was out. I introduced myself and he extended his hand.

"Nice to meet you," he said. "I'm Warren Spahn."

Oh, man. I felt like an idiot. Spahn's career win total of 363 flashed before my eyes, but Spahn, who was the Angels' minor-league pitching coordinator, was as nice as can be about it. He and I even got in a little golf together that year.

No doubt, I was a rookie back then. Working in the minors can be transient, with contracts between the teams and the radio stations often fleeting, so early in my career my time on the air doing pro baseball was intermittent. I missed the 1988 baseball season except for a handful of Pacific Coast League games on television, but it wasn't all bad — it gave Denise and me time to plan our wedding and get married. Life with a sports announcer often meant you planned trips around the games, and that was the case for our honeymoon, which came in Santa Fe while we were down in New Mexico getting ready for a football game between San Jose State and New Mexico State. Back in 1982 I'd picked up a gig doing Sonoma State football, then moved up to sjsu, and eventually I wound up calling college games for twenty-two years.

Not doing much baseball in 1988 also afforded plenty of time for reflection, and I remember thinking that although the season can be arduous, I missed the rhythm and tempo of the baseball life. At that point in my career, I really wanted to give baseball my best shot and if an opportunity arose, getting back into a full-time minor-league position would fit perfectly with my football and basketball schedule. Luckily, the Las Vegas Stars of the pcl were looking for an announcer for the 1989 season and I had a good relationship with some folks in their front office, especially Don Logan, the Stars' general manager, and Bob Blum.

Bob had moved to Las Vegas in the 1970s and eventually became the voice of the UNLV Runnin' Rebels in their heyday under Jerry Tarkanian. In November 1988, when I took a call from Bob, he was working full time for the Stars and doing a little real estate work on the side. Bob wasn't broadcasting much, save for a few innings here and there, but he was producing and engineering the broadcasts. The phone call lasted about five minutes. I basically had the job, but to make things official I flew to Vegas to interview with the team's owner, Larry Koentopp, an avid golfer. The interview went something like this:

"What's your handicap?"

"Around seven."

"You're hired."

I spent that year doing the games with Dom Valentino, who was one of the A's voices the year before Bill and Lon were hired, and for the next three years Denise and I spent our summers in Vegas and the rest of the year back in the Bay Area for my gig with SJSU.

After the 1991 baseball season the White Sox made a change on their radio team, letting Wayne Hagin go, and that opened up a part-time job doing twenty-five games with Ed Farmer when the voice of the Sox, John Rooney, was away on his CBS Radio duties. It was a great opportunity for me — a foot in the door of the big leagues. My first interview was with Mike Bucek, who had worked in the front office in Phoenix when I was doing games there and had moved on to become Sox director of broadcasting. Mike and his boss, Rob Gallas, went to bat for me, but it was a different story at the offices of the Sox flagship, WMAQ, where the brass was dead set against hiring someone from the minors: They wanted to consider only someone with major-league experience. There wasn't much I could do about that, except to point out that every announcer working in the big leagues at one point in their lives wasn't, but after a protracted tug-of-war Mike prevailed.

My first year in the big leagues couldn't have gone better,

thanks in no small part to the unbelievable support I received from Farmer, on the air and off. Ed was my tour guide around the American League. At the end of that first season in Chicago, Jim Frank, the news director of the station, approached me to say he was really pleased with my work and they should have just hired me in the first place. I resisted the temptation to tell him that it was ninety feet from home plate to first base in the minors, just like it is in the big leagues.

By then I was finally starting to leave behind some of the self-doubt that had plagued me for years. This had become a serious issue in 1985 when I was hired by KCBS, a 50,000-watt giant of a station in downtown San Francisco, to do San Jose State football and fill in on morning and afternoon sportscasts. I was coming off a good run in small-market radio, where I had fun and felt confident and never found myself tied up in knots trying to be somebody I wasn't. Things changed when I was hired by KCBS and began to obsess about my style, listening to tapes constantly, thinking I had to craft the sound of a "major market" announcer.

As former All-Star outfielder Shawn Green put it in his excellent book, *The Way of Baseball: Finding Stillness at 95 mph,* "We are so lost in the fantasies of our minds — egotistic images of who we think we are or should be." Our minds, he wrote, are "distorted by incessant judging and analysis."

That was me in my KCBS period. By the time I had dissected every word and listened to my tapes over and over, I was convinced I didn't measure up. So I would have a new approach the next week and the cycle would start again.

"Just have fun!" George Rask, the morning traffic and weather guy, would urge me, and he was right. It's one thing to work hard honing your craft, but there has to be balance. At some point you have to sink or swim being yourself. Especially in baseball, I've found, the more you try to force it, the worse it gets. I remember a *Rolling Stone* review of a Bob Dylan album where the reviewer made the point that he liked the album because Dylan had nothing left to prove.

Red Barber once told a young Vin Scully that the only unique thing you can bring to the broadcast is yourself. Barber even suggested that Vinny avoid listening to other announcers "because you don't want to water your wine." That was a hard lesson for me to learn, but in Chicago it began to sink in, and maybe that's one of the things that helped me get the nod to work alongside Bill King.

New ownership, led by Steve Schott and Ken Hofmann, took over the A's after the 1995 season. Several changes were made in the front office, and in the broadcast booth the historic partnership of Bill and Lon came to an end when Lon wasn't asked to return. Not that Lon stayed idle for long — he went back to the Giants, working a partial schedule of mostly home games, and he sounded as great as ever. Although I never talked to Bill during the selection process, I assumed at the time that he listened to my tape and had veto power once I became a finalist for the job. Unbeknownst to me, Bob Blum, in my corner again, had called Bill to tell him, "He's our kind of guy." That must have carried a tremendous amount of weight, and Bill's stepdaughter Kathleen told me much later that when Bill listened to my tape he said, "He's the one."

While Bill's "three things" edict might have made it sound like he was expecting me to do all the flexing to make the partnership work, that proved not to be the case. Before one of our first broadcasts in the spring of '96, I couldn't help but notice a legal pad that was sticking out of one of Bill's backpacks. I saw a couple of things that Bill had written in his bold, distinctive hand, like "be patient, respectful, work him into the broadcasts." I never asked him about it, but it was clear that Bill had gone to some lengths to reinforce his thoughts about how to adjust to having a new partner, about welcoming me on board.

In that first year, it helped that the A's had a fun club. The "Power Ball" A's hit 243 home runs, one of which was a grand slam by Matt Stairs in a thirteen-run first inning on July 5 on a fireworks night against the Angels. But the team, in transition, really struggled the next two years. It speaks to the futility of those teams that the call I remember most came at the end of the longest nine-inning 1–0 game in major-league history, a loss for the A's in Milwaukee on May 7, 1997, that took three hours and twenty minutes to play. The A's Scott Brosius was thrown out in a cloud of dust at home plate after a Stairs single and A's manager Art Howe came out of the dugout to argue the call.

"And Art Howe has been thrown out of a game that is over!" an incredulous Bill told listeners.

That game was at County Stadium, and one thing I came to see soon enough was that Bill loved the old ballparks, where you felt the history just walking into a place. It was the same at Tiger Stadium — "The Corner," as coined by the great Ernie Harwell.

Tiger Stadium opened the same day as Fenway Park, April 20, 1912. The broadcast booth was like none other, a cubbyhole that hung under the upper deck. To get there you walked up a ramp and then across a rickety catwalk to the booth. It was so close to the field that it was almost like broadcasting from the top of the backstop. In fact, as the Tigers' teams struggled and crowds dwindled during the last few years at The Corner, we were told several times by the A's catchers that they could hear everything we were saying.

We were in harm's way, too, especially if a left-handed hitter was up. The visiting booth was just left of home plate, right in the firing line of a foul tip off the bat of a lefty hitter. You took your life into your own hands up there and I looked forward to the games when we had former Gold Glove catcher Ray Fosse in the booth as a shield.

Harwell, the voice of the Tigers, broadcast behind a wire screen in his booth at Tiger Stadium and sometimes, because there was often an empty booth between ours and Ernie's, I would sit next door during one of Bill's innings and listen to him. Ernie's Georgia baritone was lyrical and mellow. He had the ability to project his voice but remain conversational, and he sounded so good that I think he could have said nothing in particular for three hours and people would have listened.

The A's had moved to Oakland in 1968 from Kansas City, where they played at Municipal Stadium, which is also where Bill worked Raiders-Chiefs games in the old AFL days. Hearing him talk about the radio booth there, it's easy to understand why Marty Lurie wanted Bill on his pregame shows as often as possible: "The broadcast booth was tough. The booths were sort of an overhang, down below the first row of the second deck. That was fine — you had to climb down a ladder to get there — but the roof was corrugated iron and on an afternoon game, you were in there cooking. It was like the guys who were imprisoned in *The Bridge on the River Kwai*."

In Texas when we were working together the conditions offered their own challenge, and a damned-if-you-do, damned-if-you-don't conundrum. Both Bill and I hated working in a glass-enclosed booth, so the windows were always open. This was actually a long-standing practice of Bill's — he felt detached from the action if he was cocooned behind glass, missing the buzz of the crowd. This went for football season, too, even in the frigid Northeast, according to Scotty Stirling. No matter how low the temperature and even if the wind chill was down around zero, there was no way Bill was going to close the windows.

"We would be in War Memorial Stadium (in Buffalo) or in Cleveland and we would be freezing," Scotty recalled. "So cold and the wind was blowing. Those were probably the games I talked the least because it was too cold to talk."

The summer weather in Texas was just the opposite, of course: oppressively hot, with game-time temperatures often in triple digits. But another big issue was the wind, a prevailing south wind that blew in over the right-field stands. With the windows open that wind shot straight into our booth on the third-base side. It was relentless and wreaked havoc. Bill was very organized when it came to his notes, but he often lost the battle with the Arlington wind, which would leave our booth looking like a hurricane had roared through. Game notes, score sheets, pencils, anything could be blown to the back of the booth at any time. Some of this might be tolerated, but Arlington was the Coors Field of the American

League, with long, run-filled games where a three-hour, 8–7 contest seemed like a pitcher's duel.

I'm not sure of the exact date, but there was one game in Texas that led to the only time I had to confront Bill. With the wind creating chaos in the booth and his frustration boiling over, he threw it to me for the third inning and then, one item at a time, began slamming his stuff to the ground. Scoresheets, media guides, game notes, his big yellow binder. It was like, "Here's the two-one pitch." SLAM. "Now the two-two pitch." SLAM. "Now, a ground ball to short." SLAM. Then he walked out of the booth, slammed the door behind and I wasn't sure he was coming back.

The next day I told him, "Bill, I know you were pissed, but I had a game to do."

He felt terrible about it, but that's what Texas could do to Bill. He had nothing but disdain for the Ballpark in Arlington, and of all the things I've been asked about Bill over the years, two stand out. One was Bill's aversion to interleague play and the other was his hatred of that stadium in Texas, where a game could feel like going fifteen rounds with Mike Tyson. Not only was there the wind to contend with, but it was a place that could be tough on the eyes, especially those that have aged. Bill had a hard time seeing balls in the outfield because the radio booth is a long way from the field, and during day games the glare made it very hard to pick up the ball off the bat.

Eventually, Bill would lose the battle there with the wind, the heat and his problems seeing the ball. After that blowup his visits to Arlington were limited to one series a year at the most and never in the heart of the summer. But he left behind some unforgettable calls, and one that will always stand out for me was a game played on Cinco de Mayo in 2000. The A's had a 15–7 lead going to the bottom of the seventh and were still comfortably ahead, 16–10, in the eighth inning. But Texas continued to fight back. Bill was bobbing and weaving. It didn't feel like fifteen rounds, it felt like thirty. At the end — time of game: 4:01 — Bill, nearing the mandatory eight count and exasperated, summoning every ounce of incredulity in his voice, rendered the final verdict:

" *And to the plate again, swing a drive into deep center field. Ball game over! It will go as a single, but it's a long drive plating Rodriguez and the Rangers have come from an eight-run deficit to defeat the Athletics on a night that you wouldn't conjure in your wildest alcoholic dreams! 17–16. Mike Lamb, a .182 hitter, finishes off the evening. The Texas Rangers have beaten the Athletics."*

It was in the booth at the Coliseum where we had a Bill King explosion that I thought might escalate into another Mother's Day. I had mentioned to Bill that although the team was struggling I was enjoying the interaction with the players on the pregame and postgame shows and that these were good guys who were easy to deal with. He didn't react much to this, but I learned later that my comments had him simmering.

The A's were blasted by the Yankees, 14–1, in an August 1998 game when A's starter Mike Oquist took one for the team and allowed all fourteen runs. They had no luck in the first game of a doubleheader the next day, losing 10–4, but were looking good, leading 5–1, going to the top of the ninth inning of the nightcap. Then the Yanks mounted a comeback and the A's couldn't stop the bleeding. There was a big throwing error and by the time the inning ended the A's had given up nine runs and fallen thirteen games under .500.

During one of the pitching changes I could tell Vesuvius was about to explode. Fearing another Mother's Day, I was conditioned to reach quickly for my on/off switch and had trained myself to glance over at Bill to make sure his mic was off if I thought he might say something that wasn't suitable for the airwaves. That night at the Coliseum, thankfully, his mic was off when he turned around in his chair and his voice filled the booth: "I'm tired of these nice guys who are horseshit! Give me some assholes who can play!"

Bill always stressed that no matter what the score or how bad the game was, you always had to maintain your energy. Good team or bad team, good game or bad game, you had a job to do. As Lindsey Nelson once told Hank Greenwald, "You are going to sound the way they play, and you can't let that happen."

It's probably unfair to single out announcers, because there were many guys Bill liked, but one who stood out to Bill was Gary Thorne, the television voice of the Orioles. "I love his energy," Bill said. Another is Greg Papa, who emerged with aplomb from Bill's long shadow as voice of the Raiders on radio. Bill used to listen to Papa a lot, and said, "He calls a game exactly the way I think it should be done." Hearing this provided a huge boost in confidence for Greg as he tried to forge his own identity as voice of the Raiders.

The other thing I came to see was that Bill had a keen sense of when to jack up the intensity. When I asked him about his signature "Holy Toledo," he said he wanted something that took a call to the next level so that it would really resonate and that "Holy Toledo" served as an exclamation point. But he also stressed that he usually tried to keep a little in reserve.

Cubs voice Pat Hughes, who, like me, took a transistor radio to bed at night listening to Bill, learned that you can't try to make every play sound like it was the seventh game of the World Series. "That's impossible," Pat told me. "Bill was smart enough to pick his spots and let you know when it really was truly one of the climactic moments."

A walk-off homer by Olmedo Saenz against the Giants at the Coliseum on July 15, 1999, had no trouble qualifying for the full Holy Toledo treatment from Bill:

> **❝** *Raines at second the tying run, the winning run at first base and that's Jaha but it's tough for him to negotiate that distance in very much quick time. The only way Saenz can avoid that problem is to take it deep. Nen has no idea that's going to happen. It may have happened!*

There's a swing and a deep drive way back into left-center field and it's gone! Olmedo Saenz has beaten the Giants on a three-run homer! The A's are pouring out of the dugout! The Athletics have won the ballgame by score of 11–9! Holy Toledo!! What a finish!!"

Bill avoided road interleague games, with the exception of A's-Giants matchups in San Francisco, for one simple reason: Bill hated interleague play almost as much as he hated doing games in Texas. He called interleague play a sideshow and rebelled against what he felt was an intrusion on the season. Bill was maniacal about his preparation but he hated the thought of working like crazy to get ready for three games against a team you wouldn't see for another three or four years. As much as Bill was a nonconformist he was a traditionalist as well, and he felt the only time we should see the National League was in the World Series. Anything that took him out of his routine was a serious breach and that was one reason he referred to Bud Selig — and he said this on the air — as "Bud Lite."

When you are Bill King's boss, the law of averages would dictate that the time will come when you'd hear from the authorities, as Bill rarely shied from being the provocateur. Ken Pries was certain a call would come from the Office of the Commissioner over one of those shots at Selig. No call from the commish ever came, although Ken wondered if that would have been the case if the A's played their home games in New York instead of far-off Oakland. Pries did get calls, however — from umpires.

Three or four times Pries remembers being asked by Major League Baseball to go to the umpire's room over something Bill had reputedly said. Most of the time it was a quick discussion and Pries was able to mollify the umps, but one incident stood out where a crew chief had a serious beef with Bill.

Ken was in his office when he got a call from MLB regarding remarks allegedly delivered by Bill during the previous night's broadcast. Pries went downstairs and met with the umpires before the game. The umpire explained that it was OK to be critical, but said Bill's comments "were a personal attack against me." Pries responded that he listened to the game and no doubt Bill had gotten emotional about what he thought was a bad call, but a personal attack? Ken didn't think so. He asked if any of the umpires had heard the call.

"No," the crew chief responded, "but I have friends in the Bay Area who were listening and they said Bill had crossed the line."

Pries went back to his office, made a copy of the inning in question and sent the tape down to the umpires. He told the umps to give it a listen and get back to him if they still had a problem. He never heard back, and wisely never let on to Bill about the incident. "I didn't want to antagonize him any more than he already felt about umpires," Ken said.

There was one time when Ray Fosse tried to have a little fun with Bill's loathing of the umps and brought Ken Kaiser, a frequent target of Bill's, in on the scheme. Kaiser is a huge man, a former wrestler, and he moved slowly and had a nonchalant style that included a short, often confusing jab with his left hand when he called a play on the bases.

So one time Fosse persuaded Kaiser to park his car in the F lot, which is right next to the tunnel where the players and broadcasters come out after a game at the Coliseum. He told the big guy to wait for Bill and create a scene. Bill came out and there was the ponderous Kaiser, towering over him.

"So I hear you have a problem with me, huh?" Kaiser said. "Some things I've been saying?"

Bill was eager to head home and quickly went into retreat mode, according to Ray, but it was all in good fun.

"Kaiser was so big he could have crushed him," Fosse remembered.

Marty Lurie knew all about Bill and umpires — or thought he did. One time Marty interviewed the veteran umpire Jim McKean for one of his pregame shows. McKean had been behind the plate for Roy Halladay's second major-league start, when the Tigers Bobby Higginson broke up Halladay's no-hit bid with a two-out homer in the ninth inning. Marty figured it would be an interesting story and that Bill would be impressed with his hustle.

"It was an honor knowing that he was listening every single day," Marty told me. "And it put some pressure on me, because he was such a wonderful man and a smart man and I respected him so much. Since he was listening to me, I wanted to make the shows absolutely perfect for him."

Umpires were not the ticket.

"Bill jumped out of his seat when I introduced the segment," Marty said. "I played the interview and I talked with him afterward, and he said, 'You can't put umpires on! I can't stand these umpires! They don't deserve to be on!' I realized the depth of his feeling about umpires and I never put one on again."

Another point of contention for Bill was his age, any discussion of which was basically forbidden. The mere hint of a question or curiosity would quickly be diffused. During our time together he grew tired of the questions about how long he was going to work. He was going to work as long as he was enjoying it and he was effective, which wouldn't be determined by a number. He really felt that if someone knew your age then they would have an expectation of how you were supposed to act at that age.

It was kind of like when Satchel Paige said, "How old would you be if you didn't know how old you were?"

At home with Nancy and the kids, the last birthday party came when Bill was forty. After that, any discussion of age was forbidden. "I've just very recently begun to say, 'Screw it, I'm ageless,'" Bill told the sportswriter Ron Bergman. Still, we had fun giving Bill a hard time when the A's would go to Toronto because he had to list his birthday on the customs forms. One time Mickey Morabito had to almost force him to do it.

The A's were happy to accommodate Bill on interleague games. You could say he had that kind of equity built up. In fact, Ken Pries said contract negotiations with Bill were the easiest of any he's ever had. "Our regular routine was I would call in October and ask him when he wanted to get together," Pries said. "I would go over to Sausalito and we would have lunch and just go over everything and I'd ask, 'Bill do you want to come back?' I dreaded the day when he said, 'No, I'm not going to come back,' but that never happened."

They talked about interleague play when baseball announced the schedule for 1997, the first season of AL-NL games outside the World Series. It wasn't like Bill was just looking for some time off. He was governed by his passions and if his heart wasn't in something, he couldn't fake it. That's why, I think, his interleague broadcasts were some of the worst of his career and he knew it and he didn't really want to fight it, although he did say he would do the games if the A's really wanted him to. So they worked it out that he would just do the home games and those in San Francisco — and they arranged for infrequent visits to Texas.

Not that Bill went easily into that good Texas night. "It was a badge of honor working as many games as possible," Pries said. "I remember talking to him and thinking, 'If he doesn't want to do this he must really feel strongly about it,' because I knew how much he wanted to be on the air."

He did, but the highest priority was always the quality of the broadcast. I remember the first time we did a game from the Tigers' new stadium, Comerica Park, we all found the early-inning glare to be brutal. I was on TV that night and could let the pictures tell the story, but Bill didn't have that option on radio. So before the next game, as I was back on radio with Bill, he gave me specific instructions on how he wanted to deal with the glare.

He told me how tough it had been the previous night and asked me to pick up the play-by-play and finish his calls in the first two innings. In other words, he would start the play, and let's say it was a fly ball to left. He said he would call the pitch to the hitter, but then if I noticed he couldn't see the ball, he wanted me to jump right in and say, "It's a fly ball to short left field, and it's caught by Jones."

"You've got to be kidding me," I told him. "You're the greatest broadcaster of all time, and you want me to step on your calls and finish them?"

I didn't think it would make either one of us look good, and I prevailed, but Bill didn't care how he looked. He just wanted to get it right.

One of the only other times I can remember Bill surrendering was a much less serious situation, during a spring training game at Phoenix Stadium. I believe in all those old clichés about renewal and the new season blooming like the saguaro. Bill also felt it was an important time to sell tickets and familiarize the listeners with the players. On the days we weren't broadcasting, Bill would take advantage of the nice weather and find a seat in the bleachers down the left-field line. He'd be out there with his Speedos and flip-flops soaking in the sun and the view of the desert and the Papago Buttes to his left, beyond the left-field fence and across Van Buren Street.

Bill was working with Steve Bitker on March 3, 2004, while I was doing a postseason UNLV basketball game. The A's won the game 26–3. That's right, 26–3. They out-hit the Angels 27–12 and thirteen pitchers were used. At the end of the sixth, the score was 19–3 and all of the runs had been scored in Bill's innings.

"That's it! Enough!" Bill cried out, telling Steve, "If you want the rest of the game, you can have it!"

"Really?" Steve asked.

"Take it!" Bill said.

Steve got seven runs to call in the last three innings, avoiding a play-by-play shutout. He was also in the booth for what was back then the longest game by time in A's history, in August 2002, while I was next door on television filling in for Greg Papa working with Ray. On the radio side, Bill was all business even though the game lasted until 1:20 in the morning. "Bill was the consummate professional for six hours" of toil in the notoriously cramped Yankee Stadium booth, Steve said. "He gave it 100 percent, his best effort for six hours and sixteen innings. He never took a batter off." We didn't know for sure, but we kind of had the idea that Bill was around seventy-four years old.

Beginning in 2000, the A's had four consecutive playoff appearances, and Bill was at the mic on October 1, 2000, as Jason Isringhausen looked to save a 3–0 game that was started by Tim Hudson. Bill made the call: *"Strike three called, the A's win the West!"*

Every one of those postseasons, however, ended in disappointment. Four straight trips to the American League Division series and four straight Game Five losses. The most disappointing was in 2001, when Bill and I both thought the A's had their best chance in those years to reach the World Series. But it was during the 2001 season when Bill delivered one his most memorable calls.

It came on a Sunday afternoon, August 12, as the A's were trying to finish a three-game sweep of the Yankees and extend a winning streak to eleven games. Mark Mulder and Mike Mussina had locked in a 2–2 battle through eight innings before Mussina left, having allowed only two hits. Mike Stanton, an All-Star that year, came on in the ninth and he walked Johnny Damon with one out. Another out later, Jason Giambi came to the plate as 47,000 fans squirmed to the edges of their seats.

"He was just pounding me, working three-two, working three-two, and I kept fouling off pitches, fouling off pitches," Jason told me. "In the back of my mind I thought, 'This guy is going to throw me a breaking ball for a strike right here.' He had thrown me so many inside fastballs and fastballs away that I would foul off. I just had that feeling he was going to throw that breaking ball and that he was going to throw it for a strike because I felt like he wanted to punch me out looking. And I just sat on it ... "

Ken Macha was the A's bench coach at the time and he has always remembered the description of what happened next — which he heard replayed on Robert Buan's postgame show while driving home from the game that night — as his favorite Bill call ever.

> **“** *There is a swing, a long drive hit way back into right field and Jason Giambi is THE MAN in capital letters. He has defeated the Yankees with one swing of the bat, a two-run home run and this place has gone wild! HOLY TOLEDO!!!”*

Jason Giambi is THE MAN. When Macha heard it, he thought to himself, "'That guy had to be blessed with being so creative for that just to come out of him like that.' He was blessed like that and the Oakland A's fans were blessed to have this guy as their announcer. If you are gifted like he was, it's a split second and it's just going to come out of your mouth and it did. That was an amazing call."

When I talked with Giambi about the at-bat against Stanton and his memories of Bill, we were sitting in one of the dugouts on the main practice field at the Cleveland Indians' spring complex in Glendale, Arizona. Two weeks later he would begin his nineteenth major-league season.

Jason remembered how he would rehear parts of that call when he would phone the A's office and be put on hold. Not only was it his first career walk-off hit, but it came against the Yankees, who, he said, "had kind of turned into our rivals because we lost in the playoffs the year before."

Jason Giambi is the most humble, least affected and most co-operative superstar I've met. After his homer off Stanton I raced down to the A's dugout to try and get him for our postgame show, but had wait while Jason worked through the TV interviews, which always had priority. By the time it was my turn it was often well after the game ended, and I'm sure there were times when a player like Giambi was worn out and just wanted to get up to the club-house. After closing the interview that day with Jason, I thanked him for sticking around and he responded in typical Giambi fashion: "No, thanks for asking me."

Jason was the American League MVP in 2000 and one of the keys to his success was how religiously he stuck to his pregame routine. He did very little hitting on the field before the games, preferring to spend time in the batting cage that was one level upstairs from the A's clubhouse before coming down to relax and get ready for the game. He usually found Bill in there, because Bill enjoyed socializing and the pregame spread in the clubhouse drew Bill like a magnet.

"He would always be in there milling around in his flip-flops and wanting to talk about the night before," Jason recalled. "He was such an incredible man. I had so much fun with him and he would always ask how my family was doing and I have the fondest memories of him."

Like Barry and Madden and Meschery and Beane and everyone else I interviewed for this book, Giambi's memories of Bill are of a man who enriched his life. In the empty hours before games, Bill might mention a night at the opera or symphony, and the next thing you know, "we would talk about life and all the things he had seen," Jason said. "I would ask him about the older players: 'What was Bando like or what was Reggie like?' He would fill in the gaps because we didn't have a lot of opportunities to see those guys and I would always ask him about them." Giambi saw himself as "just a baseball player," but through his conversations with Bill, he felt like more than that. "He made me well-rounded," he said.

Giambi moved on to the Yankees after the 2001 season, and every time he came to the plate at Yankee Stadium the introduction was made by the legendary and veracious voice of Bob Sheppard. "I always tell people I had the opportunity to play with two of the best voices in the game: Bill's and then of course when I went over to Yankee Stadium. Those were incredible memories."

The interview with Giambi after his home run in 2001 was in the third segment of the postgame show, following Bill's customary recap of the game. In this segment, Bill would coordinate with the studio to play highlights, which wrapped around his narrative. It was an abridged version of the game, a sort of mini Bill King suspense story that would build to a crescendo, especially after a close game. Bill's attention to every detail would occasionally drive Fosse and me crazy, especially if we were trying to catch a cab or make the team bus. We used to tell him, "Bill, you don't have to mention that a two-one pitch in the bottom of the fourth was taken for a strike." But it paid off for listeners. As Ray remembers, Roy Eisenhardt missed a game once but told Bill that catching the postgame show made him feel like he was there.

That season, 2001, was one that was about more than baseball, as the horrific 9/11 attacks jarred us from the insulated world of sports. After a one-week delay, the A's, with a fabulous club that won 103 games, advanced to the postseason and headed to New York to take on the Yankees less than a month after the attacks.

Normally, even if it is the middle of the night, there would be some talking on the team bus after we got off the plane. This time, however, we took a silent trip from Newark through the Lincoln Tunnel and into Manhattan. Nobody knew what the city would look or feel like the next morning, although I've always felt it was a credit to the resilience of New Yorkers that they tried, although angry and grieving, to go about their business.

We had two days before the start of the series, and Bill spent much of the time walking the New York streets. I took a cab down to the Village and then walked as close as I could get to Ground Zero, where a horrible smell permeated the air. For several hours baseball was the furthest thing from my mind, but we had a job to do once the series began.

Emotions were charged at the Big Stadium in the Bronx. I was told there were sharpshooters on the roof. A bald eagle soared around the field as part of a pregame ceremony and Bob Sheppard's voice, always powerful, was haunting on the public address when he asked for a moment of silence.

Finally, two great teams got down to business with the energy at Yankee Stadium, always the best in baseball, more palpable than ever. Before the series, A's Manager Art Howe had said the Yankees better bring their "A" game, prompting a tabloid headline the next day that read: "Howe Dare He." But the A's validated Art's confidence by winning both games in the Bronx before returning home for a game that will be relived forever, but the memories aren't fond for A's fans.

I called the Jeremy Giambi Didn't Slide Jeter Flip. One of the things I've never forgotten is Bill's reaction to my call of the Jeter play. Bill had a lot of pride in our broadcast team and he went out of his way to pump me up, telling everyone it was the greatest call he had ever heard. I was thrilled that he felt that way, but, trying to be objective, thought the call was OK. It wasn't the best call I've made and it wasn't the worst, either. I'll take it, it was a complicated play. I wish I had said "a flip by Jeter" instead of a pitch, a choice that must have gone back to my football play-by-play days, like an option quarterback pitching the ball to a running back. Bill told me, "I couldn't have called that play." I said, "Thanks, partner, but you could have called it in your sleep."

Many of Bill's calls are so ingrained that they have become part of our lexicon in the booth. An unexpected bunt, for instance, will take us back to the 2003 divisional playoff against Boston, when Bill delivered one of his classic lines as Ramon Hernandez won the first game with a bunt single down the third-base line with two outs in the bottom of the twelfth inning. After four hours and thirty-seven minutes, Bill King, approaching his seventy-sixth birthday (not that he would let anybody know about it), was right on it: *"The element of surprise reigns supreme!"*

I can't tell you how many times that line has been repeated on our broadcasts when a bunt goes rolling down one of the baselines.

Those big calls of Bill's weren't just confined to plays made by the A's, reflecting a belief central to Bill's philosophy of how to broadcast a game, one that fit with a West Coast approach of objectivity that I had noted since listening to games as a kid. You never heard anyone say "we" or "them" and the listeners always learned plenty about the other team from the broadcasts.

It wasn't as if Bill King didn't want the A's to win. He would be the first to admit that he was passionate about the team and that he was emotionally invested in the wins and losses. But this didn't mean that he couldn't and wouldn't appreciate a good play by the opposition. Bill had a conversation with Dwayne Murphy that he repeated many times. Murph was the center fielder on the great A's outfield of Henderson, Murphy and Armas, the best defensive outfield I've ever seen. Murphy, chafed, once told Bill: "I just heard the call you made of a home run by the team we were playing, and it sounded like one of ours."

"Murph," Bill replied, "you've just paid me a great compliment."

Bill understood that a big part of our job was to sell tickets, but he knew that would be tough to do if the announcers weren't believable. By maintaining credibility, it meant those great moments by the home team would be more powerful, more fun. It's like what Jerry West once told Chick Hearn: "You are the most unbiased, biased announcer I've heard."

Bill spoke his mind and if the A's weren't playing well he said so, which is something A's fans appreciated because they were usually feeling the same way. But it wasn't like Bill was taking gratuitous shots. He didn't need to criticize to make a name for himself. "We weren't hiring negativity, we were hiring objectivity," Roy Eisenhardt said.

Having the support of the front office is so important that it goes beyond anything you can quantify. So many announcers are on pins and needles because they fear what they say will be criticized by management. It's tough to be yourself when you are tied up in knots. In eighteen seasons with the A's I've never had anything I've said second-guessed. I've always felt that you hire someone and you trust them to do their job. That's the kind of freedom you want. In Oakland, if it is a bad broadcast it's on me.

I had a pretty good predecessor and partner from that standpoint. "He could say exactly what was on his mind and find a way to pull it off without being offensive," Billy Beane told me when I asked him for his thoughts on Bill. "He could be so blatantly honest and at the same time sound professional doing it."

Bill didn't hide behind the walls of a studio. He always said if anyone had a problem with what he said, well, he'd be down on the field the next day. By the same token, because he was so often down on the field, if Bill criticized a manager for not using a reliever you could be sure he had asked before the game who was available in the bullpen.

Bill lived for the chance to capture the big moment, and there were times he would come into the booth all excited because he had heard a great call. In August 1999, the A's were playing the Red Sox at Fenway Park, with its intimacy the greatest stage in baseball. The A's were leading, 5–3, going to the bottom of the ninth. The Red Sox had the bases loaded with two outs and the A's had right hander Tim Worrell on the mound and Brian Daubach was batting. A riveting at-bat ensued with Daubach hitting several foul balls, including one that almost hooked inside the Pesky Pole, down the right-field line. Bill's intensity matched the tension that was building in the park. Finally, on the tenth pitch, Daubach doubled off the Green Monster, scoring Darren Lewis, Butch Huskey and Jose Offerman and giving the Red Sox a 6–5 win.

Bill and I walked back to the hotel after the game and Bill was still sky high from calling the ninth inning. He talked about how it would be hard for him to tell a manager or coach how alive and engaged he felt by a dramatic moment, especially in the aftermath of a tough loss. It's not that he wanted the A's to lose that night and he certainly understood that it was painful down in the clubhouse. But he lived for those peak moments and bristled when he would hear an announcer describe a game-ending play by the opposition in a monotone like it was a mundane play in the third inning.

Nevertheless — and this might seem like a contradiction — Bill was a very good company man, and I don't mean that as a pejorative at all. As honest as he was and as emotional as he could get, he understood the need for perspective. Even after a bad performance by the A's, he would tell me that he would try to point out something positive so as not to paint a completely bleak picture. He understood that even in the darkest times, a winning streak could be just around the corner.

The A's missed the playoffs in 2004 and '05, but contended down the stretch both years. In Bill's last year they took a one-game lead over the Angels on August 11, 2005. Jason Kendall was at third base and Bobby Crosby was at first. Crosby took second on defensive indifference. Francisco Rodriguez was on the mound for the Angels. The score was tied, 4–4, and Jose Molina was catching. It was six weeks before Bill's last broadcast:

> 66 *Defensive indifference, now the ball gets away behind the mound on a throwback! Coming home to score is Jason Kendall! And on a freak play, the Athletics have won the game and the series! You would not believe it! That is one for the books! Holy Toledo!"*

If I had made a game-ending call like that one, especially in my KCBS days or even in my first few years with the A's, I would have listened to it over and over to a point where I would be convinced it was one of the worst calls ever made. I've come to understand that to a surprising degree the desire for perfection is really a sign of not accepting ourselves for who we are. As Red Barber said, you don't want to water your wine. I've tried to learn from the example set by Bill and from a conversation we had shortly after we started working together. I asked Bill if he ever listened to tapes of himself when he was a young announcer, trying to sculpt a style.

"No, I never did," he said.

When Bill's stepdaughter Kathleen heard this, she responded with a knowing smile. "Bill was not introspective," she said, which was something Bill himself used to say to me.

As time went on working with him, it became clear to me that what you got from Bill was unvarnished and not contaminated by some idea of how he *thought* he should sound. He wasn't burdened by self-doubt or trying to conform to someone else's standards. One of the reasons Bill's calls were so great was that he was able to slow everything down to the perfect combination of concentration and calm.

Like on a May afternoon at Yankee Stadium in 2000 when with Jorge Posada and Tino Martinez running, Shane Spencer hit a line drive to A's second baseman Randy Velarde. Velarde tagged Posada and then tripled up Martinez. Bill's call of the eleventh unassisted triple play in big-league history happened so fast and captured the moment with such precision that he made it look easy:

> **"** *Runners at first and second with nobody out, a three-two count, And the pitch, there's a swing and a line drive right to Velarde. Velarde tags the runner coming down from first, steps on second, a triple play!*
>
> *"The runners broke. The runner at second broke a bit later than the runner from first, who was Posada.*

But the line drive to Velarde as he was going toward second set up the triple play. He tagged the runner coming down and then tagged second base. And Randy gets the unassisted triple play. Well, that's getting yourself out of a spot!"

This is something the great athletes achieve by being in the zone when everything happens almost in slow motion. Or as John Wooden used to teach, "Be quick but don't hurry."

It takes a kind of confidence to pull that off and for all the wisdom and know-how I gleaned from Bill, maybe his greatest gift to me was his endorsement of me. I've always felt that some of our fans might have been thinking, "If Bill King thinks this guy is OK, well maybe he is OK." In a business with plenty of egos, of broadcasters looking over their shoulders protecting their turf, wary of the new guy and unwilling to share the spotlight and feeling that somehow elevating the Number 2 guy would be done at great personal expense, I never felt any of this with Bill. It's a small thing, but Bill rarely called me Ken, it was almost always "partner." That meant a lot because I had come into a potentially tough situation replacing Lon.

Bill enjoyed the banter in the booth and he was a good sport about the razzing Ray and I would give him about his eating, his clothes, his car, umpires, Texas, interleague play, domed stadiums, Astroturf, wind, etc. Sometimes the bad games were more fun than the good ones, because there were opportunities for stories and it was always great to get Bill telling stories on the air. "I think that Bill needed a little prodding," Hank told me. "It was there. But he would get so into things and the intensity level would take over. He needed somebody who could take the level down a bit so he could step back and see the humor in something. It would be a little different if we were having dinner, because, believe it or not, he didn't broadcast dinner."

CHAPTER 9

AN ARTIST OF THE AIRWAVES

If you want to do it so badly,
quit talking about it and get
the hell out of here and start painting.

I learned fast that Bill was very touchy about being bothered before a game. Once he got locked in on his preparation, his focus was such that when Marty Lurie started his pregame show around an hour and a half before the game, Bill hated any intrusion. At the time I tended to see that as Bill being a little crusty and difficult, though I always had great respect for his work ethic and was never more thrilled than when he complimented me for working as hard as anyone on preparation. But looking back I think there was a little more to it than just his being a strong personality. He loved to be on the air and put so much of himself into it, for him broadcasting became an art form. In that sense his pregame ritual almost reminded you of a jazz musician getting ready for a gig and not wanting anything to knock him out of his routine or rob him of just the right feeling of anticipation. If I ever tried to make some small talk or mention the food in the press room, he would frown and wave his hands to tell me, "Not now!" and quickly get back to work. Bill always strived to get better but never tried to change who he was. He never got out of balance with that. There was a lot of the perfectionist in Bill. If he missed a call, especially late in a game, he would be inconsolable. He would really beat himself up. He had a ton of pride and had extremely high standards for himself. He was obsessive about his preparation and was intransigent about it.

"He approached every game like an audition," said Hank.

Bill was an artist. That's all there is to it. In fact, there were times when I saw a certain madness in Bill that I thought might have made him suited to a different time, maybe back in the days of the Renaissance. He would get that wild look in his eyes, a look that made me think he would have been more comfortable centuries earlier, when there were far fewer rules and artists like Bill could flourish untamed. He was an artist in the way he went about broadcasting a game, from the intense preparation to the furious attention to detail to the joy he took in the thing in itself. Bill attached himself to everything he loved: food and friendship and conversation, sailing and Russia and jazz, baseball and basketball and football. He was an artist, also, in the most literal sense: Bill painted and painted beautifully. First he spent years absorbing everything he could about painting, visiting museums on road trips whenever he could, and then he picked up a brush and made himself a painter.

It was Nancy who gave Bill a big push toward painting when she got tired of hearing Bill talk about it. They were regulars at art museums and Bill, whether it was on road trips or when they would sit around the kitchen table, was always talking about how much he wanted to paint.

Finally Nancy had had enough of the talk and no action.

"If you want to do it so badly, quit talking about it and get the hell out of here and start painting," she told Bill.

When it came to patience, Nancy had about as little of it as Bill.

"She was pissed," Tom Meschery recalled. "Bill was always yakking away at her that he loved painting. He would get books on painting and he would always tell her, 'I can paint,' or, 'One of these days I am going to paint,' or, 'When I retire I am going to paint.'"

So one Christmas Nancy went out and bought Bill everything he needed. She got him easels, all kinds of paints and books on how to paint and basically gave Bill a shove out the door.

"Now go learn how to paint," Tom recalled Nancy telling Bill.

"If Bill gets his head around something he is going to do it," Tom told me. "And he got very serious and he settled in and started reading everything he could about all the painters."

This was back in the '80s and it wasn't long before Bill started visiting the nearby town of Sonoma to study under a couple of painters who had organized workshops. He was on his way.

"We'd be on the plane and he'd be reading books about color and techniques and the next thing I knew he was painting," Lon Simmons recalled for this book.

Time on the road gave Bill plenty of opportunity for exposure to works by the great masters. We shared an interest in art, but let me say this: I have no talent as an artist. I couldn't draw a stick figure if you paid me a hundred bucks to do it. I got a D in handwriting in elementary school. Every day my baseball scorebook looks more like something authored by a doctor writing a prescription. But spending so much time on the road broadcasting all three sports provided ample opportunity for me to get out and explore, and I found that visiting art museums was a great way to relax and get away from the day-to-day grind of being on the air. Bill felt the same way and we spent a lot of time visiting museums and talking about art, which was a good way to get a little distance from baseball. And I wasn't the only person who detached himself from sports with Bill's help.

"We all wanted to live vicariously through Bill," John Madden told me. "The things that he did, we wished we could do: Not care, not worry and just sort of do things the way you want to do."

It was Bill, with his diversity of interests, who was so able to give John, a "tunnel-vision guy" by his own admission, a respite from the pressures of coaching in the NFL.

"I was with Bill a lot as a coach when he was a broadcaster for twelve years," John told me. "So after a while, the other conversations away from the football part were a lot more interesting to me than the football part."

I can remember Bill often referring to himself as "an inconsiderate son of a bitch" for little things like failing to be the one to suggest that we do dinner together. I was never bothered by it. He could just as easily have gone out by himself, usually much later in the evening. He was fiercely independent and so I never held it against him, especially in a place like New York, which was Bill's favorite city on the road. He would take full advantage of that clause in his contract with the A's that allowed him to take time off in New York, either before or after an A's series in the Big Apple. Bill and Nancy would spend their days on the streets of the city, often stopping at the Metropolitan Museum of Art, and nights at the theater and then settle in for a "civilized" dinner around 10:30. Wally Haas still laughs about trying keep up with Bill in New York.

"I remember Julie and I went out with Bill and Nancy in New York and pulled an all-nighter," Wally said for this book. "I never would do that. It was like, are you kidding me? We went to a show somewhere and then we went to a bar and then we went to a diner. All of a sudden it was dawn. It was wonderful."

Bill also loved visits to Boston. If he had a little time before a night game a place like Boston afforded many opportunities for lunch alfresco or a trip to visit an exhibition. One time we spent parts of two days at an Impressionist still life exhibit at the Museum of Fine Arts. Bill enjoyed dining at little out-of-the-way places like the Daily Catch, where they had room for only a handful of small tables and wrote that day's menu on a chalkboard on the wall. Fenway Park was a fun place to work because of the tradition and history and also for the raw excitement of calling games there. On his way back to the team hotel after some time at the MFA, Bill would pause at a bridge in the Fens and imagine it was the famous Japanese footbridge over the water lilies that Claude Monet painted many times.

As soon as the A's schedule for the year came out, Bill would study it, thinking not only about the A's matchups but mapping out museum visits as well. He was a member of most of the art museums around the country, and as a road trip grew near he would check to see if there was an especially interesting exhibit coming up.

In the '80s, Bill became friendly with George Steinbrenner, who also took a liking to Nancy. So we'd be doing a game at Yankee Stadium, and I would look to my left and see Nancy in the Boss's box with such luminaries as the great baritone Robert Merrill, who Bill knew well enough to call "Bob."

Nancy and Bill cut such a figure as a pair, it was deeply sad for everyone when after years of failing health she took a turn for the worse in 2004. It was a long, difficult and draining ordeal for Bill. He worked as much as he could, but all of his other time was spent trying to nurse and comfort his ailing wife. When Nancy died he missed six games in Oakland against the Pirates and Reds, which under any other circumstance would have been a dream come true for Bill, given his hatred of interleague play. When he returned to the booth, Mike Baird, broadcast manager Robert Buan and I were searching for the right words to say to a grieving husband. Bill broke the ice. He entered the booth and probably knowing we were feeling a little awkward, took the initiative to say the first words: "At least she had the good sense to die during interleague play!"

⚾　🏈　🏀

I spent one summer during the season studying the work of Monet's friend Edouard Manet and eventually wrote a piece for MLB.com comparing Manet to Bill. One of my points was that both Manet and Bill resisted being labeled. Manet, for instance, was considered the father of Impressionism but resisted being in the Impressionist camp and did not care for group exhibitions. They both enjoyed the good life, which was illustrated in Manet's *A Bar at the Folies-Bergere* (1882). They both worked until almost literally the day they died, and, despite being in pain, were able to create masterpieces until the very end. And they were both self-made men who were considered nonconformists.

"Nobody who knew Bill was shocked at his irreverence," I wrote, "but winding the clock back over 100 years earlier to the mid-19th century, Manet's use of nudes in *Le dejeuner sur l'herbe* (1862–63) and *Olympia* (1863) was shocking to the artistic public — so much so that Manet was considered an abomination."

Bill would chastise me for mentioning him in the same breath as a master, but while Bill wasn't at that level he was really, really good. I admit a certain bias because we were great friends and I'm not going to equate myself to a curator at a museum, but as far as I'm concerned you could put Bill's paintings on display and people would say they belonged.

"He was a self-taught painter and a very good painter," Lon Simmons said. "I wanted to buy one of his paintings that I thought was spectacular, but he didn't want to sell any of them."

When he wasn't immersed in his off-season baseball prep, Bill would often be at work on a painting. He loved to head out from his house in Sausalito for a walk to some spectacular setting, capture the scene in a photo and use it as inspiration back home for his painting. It wasn't hard for Bill to imagine, let's say, that he was in northern France, where his idol Monet spent much of the 1880s. He loved Monet's use of color and swift brushstrokes and the way Monet's application of light could illuminate a scene, just as Bill could accent a great play in a game. That Monet broke free from the traditional mold was something the iconoclast in Bill related to, as well. I have a print of Monet's *The Cliffs at Etretat* (1885) in my office at home and it could easily be a scene from Northern California. Bill loved those settings and found inspiration from nature's canvass.

In the early '90s, Bill's great friend Howard Portnoy opened a gallery at Sixth Avenue and Delores Street in Carmel. Bill and Nancy always visited Carmel right before spring training and would enjoy long walks on the beach, checking out the little shops and restaurants, and stopping by Howard's gallery. Howard not only had an eye for art, but he was an aficionado of baseball broadcasting as well. Bill really trusted Howard's judgment and I always felt I owed Howard a debt of gratitude because he seemed to take a liking to the chemistry that Bill and I had almost from the start. It was Howard who also seconded Bill's excitement over a "Fosse day." Almost all of Howard's calls or notes to Bill would include a comment that he enjoyed Ray much more on radio than on TV, which invariably caused Bill to react with great delight.

Painting wasn't something Bill ever talked about much, let alone publicized, and as Lon said, he never sold any of his paintings. Lon and Sandy Alderson and many others asked Bill for one of his paintings, but he always found a way to refuse. He didn't want anyone to like one of his paintings because he was Bill King, and certainly not to purchase one of his paintings because he was Bill King. Howard Portnoy kept after him for years until Bill finally agreed to show some of his paintings in Howard's gallery. But even then they were not for sale. Howard wanted to see how his patrons reacted, and he was not surprised to see them reacting very favorably in most cases, not even knowing the paintings were by Bill King.

I didn't have the chance to see any of Bill's paintings until years later when I got a package in the mail from Howard with several photos of Bill's work. I was blown away. The colors were so vibrant and varied and the detail so alive that looking at the photos you could have mistaken some of the paintings for photographs of actual scenes. Bill was partial to painting landscapes. There is one painting of sand dunes that I assume depicted a scene down near Pebble Beach. Another is of the Marin coastline with the waves crashing up on the shore below the cliffs. My favorite is a painting of Bill's looking out from Sausalito across the Bay to San Francisco. He paints the reeds in the foreground with the kind of intricacy that he used to describe a complicated play on the diamond, like Randy Velarde's unassisted triple play in New York. Then the painting takes your eyes on a tour of the rippling waters of San Francisco Bay before you are led to a view of a darkening outline of The City set against a background of the setting sun, all in the various shades of reds, pinks and yellows. Bill had a passionate connection with the natural world and that passion certainly connected him to Northern California. Bill wasn't much for politics but in the case of environmentalism and the efforts to preserve the open spaces near where he lived, he was ardent in his support.

Howard Portnoy died shortly after he sent me the photos of Bill's paintings. At the time Howard sent the package it had been several years since he had studied Bill's work and the separation afforded him a new perspective. Howard had also recently put a very well received Bill King page on his gallery's website. Inside the package, wrapped around the photos was a note.

"In looking at the photos I know now why I encouraged him," Howard wrote me. "He was good, better than I remember."

Bill simply *was* gifted. He was also assiduous in his dedication. It is one thing to be gifted, but you have to have the drive as well, which Bill had in abundance. There are people who are just off-the-charts talented, and Bill was one. He was developing as a painter and getting better and better, but sometime in the '90s he quit.

"I'm too busy to paint," he used to say.

What he meant was: He was too busy keeping up with all the statistical information that was by then available on the players. He longed for the days when the pregame notes provided by the teams fit on one page. (He used to tell the story of walking into Boston Garden and seeing his old friend, the crusty voice of the Celtics, Johnny Most: "King, all I need is a cigarette and a score-book.") With the proliferation of the Internet — Bill never had a computer — and with sabermetrics there was so much more information and Bill felt compelled to keep up. So his off-seasons got shorter and shorter.

"If I don't know something," he told me, "somebody listening is going to know it."

But even after he stopped painting, those years of creating beautiful pictures helped infuse his style as a broadcaster. He always had a preternatural gift for visual description, going way back, long before he ever picked up a paint brush, but I had the feeling that his painting added texture to his broadcasts. The great American novelist John Updike, author of the Rabbit novels and one of my favorite baseball essays ever, "Hub Fans Bid Kid Adieu," originally trained as an artist at the Ruskin School of Drawing and Fine Art in England, hoping to become a cartoonist for the *New Yorker* magazine. That painterly eye always infused Updike's meticulous descriptions and I think the same was true of Bill.

As Sandy Alderson put it, "I would call Lon sort of an abstract painter in his broadcasting style and I considered Bill more a pointillist, somebody who connected all these minute dots into a panoramic portrait."

It is interesting that Sandy would compare Bill to a pointillist, because one of my favorite paintings is by Georges Seurat, who is considered the foremost exponent of pointillism. *A Sunday on La Grande Jatte* is part of the permanent collection of the Chicago Institute of Art. One of the amazing things about *La Grande Jatte*, which took Seurat two years to finish, was Seurat's painstaking and meticulous efforts getting ready to begin work on the final product. *La Grande Jatte* fills one wall in a gallery at the Art Institute, and it is surrounded by several smaller preliminary drawings and oil sketches of the scene, all part of Seurat's preparation and attention to detail. No doubt, people like Bill and Seurat had an aptitude for what they did, but great works of art, whether on canvas or over the air, don't happen by accident.

After more than twenty years of marriage, couples can begin to run out of gift ideas for each other, but as I approached my sixtieth birthday in January 2010, my wife, Denise, came up with a plan for something unique. It was a longshot, but she figured it was worth a try: Denise asked Kathleen if maybe she had Bill's paintings in storage and if, even though it would be hard to part with one, she might consider allowing Denise to give me one of the paintings as a present. Kathleen graciously obliged. She searched through the room where Bill's paintings are stored and found one she thought I would like.

We had a small birthday party one night in Las Vegas with about twenty of our closest friends. I noticed a huge rectangular gift that was wrapped and lying up against one of the seats near where I was sitting. I thought it looked like it might be a painting but, really, I had no idea.

I unwrapped the gift and inside there was a Bill King original. It wasn't even framed, just the canvas and some wooden backing, but it was magnificent, an oil on canvas landscape set in the fall, with trees changing colors and golden leaves on the ground. A wooden fence behind two trees and three bushes with blue sky above. It hangs in my office at home, a reminder of Bill, and every time I look at it I shake my head.

CHAPTER 10

TORTILLAS WITH ONIONS AND PEANUT BUTTER: BILL AND FOOD

I have a feeling of great well being.

always wanted Bill to jump in during my innings doing play-by-play and add some color commentary. He jumped in, all right, but it was almost always so he could delve into his favorite pastime: eating. I used to kid him about his eating habits and how he was a man of such worldly tastes and yet he preferred Cheetos and a Diet Coke for breakfast. This was part of Bill's morning routine unless we were in Anaheim, where he would walk down the street to a little taquería he knew and dine on calf brain tacos and Dos Equis. That's for breakfast, folks.

"I eat a balanced diet," he used to tell me. "Everything."

Unfortunately for me, "everything" included some of the strangest, most pungent concoctions you could imagine. Broadcasting with Bill required a mind-over-matter resolve to mute my sense of smell. Bill would throw it to me for the third inning and almost immediately he would dart out of the booth in search of the popcorn machine. Chick Hearn had a signature phrase whenever someone on the Lakers made a great move to the basket: "He faked him into the popcorn machine!" There were many times I wished I could have locked Bill in there. He would come back to the booth with a load of popcorn smothered with onions, peppers, tomatoes, pickles and onions and topped off with enough nacho cheese sauce to dribble all over the edges of the plate.

Bill took great delight in compiling and digging into his third-inning snack. A big smile would come over his face. I soon learned that he could do color with me and shovel down this *piece de resistance* all at the same time. This was a simple thing to do, according to Bill. "You store the food in the side of your mouth like a chipmunk and keep talking," he explained.

I think Bill would have eaten in his sleep if he could have. Roy Eisenhardt remembers times when Bill would have eaten all through the night and morning if Roy had let him. "He and Lon used to come over at night and sit and talk until two or three in the morning," Roy told me. "I'd kid him and say, 'Bill, my refrigerator is empty. You need to go home now.' He'd keep going back there and getting food out of the refrigerator."

Bill took great pride — I mean serious pride — in his ability to clear out a booth in a split second. His smile widened in proportion to the pungency of the smell he unleashed in the booth. Talk about something interrupting your train of thought. I had nowhere to go, of course, because I had play-by-play to do, which seemed to delight Bill even more. I had listened to Lon and Bill for years and now I understood the wry tone that would creep into Lon's voice when he talked about how the frogs had returned to the booth.

"You know, Bill," Lon would say on the air. "I spent all those years in the National League, and now that I am in the American League with you, I never realized that they built every ballpark next to a sulfur factory."

The *Chronicle's* Ray Ratto called it "the faint sulfurous haze." Rick Barry had fond memories of Bill except "those awful cigars and his flatulence." For a while in the early 2000s we had the gasoline company Valero as one of our sponsors on A's radio. Bill delivered the tagline to their commercial with great gusto: "Valero, gas with vroooommm!" Hank Greenwald, working with me one day, had an even better line when we came back to the broadcast live: "Nobody knows gas like Bill King!"

Bill's appetite for life was voracious. I've never seen anyone so passionate about food. All kinds of food. "He used to be able to eat a whole loaf of French bread over lunch," Scotty Stirling recalled. During football games, he added, Bill "would eat these awful-looking tortillas filled with onions and peanut butter."

Bill developed a serious allergy to wheat in the mid-'70s, and it was scary because it took time to diagnose. "He would come to games sometimes really sick and his voice was weak," said Scotty, "but he fought through it and never missed a game."

He learned to be careful and shunned some of his favorite foods. I remember many nights in my years with Bill when he would long for a pizza or some pasta, but he stayed disciplined, and this was at a time before gluten-free choices were available on menus like they are now.

One of the other things about sharing the booth with Bill was that I had to develop the ability to protect my territory. I learned early in our time together that my food was fair game for Bill. We were doing a game in Cleveland and I had taken my press room meal into the booth because I was running late and needed to finish the pregame show before I could enjoy the rest of my dinner. So I left a half-full plate in the back of the booth and was looking forward to finishing it. I came back to discover that it was empty — completely cleaned, as if someone had licked every last morsel off the plate. I looked over at Bill and without any sign of contrition at all he said, "I thought you were done."

It's funny, but whenever I say or write the word "morsel" I think of Vin Scully. Some things are indelible, like Scully's commercial for Farmer John. Anyone who has listened to a Dodgers game probably has the script memorized. "Dodger baseball is brought to you by Farmer John, the easternmost in quality and the westernmost in flavor." Vinny would stretch out that last word in Vinny-ese, as if tasting the hot dog as he was saying: *FLAAAA-VURRRR*. Then he would say something about the last succulent morsel.

Bill and I used to sit next to each other on A's flights, which was fantastic most of the time. How would you not want to spend all that time with someone as enlightened as Bill? Every flight was an education. Bill would spread out like an amoeba, newspapers and magazines everywhere, and he would clip things he thought were interesting and pass them over to me. Food was everywhere too, of course, and then with his stomach full and, tragically for me, a glass full of wine, he would fall asleep leaning in my direction. My thoughts quickly turned to dry-cleaning bills because wine stains on my shirt were a frequent manifestation of flying in the seat next to Bill.

Bill had his towns where he had his lunch spots — Nello on Madison Avenue in New York was a particular favorite — and some places were more breakfast than lunch. There is a place down the street from the team hotel in Seattle, Tulio's, that featured a frittata that he took great pleasure in devouring on Sunday mornings.

Bill was a connoisseur of fine food when it came time for dinner, but he'd eat anything. "I could give you a restaurant that was the epitome of fine dining," Mickey Morabito, the A's legendary and nonpareil traveling secretary, told me. "White tablecloth service, fine wine, a maitre d' in a tux, and he loved the little taco dump in Anaheim, so you couldn't pigeonhole him. It was the full spectrum."

It didn't take an elaborately constructed dish to please Bill; an ingredient all by itself could be a meal. He was a big lover of butter and would eat it plain. One time in Kansas City, the A's beat writers decided to have a little fun.

"We loaded a bowl with pats of butter and gave it to Bill to munch on in the broadcast booth," recalled Mike Lefkow, who covered the A's for the *Contra Costa Times*. The butter went to work on Bill's system and "made him more dangerous than usual," Lefkow said.

"By around the fifth inning, Ray Fosse had had enough. Between innings he came down to where we were sitting, yelling, 'Thanks a lot, guys. Why don't you go up and sit next to him?'"

Bill would cruise the halls of the team hotel after games looking for room-service trays with leftover slabs of butter, which he would eat at one sitting. Pedro Gomez, now a regular on ESPN's *Baseball*

Tonight, loved to go out to eat with Bill on the road in his years covering the A's for the *San Jose Mercury News* and *Sacramento Bee* and often watched Bill conduct his hallway raids. "It made me cringe," Gomez recalled for this book. "But Bill always told me, 'If they're leaving it here, you know no one has touched it. It went from their room to the hall.'"

Wally Haas can top Gomez.

"I remember one time we were on a team charter to New York," he said for this book. "There was like a deli that they put out in the front of the plane, and Bill at the end of it asked the stewardess for a garbage bag. He put all the food in it and took it to his hotel."

Bill was always on the prowl for food, especially on the A's plane.

"We would always tease him because he would always be snacking and he would dip into everything, all the food, take a little bit of this and a little bit of that, have his thongs on," Jason Giambi recalled. "But you loved him so much, you didn't care."

Steve Vucinich remembers one time seeing Bill in blue jeans, food sticking out of his pockets, walking barefooted down the aisle of the A's plane in the direction of the restroom. This was when the former Cub Billy Williams was one of the A's coaches. "Here's Billy Williams, a Hall of Famer, watching Bill go by. He sees Bill and he does a classic double take. It was classic."

There was no better entertainment than a night out with Bill King. After a glass of wine or two the stories started flowing, and that's when anyone who had a chance to enjoy the night with Bill came away with a feeling that they had just relived a piece of their childhood. He was a walking, talking history of Bay Area sports. He was such good company and enjoyed the camaraderie so much that it was almost like we needed a waiting list to join us for dinner because so many members of the traveling party had roots in Northern California and had worshipped Bill from the time they were young.

Our meals usually came after some serious negotiation between

Bill and me. I preferred to eat at, let's say, around seven on the road, but Bill felt that eating before nine was "uncivilized." I didn't have the stomach for trying to fall asleep after a big meal that late. One time Andy Dolich was talking to Bill during a rain delay in Chicago. It was a Saturday night, but Bill and Lon had thrown things back to the station to kill time, meaning it would be very late before they would get out of the ballpark, but Bill was focused on eating. Andy considered himself an adventurous eater, but with Bill, you never knew what was in store.

"Where should we go?" Bill asked Andy.

"I don't do Albanian," Andy joked.

"There is Chauchesku's on Addison," Bill shot back, deadpan. "But I think they close at 11 o'clock."

Bill would ponder the wine list at dinner like a judge considering courtroom arguments. It was very, very important that he make the appropriate choice and so, as he did with everything else, he learned as much about wine as he possibly could.

"He was not a *pseudo*-expert, but a *real* expert when it came to wine," Scotty Stirling said. "He had a collection. He knew good wine."

Raiders PR guy Bob Bestor had an uncle in Kansas City who was a high-powered lawyer with an extensive wine collection, said to be one of the best in the entire Midwest. When the Raiders were on the road in Kansas City, Bill and Scotty and Bob Bestor would always wind up at Uncle John's house to quaff some very top-level wine.

"It would be like a professional wine tasting," Stirling recalled. "John Bestor was good at it, Bob Bestor was good at it, but King was the best."

We had our rotation of places during spring training, about a half-dozen restaurants that were close to the team hotel. Sadly, one of them, a little Italian place called Pronto at Fortieth and Campbell, closed its doors three or four years after we started working together. One place fans always mention to me — because we probably gave it tons of free advertising on the broadcasts — is the Havana Cafe at Forty-fourth and Camelback. It's the place Ray and

I always talked about during any night game that we broadcast from Phoenix Municipal Stadium. Bill couldn't stand the lighting at Phoenix Muni and so he never worked the home night games. Ray and I had a little ritual around the third inning where we would wonder out loud where Bill was about then.

"He's probably pulling into the Havana Cafe about now," one of us would say, and I think we had the timing pretty much nailed. Bill's meals there started with a mojito and their signature appetizer, black bean fritters with guacamole, which sounds pretty good right now. Then for the main course he'd move on to maybe the pescado al marinero or the ropa vieja.

I wish I had a dollar for every time we were asked for a restaurant recommendation by A's fans familiar with Bill's interest in dining on the road. So in no particular order and completely unsolicited by the establishments, let me, with assistance from Mickey Morabito, offer the best recollections of the Bill King dining guide for the American League:

"In Toronto he loved old Hy's Steakhouse and in Boston, he loved Locke-Ober Restaurant," Mickey said, mentioning a colorful old joint that opened in 1875 and in its heyday was a hangout for politicians and celebrities. "He still liked Jimmy's Harborside, although it got touristy at the end," Mickey continued. "In Baltimore he loved Bud Paolino's crabs, on East Lombard," which was a place Mickey and Bill frequented with Billy Martin when Billy was managing the A's.

One of Bill's all-time choices was Tio Pepe, a Spanish restaurant tucked downstairs on one of the hills overlooking Baltimore's Inner Harbor. The management preferred that its clientele wear sports coats for dinner, which could sometimes be an issue. Bruce Jenkins of the *San Francisco Chronicle* recalled the first time he went there.

"I didn't have a coat and was presented one by management," Jenkins said. "It was a ridiculously garish, festive thing, all turquoise and flowers. We spent much of the dinner laughing uproariously at how absurd I looked. I knew right then that I had to build a whole outfit around that jacket: some kind of Halloween ensemble with orange pants, white belt, etc., to depict The Worst Guy in Town. I walked right out of there with the jacket on, and the plan was launched."

Bill wore a jacket at Tio Pepe because he loved the food there and didn't mind. Despite his preference for casual attire and his disdain for anything covering his feet, he wasn't opposed to getting spiffied up when the situation demanded. Many times he would come to the Coliseum for a day game and after the final out change into attire more appropriate for the opera, ballet or a finer restaurant. As with food, Bill's clothing choices covered the full spectrum. He could morph into a dapper gentleman and feature a coat and tie or even a tuxedo if it was a special night.

"In Chicago, we went to Eli's, which was the old-fashioned steak house before you had Morton's and the newfangled ones," Mickey remembered. "He was always loyal to Eli's — they had a little piano bar in the lounge and it was nice, a great little dinning atmosphere. In Kansas City he loved the barbeque and the rib places Arthur Bryant's and Gates — Arthur Bryant's more than Gates."

Bill looked forward to any trip to Milwaukee, because he got to dine at one of his favorite places, Karl Ratzsch's, a German restaurant dating back to the 1950s whose founder was visiting from Germany when World War I broke out and he had to stay and make a new life in Wisconsin. Ratzsch's (it's hard to pronounce even if you speak German) is on East Mason Street across the street from the hotel where the A's stayed, the old Pfister Hotel, a place with quite a reputation in baseball circles. According to legend, the Pfister is haunted. Maybe it goes back to the 1970s, when Bill was walking the streets of Milwaukee with Scotty Stirling and they ran into that woman who was certain Bill was the devil.

Everything about going to Milwaukee was fun for the broadcast team, and eating was a big part of it all. Tailgating wasn't just confined to the parking lots. The press box at County Stadium had the perfect baseball odor, thanks to the bratwurst grilling out behind where the writers worked. Bill loved German food and he could stow away bratwurst at the game and then for dinner go to Karl Ratzsch's, where he was a big fan of the schnitzel.

"I didn't go out with him that much, partly because I was scared to because of some of the stuff he would eat," Wally Haas recalled for this book. "But I remember in Milwaukee going to Karl Ratzsch's with him. First off, I've never seen any German restaurant more authentic, to the point where I thought I was going to get tapped on the shoulder and asked for my passport. *Your papers, please.* But he was a joy to be with."

There were numerous seafood choices in Seattle, but we spent most nights at The Brooklyn Seafood, Steak and Oyster House on Second Avenue, across the street from the Seattle Art Museum. Bill used to go there a lot for lunch and he would sit at one of their giant chairs at a counter by the kitchen. Shuckers, at the Fairmont hotel on University, was another favorite. As I am writing this I am thinking of some fresh halibut over a pile of mashed potatoes on a bed of asparagus. Seattle was a town where I could wait until a "civilized" hour to eat, even if we arrived late after a flight, since my stomach would start yearning for oysters and something fresh from the grill on the morning of a trip up there.

New York was another of the multiple choice cities, although Bill always had lunch at Nello, where Nello Balan is the owner and executive chef. Nello spent time in Italy as a kid (which certainly influences the cuisine), was trained in Europe and speaks seven languages, which comes in handy in New York, especially with the restaurant's location just east of Central Park on Madison. There are several outside tables where Bill loved to sit, and his food would be accompanied by a glass or two of white wine. Then he would head back to the hotel for some prep for the game and a power nap and he would be set to go for the team bus to Yankee Stadium. A caveat, by the way: If you are going to Nello, bring plenty of money. It's not cheap.

"In New York," Mickey told me, "he would rush to get out of there after the game to try to get to the Russian Tea Room. Bill loved all the cities, except Texas."

Well, actually, in fairness to the bane of Bill's existence on the road, he liked a chain restaurant called Pappadeaux Seafood Kitchen that was walking distance from the Ballpark in Arlington. He'd have a little blackened seafood with an etouffee sauce and maybe a layer of crab meat on top.

The only good thing I remember about the A's 2002 playoff trip to Minneapolis — the A's lost both of the games at the Metrodome — was dinner the night before Game Three at Oceanaire, where Bill always ordered the side of scalloped potatoes. The sides at Oceanaire were big enough for a party of four, which meant they were actually the perfect size for Bill.

Until the recent past the A's stayed in downtown Detroit in Greektown, which has several restaurants lining Monroe Street and a Cajun place called Fishbone's. There is also a bakery called the Astoria Pastry Shop where I gained ten pounds on every trip loading up on their apricot tarts to have with coffee in the morning.

Mickey said Bill would find places in downtowns where others would never have ventured. The Warriors used to stay at the Book Cadillac Hotel in Detroit, which was closed for many years but, as Mickey told me, has reopened as a Westin and some of the American League teams are staying there again. The London Chop House was on Congress Street downtown around the corner from the Book Cadillac and opened in 1938 and was a favorite of Bill's during the NBA days and his early years with the A's. He ate there many times with Meschery and the gang, and Mickey happened to be there with the Yankees when he was their PR director on the day they had a magic number of one to clinch the pennant after playing earlier at Tiger Stadium. George Steinbrenner told Mickey to gather the team at the Chop House to wait for the end of the Red Sox game at Baltimore. Mickey was on the phone with Bob Brown, the old Orioles PR man, getting play-by-play of the game from the press box so the Yanks could celebrate if the Orioles won, which they did. The London Chop House reopened early in 2012 and is making a comeback. "It was a great, fine dining place and Bill loved it," Mickey recalled.

"My greatest memories were the three-hour dining experiences with Bill King," Mickey said, reminiscing on the twenty-five years he traveled the American League with Bill. "Sitting there sometimes it would drive you crazy — you'd be done — he would eat so slowly and drink his wine and it would take you three hours to get through a dining experience with Bill, but it was never for a loss of great stories. I loved the old NBA stories of doubleheaders in Boston and stuff like that. I was fascinated to hear those stories. It was incredible to be in his company in that kind of environment and I'll never forget those dinners with him, it was marvelous."

Bill hated the hassle of driving so much that he and Lon used to kid about their dream arrangement. They were going to ask the A's if they could work it out so that Lon would do all the home games and Bill would do the road. The road is where he felt the most free during the ten years we spent together. There were no bills to pay, no responsibilities except the games, the phone didn't ring, there were no errands to run and he was totally relaxed. He didn't change his routine that much from when he first started traveling with the Warriors. Maybe the nights were shorter because he needed a couple more hours of sleep and he obsessed a little more over his homework, but he never really slowed down. Those glasses of wine and all of the different food tasted as good when he was seventy-five as when he was just starting out. He certainly had his quirky habits when it came to food, but I'll say this, every meal with Bill was an experience.

For the big groups along for these dinners, it was like a trip back in time as Bill brought to life people like Wilt and Barry and Stabler and Davis. Every story, like the way Bill savored his food, was an event. Then Bill had a little tradition that followed every meal. Content, he would pull himself back from the table and exclaim, "I have a feeling of great well being."

CHAPTER 11

THE STREAK

*Swung on, there's a high drive, hit way back,
right-center field. That one is gone, and it's
twenty consecutive victories for the Oakland
Athletics on an unbelievable night when they
lost a 11–0 lead and now they win it!
The crowd comes back to insane life.
Crazy, just plain crazy!*

ill King had been a broadcaster for more than forty years and had borne witness to the full range of drama that professional sports could offer, describing the indescribable as it unfolded in the stadiums of the NFL, arenas of the NBA and ballparks of Major League Baseball. Did I say full range? Correction: What happened in late summer 2002 stretched the boundaries, more and more with each subsequent game notched in the "W" column. *"Crazy, just plain crazy! How do you explain it?"* Bill cried when the fabric of reality finally broke and the A's had taken possession of an American League win-streak record that was more than a century old. You could say it was all the more remarkable because the A's in late May had been six games under .500 and ten games out of first, and that in the recent off-season they had lost Jason Giambi to big Yankees money, not to mention Johnny

Damon to big Red Sox money, and that their hearts had been broken by Derek Jeter in the playoffs the fall before, and that another bout of baseball labor strife was lying in wait to derail the whole thing — and you'd be right. But the beauty of the Streak — like all the great streaks — was how remarkable it was strictly on its own terms, apart from any larger context, unfolding day by day with twists and turns like a great suspense novel that had you hungry for the next page.

Barry Zito started the streak on August 13, although of course no one realized it at the time. He struck out seven, working eight innings to earn his sixteenth win of the season, a 5–4 decision for the Athletics that kept them 4½ games behind the Mariners in the American League West race, with the Angels sandwiched between the two teams, two games out of first. Tim Hudson picked it up the next day, winning 4–2 over the Jays. Then for win Number 3, Cory Lidle and the bullpen combined to shut out the White Sox. The offense got going in back-to-back laughers to close out the homestand, and by then it was a noticeable if still modest streak for the A's, at five in a row.

The A's took to the road for a ten-game trip, beginning at Jacobs Field in Cleveland where they proceeded to take four games straight from the Indians. None of them was close — 8–1, 6–3, 6–0, 9–3. The highlight of the sweep was a one-hitter by Lidle in the third game of the series. Bill:

> **"** *Bouncing ball softly hit right side, tough play for Ellis, shovels it over in time to Lidle covering, ball game is over!"*

Momentum really began to build on that road trip. It was exciting to work those games, but I had one eye on the standings and the other on news of the labor situation. The owners and players were headed to an August 29 deadline to reach an agreement, trying to avoid a repeat of 1994, when a strike derailed the season on August 12. If it happened again, we were all thinking, the fans were unlikely to be so forgiving.

The A's came closest to losing on the trip on a Sunday, August 25 in Detroit. They were trailing 7–3 before breaking through for a five-run eighth. Here's Bill's call:

> 66 *Mabry hits one, deep to right-center field, racing back Fick can't get it, it bounces to the wall by the scoreboard. One run is in, two runs are in. Mabry, on one pitch, has shot the A's in front!"*

They scored two more in the ninth, but were holding on for dear life when the Tigers loaded the bases in the bottom half with Brandon Inge at the plate. Billy Koch was on the mound: *"Strike three called! Twelve straight wins for the Athletics. Man alive, was it hairy!"*

After winning three in the Motor City, the A's moved on to Kansas City. Bill, at the end of the middle game of the series: *"That's the sound of fourteen straight victories!"*

On the off day before Number 16, I played golf with Art Howe. Art's a heck of a golfer and in those days we had some serious battles on the course, but that day our attention was diverted out of fear there wouldn't be a game the next day in Oakland. "Everyone was on pins and needles wondering if there was going to be another work stoppage," Art recalled. Sometime on the back side, Art's phone rang with news of an agreement between the players and owners. Relieved, we could relax and enjoy the golf for the rest of the day.

Months earlier, Bill had planned on taking Labor Day weekend off. At this point in his life Bill looked forward to taking vacation time during small segments of the season. I hope I have made the point in this book about Bill's class and graciousness toward me. This was perhaps the greatest example.

I imagine many of my peers, some driven by ego and insecurity, would have canceled their vacation plans. After all, the A's were now on the doorstep of history. They needed three wins to set a franchise record and five in a row to break the American League mark.

Broadcasting the ninth inning is like a trophy in our business. There is a certain status that goes with it, and the reality is that most of the dramatic moments come in the ninth. Bill had friends who told him that surely he should cancel his plans so that his voice would be the one of record if something truly memorable happened over the weekend. Honest, I wouldn't have blamed him if he had worked.

At home the night before game Number 16, Bill was asked if he might have a change of heart. He was resolute, telling Nancy and Kathleen, "No, those games are Ken's." Steve Bitker filled in for Bill.

There was a huge walk-up crowd at the ballpark on Friday night for the A's win over Minnesota. The next night Eric Chavez's broken-bat single in the eighth off J.C. Romero secured the seventeenth win.

But on Sunday afternoon things looked dire. It was Eddie Guardado on the mound with two on and two out in the ninth and the Twins leading by a run. Miguel Tejada, burnishing his MVP résumé, drilled a one-two pitch into the left field seats and pandemonium broke out at the Coliseum. The planets were aligning for the A's.

"We never hit Eddie," Art recalled eleven years later. "He could throw his glove up there and we couldn't hit it."

I've always felt my call was over the top — I was screaming at the top of my lungs — but it was what I was feeling at the time. The A's had broken the franchise record set in the Connie Mack days back in 1931.

Robert Buan and I went to see Jackson Browne and Tom Petty that night, but I left after Jackson's set thinking it wouldn't be a bad idea to get some rest for the afternoon game the next day.

On Labor Day with the Royals in town it came down once again to Tejada in the bottom of the ninth. Tony Pena was managing the Royals and he tried everything, even employing a five-man infield, but there was no one over the bag at second when Tejada hammered a Jason Grimsley sinker into center field. A's, 7–6.

I've been asked a thousand times what it was like to be in the Coliseum for game Number 20. My answer is always simple: "I wasn't there." I had planned on taking the game off, since Labor Day had caused an anomaly in the schedule. The A's series with the Royals was a two-game set, but because the A's wanted the home date on the holiday, the teams played on Monday and had Tuesday off. Game Number 20 was on a Wednesday night and the A's had the next day off as well before beginning a series in Minnesota. In those days I tried to take a day or two off around the first of September to be home for our wedding anniversary and Emilee's first day of school. So by missing the second game of the Royals series I got three days off in a row.

Denise and I talked on the phone about how I had broadcast the first nineteen games of the streak and that maybe I should consider staying and working Number 20. Ray was going to be in the booth that night — there was no local TV because ESPN was carrying the game — and it was also going to be Bill's first game back after his mini-vacation. Taking my lead from Bill, I decided to leave the game for Bill and Ray to broadcast.

In the movie *Moneyball* there is a scene where Billy Beane and Ron Washington go to Scott Hatteberg's house to recruit Scott to join the A's and make a position change from catcher to first base. Obviously, the home visit never happened in real life. I asked Scott, who had signed with the A's ostensibly to replace departed superstar Jason Giambi, if the trepidation at playing first, as depicted in the movie by Chris Pratt, was accurate.

"I didn't want a ball hit at me," he told me. "I was nervous. I hadn't picked up a ground ball until I got to the big leagues that year. I was a catcher my whole life. It was hard. I thought those things, but I didn't let anybody know them."

Scott wasn't concerned about playing first base on September 4. He wasn't in the lineup and was certain he would have the entire night off once the A's built an 11–0 lead with their ace right-hander, Tim Hudson, on the mound. With all the September call-ups, the dugout was crowded and so Scott was up in the clubhouse drinking coffee, thinking there was no chance he would be playing and looking forward to celebrating with his teammates.

Upstairs Bill had the same feeling: "I think my recap will be simple," he told his audience. "The A's scored six in the first, one in the second and four in the third."

Fosse, knowing Bill's postgame recaps were usually only slightly shorter than *War and Peace,* had the perfect retort: "And people would be shocked if you just did that."

Down in the dugout Art Howe, who had endured the stress of the ninth-inning dramatics of the previous games, was finally able to exhale. That was his big mistake.

"I take the blame for what happened," Art told me. At the age of sixty-six, he is still trim and athletic and not at all like the schlubby character portrayed by Philip Seymour Hoffman in the movie. "I did something that was taboo. I told (pitching coach) Rick Peterson that we finally had a laugher." Apparently, the baseball gods didn't take too kindly to that. The Royals began pecking away and by the time the ninth inning began, to paraphrase Scully's call of Gibson's home run: On a night that was so improbable, the impossible was happening.

"It wasn't all Huddy's fault," Art recalled. "We kicked some balls and didn't make some plays behind him that we normally make."

Hatteberg's head was back into the game at this point. The Royals had scored five in the fourth and another five in the eighth to make it 11–10, and as the game neared the ninth, he headed to the indoor batting cage that is up the steps from the A's clubhouse adjacent to the Raiders' locker room. He was there with another left-handed hitter, Greg Myers, taking some swings and watching the game on a little TV and thinking, "We're letting this fall right through our fingertips. That was a pretty hollow feeling."

There was a phone nearby where Howe would often call late in a game to tell one of the hitters to get ready. Grimsley, who had been victimized by Tejada on Labor Day, was warming up in the bullpen. Howe was going to have either Hatteberg or Myers pinch-hit in the bottom of the ninth.

Up in the radio booth Ray Fosse had a plan as well. On the days when it was just Ray and me or Ray and Bill in the booth, Ray did play-by-play in the third, fourth and seventh innings. He also had the tenth if the game went extra innings. Fosse is one of the most insightful analysts in baseball, but play-by-play, by his own admission, is not his forte.

When the ninth inning began he told Bill that if there was a tenth, that Bill should do it. He was going to leave the rest of the action, no matter how long the game lasted, to the master.

It was 11–11 when the bottom of the ninth began, after Luis Alicea's two-run single had tied the game in the top half. Howe had called up to the cage for Hatteberg and Scott knew he would be up second, batting for Eric Byrnes. The Coliseum crowd, the largest ever for a regular season game there, sat in stunned silence, a major mood swing from earlier in the game when jubilation engulfed the place.

Hatteberg knew what he was going to get from Grimsley, a pitcher he had had little success against in the past.

"It was 98 mph sinkers, bowling-ball sinkers," he said. "It was very, very hard to get the ball in the air off him. It just goes down so hard that contact always ends up in the ground and he gets a lot of ground balls. I was thinking, 'Make him get the ball up,' something I can get into a gap, maybe get a double and get into scoring position and we'll have a shot at it."

Grimsley left one of those sinkers up a little bit, and Hatteberg was able to get just enough of the bottom half of the ball to achieve enough elevation to send a majestic drive toward the right-center field seats.

In the broadcast booth, Bill King, focused as always, a little over a month away from his seventy-fifth birthday, was poised to deliver the call of a lifetime:

“ *This year Hatteberg in pinch-hitting roles is one for five. Two-sixty-nine average. He's gone deep a dozen times. Now the pitch. Swung on, there's a high drive, hit way back, right-center* *field. That one is gone, and it's twenty consecutive victories for the Oakland Athletics on an unbelievable night when they lost a 11–0 lead and now they win it! The crowd comes back to insane life. Crazy, just plain crazy! How do you explain it? Hatteberg is mobbed at home plate. In 103 years of American League baseball, the Athletics have accomplished what no one has before. They have won twenty consecutive games!"*

Bill's voice tails off at the end and I wasn't there, of course, but I'm guessing he was choking up a bit. It wasn't unusual to see Bill tear up, either during a poignant pregame ceremony or while he was calling a special play. It wasn't just that he wanted the A's to win — "He wanted us to do so well," said Art — but he was so immersed in every moment. He was describing the emotions unfolding before him, but he was also feeling them.

Hatteberg heard nothing, despite the madness in the ballpark. "I was running around like an idiot. It is kind of a numbing click when it happens and you don't really hear the crowd. I don't think I heard anybody until about second base. I was hearing my own screaming and the bells and whistles in my head. We had fifty-some thousand there that night — it was packed — it shook you, man, it shook your chest."

Now, eleven years after one of the most famous home runs ever hit, Hatteberg remembers that he knew he hit it well and, even though the Coliseum is a pitcher's park, especially at night, he was pretty certain it was going out.

Art Howe was sure as soon as the ball left the bat. "Grimsley had that power sinker and when Hatte got him he got the sinker up a little and he didn't miss it. That's what is great about hitting, when you get that one pitch you've got to be ready."

Oftentimes during games Billy Beane would get so intense that he would turn nomadic, unable to watch the action in person. During a game of such roller-coaster emotions he was all over the place.

"I'm not even sure where I was when that happened," Billy told me when I asked him about his memories of Number 20. "That night, you could have written a book on that night alone. They could have made half the movie if they had just followed me around with the GPS. It was such a long night, because the game itself was long and it was an incredibly surreal evening."

Scott Hatteberg retired in 2008 and has worked in the A's front office for the last two years. He also works on A's television, about 20 games a year beginning in 2012. He was sitting in the home radio booth before a game early in 2013, about two feet from where Bill made the famous call, when I asked him what he thought the first time he heard it.

"It was a game that really was going downhill," Hatteberg told me. "It was depressing what we were doing — it was falling apart."

When he went to the plate that night, Hatteberg wasn't thinking about making history.

"It was just a pinch hit with nobody on. It wasn't a dramatic moment," he said. And yet when Scott struck the big blow, Bill was poised to seize the moment and freeze it in time.

"All of a sudden, fireworks! It happened, we win, and to have the wits about you to grasp the situation so well and put it into words … " Hatteberg said, shaking his head in wonder. "To just absorb yourself in it and let it come out and to do it so profoundly. I don't know. It is pretty cool. Masterful."

Michael Lewis was probably going to have a best-selling book whether the A's won twenty straight or not. After all, *Moneyball* was as much about economics as baseball. Michael spent a good part of the '02 season traveling with us. What resulted was a seminal examination of Billy Beane and the A's approach at that time. It would be a stretch to say the book changed the game, but it is not an embellishment to point out how much the game has changed in the last decade. *Moneyball* was about finding value and maximizing resources and breaking heretofore barriers when it came to evaluating talent.

I was doing a game early in the 2013 season in Houston when I made the point, only half in jest, that you couldn't work for the Astros unless you graduated from Harvard. The Astros literally have a rocket scientist in their player personnel department. The whole debate of old school versus new school and the importance of scouts came to the forefront after the publication of the book. I don't think there is much debate now that the best approach is a combination of the two, and that six postseason appearances in thirteen years beginning in 2000 validated the stamp Billy Beane made on the franchise and the game.

It wasn't long after the publication of the book that word began to filter out that they were thinking about making a movie. Was Hollywood nuts? How could you possibly make a movie out of an economics of baseball book? Multiple scripts were written until they centered the movie around the twenty-game winning streak.

"That's when they were able to come up with a script," Billy told me. "When the screenwriters actually focused on that game and then worked out from there, that was when they got a script that the director and Sony and everybody was happy with. It was six or seven years of writing it and rewriting it."

At the culmination of the streak, the producers of the movie had something golden: the perfect exclamation point provided by Bill King.

"It was fitting given his history and it will go down," Billy said. "Heck, it is cinema now forever, and that's a good thing for the people who follow the A's. And the punctuation mark was Bill's call and I know the first time I saw it and heard that, I went, 'Wow!'"

The producers of the movie combed through hundreds of hours of A's radio and television archives. You hear many voices in the movie, including that of Greg Papa, who was the television voice of the A's in 2002. Greg recorded some voice-overs and shot several scenes for the movie with the A's current TV announcer Glenn

Kuiper. I spent an hour shooting a scene with the director, Bennett Miller, that landed on the cutting room floor.

All the stars were there at the movie's Oakland premiere in September 2011, including Brad Pitt and Jonah Hill, a favorite of Emilee's. Television production trucks and satellite dishes lined the streets outside, as did fans who waited for hours to get a glimpse of Hollywood royalty. The Paramount Theatre was packed and many A's players were on hand. The balcony was filled with A's fans who roared during the scenes of the winning streak as if it were happening all over again.

Hatteberg was there, watching Chris Pratt play him on the giant screen. As an athlete, Hatteberg had never been impressed with Hollywood's ability to capture the essence of sports.

"They always screw up baseball movies and they never seem as dramatic and never look as good on the screen as they do in person," he told me. This time, though, Hatteberg thought they nailed it.

"I lived it and we lived it as a team. For them to get even remotely close to the drama that we had was going to be a tall order but my gosh, it gave me goose bumps and it still does," Hatteberg said. "It was a great moment and Bill's voice right on top of it is the perfect soundtrack."

When the movie focused on the final games of the streak, my voice boomed over the loudspeakers in the theater. It was a surreal feeling and I fought my usual impulse to self-consciously analyze whether the calls were any good or not. Emilee was sitting in the middle, with Denise to her left and me on her right. After the scenes of the nineteenth game had ended, Emilee turned to me. The fans in the theater were going crazy and we looked at each other, our eyes a little damp, sharing a very special father-daughter moment. "Dad," she said, "you had a pretty big part there."

It took less than a split second for my thoughts to turn to Bill and how gracious he was, and that the only reason my calls made it into the movie was Bill's selfless act to stay away during games sixteen through nineteen. Every time I think about it, even now after all these years, I find myself getting emotional. I would probably have lasted eighteen years with the A's without working those ninth innings and without the movie, but it didn't hurt. Those highlights have been forever etched into the memories of everyone associated with the A's. Putting the movie and what those calls meant to my career aside, the once-in-a-lifetime experience of being on the air in the ninth inning as history was being made will stay with me for the rest of my life. As a broadcaster, you live for those moments.

The movie was a huge success at the box office as well as critically. It received six Academy Award nominations, including Best Picture, although it was shut out when it came to the Oscars. The detractors of the movie point out, with good cause, that it didn't really focus on the stars of the team like Hudson, Mulder, Zito, Tejada and Chavez. There was much Hollywood license taken with the facts, but I have always thought that the movie was basically true to the premise of the book.

Bill's call has taken on a life of its own. Back in 2003, the A's gave their season-ticket holders Bill King bobbleheads: Push the button on the base of the bobblehead and, presto, several of Bill's great calls are heard, including, of course, Number 20. The A's also produced a bottle opener that when you pop it you hear audio of the call. What will they think of next? Scott Hatteberg and Bill King will be linked forever, the player and the broadcaster combining for one of baseball's most memorable moments. It was like a composer providing the music to a virtuoso conductor.

In 2012, the A's celebrated the tenth anniversary of the streak with a Hatteberg bobblehead giveaway. Bill's call is part of that one, too, broken up into three audio segments. "That was totally cool," Hatteberg said. Scott has three kids and each has a bobblehead in their room. "People come over and they are always pushing it. We have one of the bottle openers and we've gone through batteries with all those calls. I don't get sick of it for some reason."

Art Howe and Bill King spent seven years together recording the pregame manager's interview. From time to time they chose historical places in the various ballparks, like the red seat at Fenway Park that commemorates a prodigious home run Ted Williams hit in 1946. Art has the Bill King bobblehead at home in his office as well. It's a reminder of all those early evenings and afternoons they shared. "I miss him to this day," Art told me. "I push the button from time to time just to listen to his voice."

CHAPTER 12

LOSING A PARTNER

*Alas, he was, like the Golden Gate Bridge,
a treasure all ours, to be dispensed
in portions but too magnificent to share.*

I have this vision of Bill's first appearance in the spring. He usually arrived in Phoenix a couple of days before our opening broadcast and he would come straight to the A's offices at the stadium. He'd enter through the front door and cross the hall to the room where some of the broadcasters and PR people would hang out. He always had two old ratty knapsacks on his shoulders and he lugged a briefcase that looked like it was produced before Samsonite was founded. He would be wearing blue jeans and his signature flip-flops were on his feet. We didn't usually talk much during the off-season, but once Bill came on the scene each spring it was like it normally is with good friends. You pick up right where you left off.

Bill's health was generally good when the 2004 season ended. He did slump over a bit when he walked and had a hitch in his gait, the result of an old hip injury. He'd had a hip replacement during his time with the Raiders in L.A. and now he was seventy-something, but I thought he had a great year on the air in '04 and for thousands of A's fans, tuning in to the first spring broadcast and hearing Bill's voice once again was a sign that everything was right with the world.

That world turned upside down when Bill tripped on that old briefcase in his hotel room during spring training in 2005. Mickey always lined up the same room for Bill at the Doubletree Hotel, one that faced west, "so I can see the weather coming in," he used to tell me. He loved clouds and he would go into rhapsodies about clouds on the air.

Luckily Ken Pries was in town the day of Bill's accident and rushed to the hotel to take Bill to the hospital. Ken called me later that day with the news that the injury was serious since Bill had wrenched the hip that had been replaced, dislodging some of the work that had been done. Bill was in a lot of pain and had a decision to make: The doctors said he could have surgery right away or wait until the end of the season. How do you tell someone like Bill what he should do? They talk about the immovable object and the irresistible force. Bill was both. Determined to work and assured by his doctors that he couldn't damage the hip any more, Bill decided to put off the surgery to avoid missing a couple of months of the season.

"I'd go nuts missing that many games," Bill said, wary of the feeling of becoming detached.

"Broadcasting was his oxygen," Ken told me.

That was true, but it wasn't that he had to work for the ego gratification or adulation. He never lost the love and desire to be on the air and never stopped taking joy in every aspect of calling a game.

"That's what he loved," John Madden told me. "I think he enjoyed the camaraderie that goes with it. I think he enjoyed being around the teams. I think he enjoyed being in the arena, at the stadium."

At this time Bill said something amazing to me that might have come from his old underdog mentality or from the work ethic and toughness that was instilled in "The Greatest Generation," the heroes Tom Brokaw wrote about in his moving portrayal of those who came of age during the Depression and served valiantly in World War II. Bill said he was concerned about losing his job if he missed too much time. I told him he was crazy on that point, but that was Bill. Very often he made self-effacing comments. I can't tell you how many times he told me, matter-of-factly, "When I'm gone, there'll be a game the next day."

So he worked only home games. Despite being in pain he was much more relaxed than usual upon arrival at the Coliseum, thanks to Kathleen, who drove him to the park and back. It was very important and meaningful for Kathleen and Bill to spend so much time together, especially so soon after Nancy's death less than a year earlier. They needed that time together. They shared a lot, caught up a lot, grieved a little — and Bill taught Kathleen about baseball.

"Bill was so pleased and proud when I taught myself to score the game," Kathleen would recall. "I would arrive to pick him up fifteen minutes early so we could go over my score card from the day before and he would answer my questions, which were many, because I had suddenly discovered how complicated this seemingly simple game really was.

"We'd talk from the moment I picked him up to the moment I delivered him to the radio booth. And after the game we'd repeat the routine all over again on the way home. Those eighty-mile round-trip drives went by in a flash. Of course we'd talk about baseball. I had so much to learn.

"There were some scary moments driving sometimes, like when I would ask him to explain how a certain pitch was made and he would use his hands to show me and I would try to watch how he was holding the imaginary ball and drive the car at the same time. But we also would talk about everything under the sun. I honestly don't know how we got to and from the game sometimes because we were all over the map. One day a question I asked led to a conversation about the *Mutiny on the Bounty*. And then I read the *Bounty* trilogy and a pile of other books on the subject that Bill lent me. And then we'd spend the next few weeks in Tahiti and on Pitcairn Island. Another time a conversation about Cannery Row led to a conversation on John Steinbeck and I would read every Steinbeck book I could get my hands on and then we would spend weeks in Monterey and in the Salinas Valley.

"Once in a while he'd get in the car and he'd say, 'Let's listen to this,' and he would put the opera *La Traviata* in the CD player, or arias by Anna Netrebko and we would drive in complete silence — enthralled by the music. We never ran out of things or people to talk about — or music to listen to."

Before 2005, about the only time I think Bill really wanted to take advantage of being the *éminence grise* was when he threatened (and this happened often) to ask the A's to provide a driver as part of his contract; not to show off, but for the peace of mind because enduring Bay Area traffic was driving him nuts.

Bill arrived in the booth on crutches during the 2005 baseball season, but once the mic was turned on he still had it. The passion was there and in the final analysis, as much as it's easy in hindsight to say things might have been different if he had had the surgery earlier, he wanted to work. How do you convince him otherwise? It would have been like trying to pry an onion-and-peanut-butter tortilla out of his hands.

Hank worried that Bill was working too hard and that he wasn't having any fun away from the park. He thought Bill might have been dealing with that old thing about if you quit working you're going to die.

"You and I both used to talk about our concern about how deeply, in his later years, he was getting into his preparation — to a point where he was getting so consumed that he was shutting himself off from all of his other interests," Hank told me. "He used to love to read books about various other subjects and it was sort of like he thought he had to work harder and harder and what it gets down to is how much of it really matters? I know that worried the two of us. Maybe he felt because of the age factor that he had to show he could still do it and keep up and be more prepared, but there is a point of diminishing returns, I think."

Hank, whose introduction to Bay Area radio came because of Bill, joined me to broadcast the A's opening series in 2005 from Baltimore and Hank and Steve Bitker rotated on the road filling in for Bill.

By the time the season was nearing its end Bill had his eyes on

2006 and a fresh, healthy start after getting the hip surgery out of the way. He was looking forward to working a full schedule and he sounded a lot like Dick Enberg, when Dick, in his early seventies, wrote in his autobiography: "It is a narcotic, my occupation, and right now I enjoy my work as much as ever. The time I might want to consider hanging up the mic is when I don't look forward to my assignments — when the passion is gone. So far that hasn't happened."

The legendary scout Gary Hughes, who went to Serra High in San Mateo and to San Jose State and started listening to Bill in the early '60s, has been a fixture at ballparks for fifty years. At the end of 2005, Gary was working in the front office for the Cubs. Like Bill, Gary's hip had been replaced. In fact, he talked a lot to Bill about Bill's original surgery before Gary had his.

"Bill was all pumped up about going in for hip surgery after the '05 season," Gary told me. "He was really feeling positive and sought me out to talk about it, which was really neat for me."

Bill never left the hospital. Ken Pries called me the next Tuesday, October 18, to tell me that Bill had died of a pulmonary embolism. I was numb like everyone else in the Bay Area, including two old friends of Bill's who shared a poignant but awkward phone call that day. Greg Papa and Al Davis had become very close, especially in Davis' later years. They talked on the phone at least three or four times every week, but the phone call that came in October 2005 was one that neither man was prepared for.

Davis observers have talked often about how he had such a difficult time with death.

"He said it was the one thing he couldn't dominate," Greg told me.

Davis called Greg Papa on the day Bill died. Greg and his boss struggled with what to say. For three or four minutes no words were spoken. Then, Greg felt the anger in Davis. "'How could this happen?'" Greg recalled Davis asking. "He was so upset. The day Bill died — that really, really affected him."

The outpouring of love and admiration for Bill came flowing out of every article and every obituary in the papers over the next few days. The sheer volume of the tributes was mind-boggling but one line that really stood out for me was penned by Monte Poole in the *Oakland Tribune*: "Alas, he was, like the Golden Gate Bridge, a treasure all ours, to be dispensed in portions but too magnificent to share."

I asked Monte how he came up with the line.

"My thought was this: Bill, on a national level, doesn't get what he deserves because he was not national and that hurts him because I can't believe that anybody who heard Bill King doesn't believe he belongs in the Hall of Fame. Those of us here who heard him know it. There is something real about that because — and I'm sure Bill had opportunities if he wanted to explore the national market — but he had a lifestyle and also I'm sure there were some people who wouldn't want to hire him or would be afraid to hire him because he might do or say the wrong thing and he wasn't just going to be a cardboard cutout behind a mic. That's what endeared him to us and probably scared him away from other people out there. Fine, keep him here because we're OK with that. It was just good to know he was the same guy that I listened to as a kid when I met him as an adult."

A memorial service was planned for the Oakland Coliseum Arena, where Bill had broadcast so many games. Greg Papa remembered Davis being overcome with sadness but that he was also thinking about the best way to pay tribute to Bill. When Ken Pries called Davis' secretary, Fudgie Otten, she said Mr. Davis would do whatever the A's wanted.

A week later, Bill's friends and professional associates gathered for a service that was closed to the public but a huge crowd was there. It had been determined that representatives of the A's, Raiders and Warriors would deliver a eulogy. Davis spoke for the Raiders, Al Attles and Franklin Mieuli for the Warriors and the A's asked me.

Sandy Alderson and Roy Eisenhardt were there. So were Tony La Russa and Art Howe, who flew in from Houston. Rick Barry, Nate Thurmond, Tom Meschery, Jim Barnett and others were there from the Warriors. The Raiders were represented by Ben

Davidson, Tom Flores, Jim Otto and Jim Plunkett and several members of their front office. Virtually the entire A's staff was on hand, including the team's owner, Lew Wolff. A "Who's Who" of Bay Area broadcasting and newspaper talent showed up. Hank Greenwald served as emcee.

A stage was set up on the floor of the arena and a bottle of wine was placed at every table, but there was no food.

"Bill came in and ate all the food," Roy Eisenhardt said.

Franklin talked about their shared love of sailing and Bill's "mania for preparation." That was one of the great themes of Bill's life. He had all of these interests but they never compromised his dedication.

"There was nobody better than Bill," Al Attles said. "And I'm better for knowing him."

Michael Smuin picked a couple of dances he thought Bill would have loved. The Smuin Ballet opened the service, fittingly reflecting the many facets of Bill, and shortly thereafter Hank played the Mother's Day tape from 1968.

Davis was frail and I remember thinking how weak he looked as he walked to the podium. Then the stage became a vehicle for a trip back in time. All of a sudden it was Davis commanding the room like it was 1970, talking about "Pride and Poise" and about his dream of a million fans watching a Raider game, but that it wouldn't feel right unless Bill King was doing the play-by-play. Davis said Bill was the only person who could bring the Raiders, A's and Warriors together in the same building. Then in a pronouncement only Al Davis could have made: "I give him the cloak of immortality."

I don't usually work from a script when I speak in public, but I did this time. I wanted to get it right, but more than anything, I thought having a script might help me focus so I wouldn't lose it up there. At the end of my eulogy I told the story of the three things I couldn't say. I couldn't say "grand slam home run" or "early on." I couldn't thank him when he threw it to me. Then I violated Bill's rule and thanked him.

A couple of days later another service was held at the Sausalito

Yacht Club. It was a wonderful day with similar thoughts and emotions. It was with a different group of people, but the common denominator was Bill and how much he would be missed and how he had enriched so many lives, sentiments that were eloquently expressed in a poem Tom Meschery wrote and delivered at the occasion.

It was a tough first year without Bill and he will always be missed, probably as much now as back in our first year without him. One of the things that cushioned the blow for me back in 2006 was the knowledge that our fans were missing him as much as I was. But I couldn't be Bill King and knew I shouldn't try to be. One of the lessons from Bill is that you had to be yourself. In the ten years we worked together he was always the same guy I had listened to on the radio in my bedroom when I was a kid. He never wavered from who he was and that was one reason he endured. I've tried my whole life to find that kind of singular fortitude, and what a great role model to have. Bill never lost confidence in himself and in a business that can be rough and transitory he never gave in to the temptation to fit into someone else's mold.

"The most important thing is he didn't compromise who he was," Al Attles told me. "He was just a great man. The thing that I really, really liked about him, you always hear people say you want the honest opinion about things — no sugarcoating. He had to be Bill King, he couldn't be somebody else."

He was one of a kind. He knew it, we all knew it and yet he treated everyone as if he was just a guy who had a job to do; albeit one he did with a talent and verve that was unmatched.

I still find myself thinking about him, especially on the road. "Man, Bill would have loved this place," we'd say after a good dinner. It was hard on the bus rides. I can't tell you how many times, even now, I'll look across the aisle and want to tell him something.

We've talked about him on the air. The stories are still fun to tell and I thought it was good therapy, especially in the first couple of years for Ray and me and above all for the fans. Ray and I got to go to the memorials, but the fans, who felt they knew Bill as well as we did, never really had the chance to say goodbye.

Bill left it all on the field, as they say. He had no regrets about his career and he was secure in his legacy. Hank Greenwald knew him best.

"There is the great story of how he made a success of himself without having gone to college," he said. "The inspiring part is that Bill never stopped, even though he attained the level that he did. He approached it like every day was an audition. That was the lesson, that as good as you are and as prominent as you are, you are putting your ass on the line every day in this business, because you are only as good as your last broadcast. He never became a caricature, like some guys at the end of their careers. He never stopped trying to get better."

Bill King was the greatest sportscaster this country has ever produced. He was the most erudite person I've ever met. He was the most intelligent, the most ardent and the most unalterable. In fact, if you write the word "most" and put Bill King next to it, it's probably going to fit.

"He was a smart guy," Madden told me. "He was so multifaceted. Before football would start, he would go sailing all over the world or some doggone thing, and then he'd come back and tell you where he'd been and what he'd done. He'd kind of get away and open his mind up and refresh it, so that he could open his mind up and put a lot of stuff in it. There was a lot of stuff in his mind. He was a brilliant guy. And that stuff would just come out. He didn't have to read anything or have any notes. He just talked and reacted. He was just so natural."

There is no doubt Bill was set in his ways and could be a real stickler. There was the time I used the word "forte" and pronounced it for-*tay*. He gave me one of his serious Bill looks.

"I thought you knew better," he said.

"What's that, Bill?"

"For-*tay* is OK to some people, but *fort* is the proper way to say it," Bill replied. "If you want to get it right, the way the word was meant to be said and should be said is *fort*."

I haven't said for-*tay* since.

Bill was very demanding. It's like if you enroll in an honors class, you know the standards are going to be very high. Marty Lurie said that he made every one of his broadcast partners better.

"You couldn't have a discussion with him unless you were prepared, and that's how he affected everyone," Marty told me. "You didn't sit down with him and work with him unless you were ready to go as well, and that's what he did for people."

Bill was vigorous in everything he did. I've often felt he left a little bit of that spirit inside generations of listeners, including myself, who were fortunate to hear his voice coming out of their radio.

Hopefully, a book project brings some introspection. I've asked myself, seven years after his death, if I think of Bill as a father figure. We've all had roadblocks in our lives and difficult circumstances that we've tried to overcome. I lost my mom when I was twenty-one. My dad, though, is still going strong at ninety-four. He's been a rock and a consistently positive force in my life. I'm not sure I've known anyone who engenders any more respect than my dad. It's a thrill to know, thanks to satellite radio, that he's at home in Los Angeles listening to our broadcasts.

My mom took her own life on April 24, 1973, when she was forty-eight. She had a debilitating and extremely painful back condition and was bedridden much of the time toward the end of her life. She adored her father but she also had a very complicated and unresolved relationship with her mom. I don't think she had the strength to carry on.

One thing I know for sure: Losing a parent, especially so suddenly and without the chance to say goodbye, has made me appreciate my dad and Bill and my old friend Bob Blum even more. Like any great broadcaster, Bill King was a member of the family for thousands of his listeners. He felt like family to me, too, although he always referred to me as "partner." And if someone being a father figure means hoping you've made him proud and that you've tried to do justice to his legacy and that you wouldn't be where you are without him and that you regret never having that talk when you tell him how much he meant to you — my relationship with Bill was all that and more.

He hardly traveled in his last season, but he made the trip to

Seattle for the final games of the year. We were in the booth when he pulled me aside before the first pitch of what would turn out to be his last broadcast. He told me that if I ever left the A's he would hang 'em up. His eyes were teary. So were mine. Forty years earlier I listened to him for the first time. Al Davis said it right at the memorial service. Time never stops for the great ones.

HALL OF FAMER

You know a Hall of Famer when you see one. It's like if you walk outside when it's a hundred degrees: You don't need a thermometer to tell you it's hot. A Hall of Famer, no matter the sport, has an aura. Just hearing the name inspires an instantaneous reaction: *Rickey Henderson. Willie Mays. Sandy Koufax. Bill Russell. Johnny Unitas.* All of them have the Hall of Fame aura, no doubt about it, and that's how it should be. Entry into the Hall of Fame should be reserved for the elite of the elite, the all-time greats, the figures who loom large over their sports. And even with that lofty standard, it's obvious to me that Bill King was a Hall of Famer. Nobody who ever heard Bill has doubted his greatness. Just mentioning his name to his peers elicits the kind of reaction you get when you mention Hall of Fame players. Bill has that kind of veneration.

"I can say without any reservations that without doubt Bill King was the greatest radio broadcaster in the history of the United States," Greg Papa told me.

Those thoughts were echoed by many, many people I talked to doing the research for this book. Pat Hughes, who has been the radio voice of the Cubs for eighteen years and before that was Bob Uecker's sidekick in Milwaukee for twelve, told me: "Bill King is the greatest radio play-by-play man, and I'm talking all-around — football, basketball, baseball — in the history of our country. He is the best all-around radio play-by-play man and I will tell you the truth, I don't think there is anyone who is even close."

Actually, odd as it sounds, Bill's "multiversity of skills," in Roy Eisenhardt's colorful phrase, has worked against his candidacy for the various halls of fame. He was so great in three different sports that he wasn't solely identified with one.

"I don't think I've ever met a more versatile announcer than Bill King," Marty Brennaman, the longtime radio voice of the Cincinnati Reds, told me. "He did the Oakland Raiders! He did the Oakland A's! He did the Warriors and the guy never missed a beat! And he was as good as they come on all three sports. You and I are forever going to be identified solely with major-league baseball and a team. Bill King is associated with three teams, and while you marvel at the fact that this guy was so good in every sport he did — and make no mistake about it, for people reading this, he was as good as it got — I think that can hurt you a little bit, I really do."

Almost all of the Frick winners were strongly identified with baseball, but even in the Bay Area many people still think first of the Warriors and Raiders when they think of Bill. "What hurts him as far as the Frick Award is that he was so good in basketball and football," baseball broadcasting historian Curt Smith told me. "People don't think of him as primarily a baseball announcer."

Bill's arguments with Tom Meschery matched two brilliant but obstinate minds. When the two would work their way around to debating which sport was Bill's best, it was Bill who argued that it was baseball. Meschery never doubted that baseball was the love of Bill's broadcasting life, but being a basketball guy he argued that basketball was Bill's best sport.

"I don't think there has been any announcer who has been able to create a visual landscape of the game like Bill, and that includes all of the greats," Tom told me. "He was the absolute best basketball radio guy I've ever heard. There was nobody like him."

"He should certainly be in the Hall of Fame," Rick Barry, inducted into the Naismith Basketball Hall of Fame in 1987, told me.

"I'm sorry, but he's better than Chick Hearn. Chick was amazing at what he did and outstanding in his own way, but I've never heard anybody better than Bill. It's a travesty. I didn't follow baseball as much, so I can't say, but I did follow football and I've listened to many football people and what he did all those years with the Raiders and what he did with the Warriors, to not be in the respective hall of fames for both of those — he should've gotten the awards."

Rick has done some lobbying for Bill for the Curt Gowdy Award, which is presented annually to a basketball broadcaster for contributions to the sport. Those contributions, in Bill's case, included his influence on people like me. I broadcast twenty-two full seasons of college basketball and I remember doing games when I would say something like, "Down the middle, draw shot, ten-footer, tough roll," and I would think, "That sounds like something Bill used to say." It wasn't a conscious effort to copy him, but I had listened to hundreds of hours of Bill doing basketball. His calls were so ingrained that sometimes they crept into my play-by-play.

Sportswriter Susan Slusser, who covered the Orlando Magic in the '90s as a beat writer for the *Orlando Sentinel*, got her start working for the *Sacramento Bee*, where she covered the Sacramento Kings. Like me, she grew up listening to Bill doing basketball and remembers many nights when she would have an ear next to the radio with the sound down low, hoping her mom wouldn't overhear and tell her it was time for bed.

"Everybody who has listened to Bill will say he was the greatest basketball announcer ever," Susan told me. "There is just no doubt about it. He had an ability to bring out the color and the drama, the smallest details. He made everything pop. Despite how fast-paced the NBA is, he didn't miss a trick. I have not been able to listen to basketball since Bill stopped doing the Warriors. There has been nothing like it."

The winners of the Pete Rozelle Radio-Television Award, handed out yearly by the Pro Football Hall of Fame since 1989, have included Chris Schenkel, Curt Gowdy, Pat Summerall, Frank Gifford and Jack Buck. That's quite a fivesome. John Madden was honored with the award in 2002 and he's clearly one of the all-time greats. Think of the parlay of a career John has had: He is one of a very select few to have been brilliant on the sideline *and* in the booth. One thing, though, about the football broadcasting award: The tendency is to honor national figures. Bill loved the Bay Area and the fans loved him back, but Madden demurred when I asked him if the fact that Bill worked most of his career in Northern California somehow helped to foster his success.

"I think Bill King would have been successful in radio any place he went," John told me. "He was the best. He had too much talent to say that he needed an area to be a star. I honestly believe that Bill King could've done it anywhere."

Former sportswriter Josh Suchon's current career as a network broadcaster wouldn't have happened, he told me, without inspiration from Bill King. "For my high school friends and family members, they'd always ask me 'What's Bill King like?'" Josh told me. "They did it way more than they'd ask about any player or Billy Beane."

Josh grew up listening to Bill and got to know him as the A's beat writer for the *Oakland Tribune*, beginning in 2004.

"One of my all-time favorite days as a baseball reporter was in Cleveland, of all places," he said. "On a Saturday morning I rented a car and drove from Cleveland to the Football Hall of Fame in Canton, Ohio. Throughout the day, I wandered through the halls and saw all this football history. There's lots of interactive displays where you can view famous plays and players. Naturally, all I did was look at the Raiders players. That meant I heard the voice of Bill King, over and over, from the 'Holy Roller' call to 'Old Man Willie' and so many more. Then I show up at the ballpark for the A's-Indians game. After spending some time in the clubhouse collecting some notes, I walk out to the A's dugout. There's Bill King just sitting there on the bench and he says hello to me. I got goose bumps. I told Bill about my day and how I'd heard his voice so many times over the last few hours. Ever the self-deprecating man, King replied that I must be sick of his voice and vowed to shut up."

Judging anything is, by definition, subjective. It's that way with the Frick Award, which is presented annually by the Baseball Hall of Fame to a broadcaster for "major contributions to baseball." On the Hall of Fame website, fans are encouraged to vote for their favorite announcers each year. The top three vote-getters are added to seven other finalists who are selected by a Hall of Fame research team. The living Frick Award recipients and a select group of five historians and veteran media experts chosen by the Hall make the final vote.

On the Hall website, these guidelines are listed for the fan ballot:

Fans have the opportunity to help influence the final ballot by voting for their favorite broadcaster on Facebook. Fan voting will select three candidates to appear on the final ballot. A minimum of ten years of continuous major-league service with a club, network or combination thereof is required to appear on the ballot. Electors are asked to base their selections on four criteria: (1) longevity; (2) continuity with a club; (3) honors, including awards and national assignments, such as the World Series and All-Star Games; and (4) popularity with the fans. All of the living Frick recipients and the group of five experts are given ballots. They are asked to list their top ten choices, so that everyone on the ballot gets a vote, beginning with the top choice getting the equivalent of one point. The person with the lowest total wins.

I don't have a vote for the Frick Award, but if I did, I would ask these questions in considering the candidacy of Bill King:

Did he love and respect the game and was he diligent in his preparation? √

Did he call a good game and was he descriptive and accurate so that he kept up with the action and painted a clear word picture? √

Did he keep me entertained during the time between pitches? √

Was he articulate and did he respect the language? √

Was he good when the game wasn't? √

Did he work well with his partners? √

Was he a baseball historian? √

If you were to consider the history of a franchise,
how much did he contribute to that legacy? √

Was he a good interviewer? √

Did he have a voice that sounded like baseball? √

Did the fans think of him as a member of the family? √

On every count, Bill King scores an A+.

"He was the best baseball announcer I've ever heard," Susan Slusser told me. "I'm astonished he hasn't won the Frick."

Susan, longtime *San Francisco Chronicle* A's beat writer, is president of the Baseball Writers Association of America. She said she doesn't think East Coast bias is the culprit in the voting for the Frick.

"But I don't think people were as aware of Bill as they should have been," she added. "Everything about him was so perfect. He had a great voice and his knowledge of baseball history has been underappreciated. Some people think the other sports diluted his baseball, but I think it is crazy that people think that. He was such an omnivore with everything else in terms of his knowledge and so he was sort of dinged for being this basketball or football guy. I couldn't disagree with that more. He knew as much about baseball as any broadcaster I've ever listened to.

"He was so well suited to the Bay Area. The Bay Area likes a smart broadcaster, someone who doesn't talk down to the listeners, and Bill absolutely never would have talked down to the listeners. He was so good and so good at conveying himself. He injected his own personality and he wasn't afraid to make fun of himself — the way he dressed, his eating habits and all the quirky things about him. You got a sense of Bill. You felt like you knew him and felt like you loved him."

Billy Beane grew up in San Diego and as a Chargers fan, and

therefore always hated the Raiders — and always associated Bill with the hated enemy. But after he joined the A's, Billy came to see how special Bill was.

"He was *so* good at what he did," Billy told me for this book. "When the Ford Frick award comes up I'm more shocked that it's taken this long, to be honest with you. There are a lot of people who do that job that are considered really good that I think he is much better than, some who may have received the award. I've heard a lot of announcers. I've grown up around the game for thirty-something years and heard plenty of guys who are in there and all usually deserving, but he is as good as anyone I've ever heard. He was great at what he did."

Bill was so thorough in everything, including his preparation for the manager's show. He took that five-minute pregame interview very seriously. He was studious in the way he would analyze the previous game and set the table for the game that day. He didn't write out the questions, but he would jot a few notes on a pad as a reminder before starting the interview.

"It was just amazing," former A's manager Ken Macha told me for this book, saying that Bill's preparation and knowledge of the game packed his questions with so much insight, he was in a special category. "Your knowledge of what you want out of this guy — by the questions you use — just comes flowing out of the person you are interviewing. Bill had a unique way of doing that. I got an education and I didn't have to pay for it."

People somehow hold it against Bill that he was great at broadcasting three sports — and they sometimes also nick him on the longevity issue, an argument that to me is another nonstarter. Who cares if he *only* did twenty-five years with the A's and four years with the Giants? For those nearly thirty years he poured his heart and soul into his work. I never felt he was a "basketball guy" or a "football guy" who was doing baseball. He was a baseball man. He lived the life, he loved the game and the fans loved him back. Shouldn't the quality of time be as important as the number of years?

I give credit to anyone who has broadcast more than thirty years in the big leagues. They had to have done many things very well to have had a career that lasted so long. But would you rather have Bill King or someone who does thirty-five years but rarely goes down on the field before a game? Who made more of a contribution, someone who had more longevity than Bill but coasted, or someone who prepared like crazy the way Bill did? There are people in our business who abuse the privilege. They think preparing for a game is getting off the team bus, going to the press room to dine and then perusing the game notes. Bill never worked from a media guide. He had his own guide in the form of that giant, ten-inch-thick yellow binder where he kept bios on the players, statistical information, stories, anecdotes and anything else he found interesting. There were no off-seasons for Bill. Keeping up on his yellow binder was a full-time job.

Give me Bill King, who loved and respected the game and the tenets of his profession so much that he felt it was his obligation never to cheat the listeners. When you listened to Bill, not only did he tell you what was happening on the field, but he filled in all the gaps between pitches as well. You knew what was happening with the A's *and* the opposition because he was so informed. This was an ethic the great broadcasters share.

Take Scully. We were in Los Angeles for an interleague game in 2009 and Vinny came down to our booth before the game to chat with my broadcast partner Vince Cotroneo and me. He was on a mission to find some information about Curt Young, the A's pitching coach, specifically the details of Curt's appearances in the 1988 World Series. I felt bad that I didn't have all of the info on the tip of my tongue, and then while Vince did the research on his computer, I had a little fun with Vinny.

"Man, you're really grinding here," I kidded him.

His reaction reminded me a little of Bill, when we had that first dinner and he told me the three things I couldn't do.

"This is what we do," Scully said, giving me a stern look. "We tie it all together. How could I go on the air and not know when Curt Young pitched in the Series? Now when he goes to the mound for a visit I can talk about how he pitched here in the Series and now he is back twenty-one years later mentoring the A's young pitchers. It's what we do. We knit it all together."

He was eighty-three years old then and he was kicking our butts in his preparation. One of Curt Smith's favorite quotes is from Scully. It's a beauty and goes directly to how he crafts his broadcasts so that they reach far beyond the mundane: "People who over-rely on numbers are like the drunk who depends on the lamppost for support and not illumination."

I grew up, of course, listening to Vinny and Bill and each has had a profound impact on me. At first glance it might seem odd to equate the two: Bill was flip-flops and Speedos and Vinny a coat and tie and on the surface their differences were as stark as the contrast between Northern and Southern California. But at their core, each had a total commitment to his craft and a passion and virtuosity that transcended baseball or, for that matter, broadcasting. They were iconic figures, members of the family, larger than life, and were so deeply woven into the fabric of their respective regions than anyone who listened to them felt like it was almost a cultural experience, like visiting the Louvre or the Metropolitan Museum of Art.

My friend Curt Smith, a former speech writer for George H.W. Bush, is the foremost authority on the history of baseball broadcasting and the author of numerous books on the subject. He is also one of the five historians/media experts who vote for the Frick.

"My Number 1 criteria, and this doesn't apply to everyone, especially the younger guys, would be a question: Would baseball broadcasting as a craft be the same without that person?" he told me.

"Number 2 is the voice, not that it has to be like James Earl Jones, but it has to be distinctive and, as Charlie Steiner said, 'cracks through the ambient background noise.'

"Longevity, but for me this is not the most important. Continuity, also not the most important, but you don't want someone who jumps from one team to another. Network assignments always help. Awards, popularity, the intangibles — like some of the calls — and the use of the language. Take, for instance, Scully and Dizzy Dean. You couldn't find two people who used the language more differently. Scully facilitates the language and Dizzy incinerated the language. But they both made you listen and that is the ultimate goal, and both were unbelievably popular and that makes a difference."

Barry Horn, media columnist for the *Dallas Morning News*, also has a Frick vote. His criteria?

"As defined: The Ford C. Frick Award is presented annually to a broadcaster for 'major contributions to baseball.' I can only say that the parameters are so vague that the voting becomes so subjective. Is there a better explanation than, 'I know a Frick-worthy winner when I hear one?'

"In reality there should be at least one Frick-worthy candidate currently working in every market — a voice that the fans know intimately, a voice that is *the* direct link to their team. The voice, if you will, that they trust to be their eyes and their ears. A voice that understands them. A voice that more often than not knows their pain and sorrow and ultimately can describe their joy. That kind of bond can't be bestowed. It has to be earned. Earned over seasons. Many seasons. It is a lifetime relationship....

"In voting, where they are so many outstanding candidates, I do take into consideration how many Frick winners already have come from a particular market. (And I would imagine) that is where people would quibble with me most. A contribution in Milwaukee has to be equal to a contribution in New York or the whole magic of baseball is flawed."

If there was a Hall of Fame for pregame hosts, Marty Lurie, who has spent sixteen years doing shows for the A's and Giants, would be a charter member. With all the interviews he's conducted, his archives comprise an audio history of the game. As a former criminal defense attorney, he knows how to make a good case for Bill:

"He was an unbelievable baseball historian. People say he only did twenty-five years, that's not enough, but that is the tip of the iceberg and this is the point about Bill King: It's the tip of the iceberg as to his depth of baseball knowledge. It's his passion for the game and what he brought to the game. He goes back to going to games and listening to games in the '30s and '40s, and with an encyclopedic knowledge of baseball.

"You can give me all the people who received the Frick Award and maybe broadcast for thirty to forty years for a certain team and nobody had the passion this man had for baseball. Whether it was Burleigh Grimes, Jimmy Foxx or Gabby Hartnett, Bill King lived baseball his entire life. The broadcast part was outstanding, as well as anyone could ever do it, but the depth of his knowledge went beyond anyone I've ever come in contact with in baseball. That's why he should get the Frick Award. That's what people don't know about him.

"It's not just his body of work with the A's or his time with Russ and Lon with the Giants in the late '50s and early '60s. Bill King was more than that in baseball. Bill King to me was as significant in baseball as a Leo Durocher, a Walter Alston and a Bill Rigney. He was someone like that who knew the game and lived the game. He lived the game every day, and to me it's the greatest thing I can say about him. If he told me something about baseball, I could take it to the bank. That's the highest compliment I could give him."

Bill would probably say that we are making too big a fuss about how much he deserves the Frick. He didn't need the kudos to justify his existence. But even though he deflected attention away from any discussion of the Frick, he would have been honored and thrilled to have received it during his lifetime. How could he not be, especially considering his deep appreciation for the history of the game?

I've always thought Marty Brennaman had a lot in common with Bill. Like Bill, Marty dances to his own beat and is defined by his integrity. Marty is still going strong after forty years in Cincinnati and he reached the baseball broadcasting pinnacle when he was a richly deserving recipient of the Frick Award in 2000. I asked Marty for his criteria when he votes for the Frick:

"Well, I have two," he told me. "I think longevity obviously has got to be Number 1. I mean you can't get into the broadcasters' wing and serve a team for five or six years, you've got to be around for a long time. And the other thing for me is popularity. ... If there's a pure art form to what we do for a living, this is the sport. It's not football, basketball or hockey, it's this sport right here because it is the single most difficult sport of all to do well. And so you've got to be able to, in however you approach your craft in terms of broadcasting a baseball game, sustain to the point where not only are you around for a lot of years, but you are around to the point where people think, for want of a better term, that you hung the moon, that you're the guy. You know, we turn the radio on to listen to the A's games, and we love Bill King, or we love Ken or Ray or whoever it is. So to me the top two things are longevity and popularity."

One of the other things to consider is that Bill did twenty-five consecutive years with the same team. It's one thing to get a job, but it's another to keep it. You have to wear well over time and there are plenty of guys who become broadcasting itinerants, drifting from market to market. Bill got a late start broadcasting full time in the big leagues. He was fifty-three when he was hired by the A's. It would be fun to have a poll and ask who was the person who made the biggest impact on the fans in the history of the Oakland A's, one of the most storied franchises in baseball.

Rickey Henderson might win it and he would be a great choice. Susan Slusser said the top three, not necessarily in order, would be Bill, Rickey and Billy Beane. Rickey is in the Hall of Fame and Billy might make it himself one day. Jay Alves said Bill might be the A's all-time fan favorite.

Mickey Morabito talked about going to A's functions that Bill would emcee. Fans would flock to Bill for autographs and it was always the same everywhere they went. No matter how many players were there, even if they were the big stars, it was Bill, by far, who was the person the fans sought out first.

Bill didn't have a national profile, but with XM Radio and the Internet making all broadcasters more accessible, the emphasis on "local" vs. "national" seems to be fading. And the committee deserves great credit for selecting announcers like Dave Niehaus and Lon Simmons, who made their mark locally. I've always felt that a broadcaster — or anyone in any line of work — should be judged by the quality of their work and not the level they reach. Bill was certainly talented enough to work nationally, but that was never a motivation for him.

"Bill never gave a damn about network television or network radio," Pat Hughes told me. "He loved doing games on a local basis on local radio in the Bay Area and I don't think he gave a damn whether they knew him in Philadelphia or Miami or Dallas."

As a way of summing up how unjust it is that Bill has not been voted into a Hall of Fame yet, stop for a moment to consider great broadcasters who forged the strongest links with the listeners in their cities. To get some perspective I called up the great Murray Olderman, now ninety years old, who is in both the National Sportswriters Hall of Fame and the National Sportswriters and Sportscasters Hall of Fame. Murray has written a dozen books and his articles and iconic cartoons have appeared in over seven hundred newspapers and publications like *Sports Illustrated* and *The Saturday Evening Post*. Here is the list Murray compiled for me, in no particular order, of the broadcasters he felt were the most synonymous with the places where they worked.

Bill and his relationship with the fans in the Bay Area.

Mel Allen of the Yankees.

Red Barber of the Brooklyn Dodgers.

Vin Scully of the Dodgers.

Russ Hodges of the New York and San Francisco Giants.

Lon Simmons of the Giants.

Bob Uecker of the Brewers.

Marty Brennaman of the Reds.

Harry Caray of the Cards and Cubs.

Jack Buck of the Cards.

Curt Gowdy of the Red Sox

Ernie Harwell of the Tigers.

Harry Kalas of the Phillies.

Chick Hearn of the Lakers.

Marty Glickman of the Knicks.

Myron Cope of the Steelers.

Of the sixteen names on that list, fully twelve — all but Bill, Cope, Glickman and Hearn — are recipients of the Frick Award. Hearn and Glickman are in the Naismith Memorial Basketball Hall of Fame as Curt Gowdy Award recipients. Cope received the Pete Rozelle Award, the NFL's answer to the Frick Award. Bill hasn't been honored by any of the three sports. Alone among the names on the list he hasn't been honored by one Hall of Fame. There's a part of me that doesn't get too worked about these slights to Bill, even if they are ridiculous. *I* know how great Bill King was and I don't require even an institution as august as the Hall of Fame to confirm it for me — he's the greatest ever, period, end of story, as I've said. But I also know how much the Frick Award would mean to Bill's family and so many of his friends. And more than anything, I know how much the award would mean to the fans, Bill's listeners, who still hear the great calls ringing out in their memories and who cherish all he gave them. Bill deserves this honor, and so do they.

DESCRIBING THE INDESCRIBABLE

G **REG PAPA**, voice of the Raiders

I called them the Three Tenors, Lon, Hank and Bill, the three greatest broadcasters in Bay Area history. They were the guys we strived to be. Bill was better than all of them. He was unmatched. Bill was the single most important voice in the history of the Bay Area. He had more impact on people's lives. Nobody could have had more of an impact on the medium of radio. He had a different style — maybe not the greatest voice — but it was more the cadence and the word choice and the ability to broadcast a game and not sound like he was broadcasting a game. To encompass all three sports the way he did, no question he was the greatest sports radio broadcaster in the history of the United States.

Sometimes I feel like I am twelve years old again collecting baseball cards: What kind of life is this? And what kind of talent do we really have? We never grew up. We're still children. When I was a young broadcaster I really struggled with this: I didn't think broadcasting was a noble profession. At a party or social function I would wonder, 'Why would you want to talk to me? I'm not that interesting.' But Bill was a man of superior intellect in every way — a man of the arts — obviously a very well read man, and so when I was around Bill I felt much better. I felt better about my chosen profession that this great man and this great mind would choose that same profession. Here was a man who truly was interesting and he chose it, so maybe it's not that bad. Maybe it is noble.

TIM KEOWN, best-selling author and senior writer, ESPN *the Magazine*

I grew up listening to Bill on the Warriors and Raiders before he started doing baseball. Nobody I've ever heard could make you see a basketball game on the radio the way Bill could. He had a verbal dexterity that went beyond mere talent; it was art. My father and I would sit and watch the games that were simulcast on television, and my dad was convinced there was trickery involved. There's no way he can keep up with the game that well, he would say. Bill would tell you who was going to catch the pass on the wing before the ball got there. It was like sorcery.

To me, a sports-crazed kid in the Bay Area with designs on becoming a broadcaster, Bill King was bigger than any athlete, bigger than Rick Barry or Nate Thurmond or Kenny Stabler. When I ended up writing for the San Francisco Chronicle, *I was around Bill occasionally in the mid- to late-1990s. It sounds strange, but I never spoke with him. I was a grown man, and I was still in awe of him. I could walk right up to Barry Bonds or Joe Montana or Mark McGwire, but not Bill King. I'm sure there was something weirdly psychological going on, but I think it comes down to this: He was bigger than life, and I preferred to keep him that way.*

BRUCE JENKINS, *San Francisco Chronicle* columnist

A typical A's team charter in the Billy Martin era: You're heading east, it's mayhem, Billy's in his cups, wicked card games in the back, two completely buxom, comely stewardesses with their tits hanging out, and up front Bill King, barefoot, immersed in Russian literature, and oblivious to it all.

TONY LA RUSSA, former White Sox, A's and Cardinals manager

On the plane, he'd take off his shoes, put on his thongs and his shorts and he'd be sitting there with a bunch of reading material. He was his own man.

SUSAN FORNOFF, former A's beat writer, author

He was such a character! A cultured man, yet, on a hot day he'd be almost naked in the radio booth!

JOHN MADDEN, Hall of Fame coach and football analyst

I think Bill King would have been successful in radio any place he went, because he was the best. He had too much talent to say that he needed an area to be a star.

JON MILLER, voice of the San Francisco Giants

Nobody has ever been able to rise to an exciting moment and bring the excitement into the sound of their voice like Bill. It's not just shouting, but the theatrical flair that he brings to it. Sometimes in an exciting moment, I find myself trying to do Bill.

KEN PRIES, A's VP for broadcasting and communications

Bill was not only a friend but bar none the best all-around announcer I have ever heard. There is no one else in the world I would want to hear describe a one-run game in the ninth inning with two outs and the bases loaded other than Bill.

SCOTT OSTLER, *San Francisco Chronicle* columnist

Some guys are cool. Miles Davis, Joe Namath, Derek Jeter, John Madden, The Most Interesting Man In The World. They are guys you want to listen to, guys you admire and seek out. Bill King is on my all-time All-Cool team.

I grew up in Southern California listening to classic announcers Vin Scully and Chick Hearn, and I didn't catch Bill King until near the end of his career. You bond with the announcers you grow up with, but when I moved to the Bay Area it didn't take me long to recognize that Bill was special.

When you're cool, it's never just in your job. I got on to an elevator with King one day at the Oakland Coliseum. I knew he was an opera buff, and I asked him a question about it. He gave me a lively, interesting, informative and charming take on opera, without sounding the least bit hoity-toity.

Cool is a gift, and it's great that Bill chose to share his with us. He made the sports world a cool place to be.

BRUCE JENKINS

Football, he's definitely the best ever. Just ... period. If anybody doesn't get that, they're out of their minds.

JOHN HICKEY, A's beat writer

Bill King had that rare ability to transform images into words in a way that kept the listener taut and mesmerized and completely in the moment. No one was built for radio in quite the same way as Bill.

BRUCE JENKINS

He's the best basketball announcer that there ever was. I grew up with Chick Hearn. Chick called the action really well. But Bill King called the action even better than Chick and in an incredibly lyrical and opinionated way, never a word out of place, just never: Write it down, it looks great.

TONY LA RUSSA

When you look at the different sports, one guy who could do all of them and just excel, he's right at the head of the class. His broadcasting was very unique and he and Lon Simmons together, I don't know how you could have a better pair.

JOHN ENGLISH, via the *Holy Toledo* Facebook page

Bill King wasn't just a sports announcer, he was an artist. No other in his field that I've heard has displayed the same ability to paint a picture before your eyes, a truer vision of what's going on in front of his. From the sounds of the ballpark to the crack of the bat to the thrill of the crowd, Bill brought it all home to wherever the listener was. For an eight-year-old boy discovering the game of baseball, this was magical.

MARIA ESCORIO, via the *Holy Toledo* Facebook page

When I heard Bill King's voice I knew I was home, even if I wasn't physically in my house. His voice was as familiar to me as my own parents'. So many nights when I was in middle school and high school, his was the last voice I would hear as I fell asleep listening to an extra-inning night game. It was like a baseball bedtime story read by an old friend. Many times I took a radio to the games with me so I could hear Bill and Lon's commentary as the play unfolded on the field.

DAVE HENDERSON, A's player from 1988 to 1993, who grew up in the San Joaquin Valley town of Dos Palos

Down in the valley, remember, these were farmers and workers that didn't have the money to go to games, so they listened on the radio. They equated Oakland A's baseball with Bill King. If they heard his voice, baseball was going on and it was summertime and everything was rosy. He gave everybody that feeling that everything was okay, Bill was on the radio, nice warm day, baseball was going, everything was fine in the world.

HOWARD BRYANT, ESPN senior writer, author

When we think of the game, we immediately drift back on the currents of memory. For me, a Boston guy, sports is a Bobby Orr end-to-end rush, Bird to Parish back to Bird. A fan of Dave Winfield, it was the big man striding to the plate, facing Roger Clemens at Yankee Stadium.

Then, somewhere, the truth settles in. These snapshots are formless, wide swaths of fabrics without seams, without stitching. It is then that you realize a layer below, that it isn't what's on the field that gives the game life, but the strength of its narration. The narration is the voice, because, especially in baseball where the game becomes the wallpaper of our summer lives, so much of the game is what we hear and do not see. The voice is the stitching. It wasn't just Winfield ripping a double, but Bill White and Phil Rizzuto saying so. It wasn't Jim Rice getting hit in the back with a Matt Keough fastball, but Ned Martin and Bob Montgomery on the call. My favorites were Fred Cusick and

Johnny Peirson, the voices of the Boston Bruins on WSBK TV-*38 in Boston. All these years later, you hear them more than you can see Orr on the ice.*

In the Bay Area, that voice was Bill King. It wasn't just Rickey taking off for second that created the magic, but Bill King's voice telling you that he had. There is no universe where words and deeds become one more than in sports and when you sit for a moment you realize that the wins and losses, home runs and strikeouts did not exist by themselves, after all, that it wasn't just the story, but who was telling it. For the child in us, Bill King read us a thirty-year bedtime story with a different ending every night.

DOUG GREENWALD, voice of the Class AAA Fresno Grizzlies

Bill King I always considered as my American League father. He defined the East Bay sports scene as he was the A's, Raiders, and Warriors rolled into one. People often ask if I could go back in time and choose any Bay Area team to follow. It would have been the great Raiders teams of the '70s, and the reason is Bill.

RHAMESIS MUNCADA, via the *Holy Toledo* Facebook page

To me, Bill King was the grandfather I never had. As the son of immigrants who had little knowledge of baseball, I learned much of the game from Bill and Lon. As an awkward kid with a funny name, I turned to baseball on the radio to help me feel more American. Thanks for raising me to be a good baseball fan, Bill, even if you never knew you were doing it.

RICH WALTZ, Miami Marlins TV voice

Growing up in the San Francisco Bay Area, Bill King was the definitive soundtrack to my world. Not as an aspiring broadcaster, but as an athlete and sports fan. I grew up in the '70s and the '80s when Bill was the voice of the Raiders, A's, and Warriors. As a point guard, shortstop, and QB/WR *I was either on the playing field, practice court, or backyard; and Bill's voice was in my head.*

A fall Sunday was not complete without King's narrative of Stabler, Branch, Plunkett, Casper and the rest of the Raiders. Winter nights were spent with Rick Barry, Jamaal Wilkes, Phil Smith and an occasional appearance by Mendy Rudolph (Bill was always happy to offer a critique of NBA *officials). From Billy Ball to the Bash Brothers, Bill and Lon Simmons were with me as I played* HR *derby vs. my brother against the barn. If I did something on the playing field or backyard, I did it to Bill King's voice.*

RICK TEIXEIRA, via the *Holy Toledo* Facebook page

His voice was the sound of summer. As a child I thought he was so much more important than any player on the field. Who can forget his exotic stories about sailing and Russian literature and calf brain burritos? Bill could have easily come across as an intellectual snob, but he never crossed the line. His love for life and passion for the games always made his broadcasts feel like an intimate conversation with a favorite uncle.

LOWELL COHN, Bay Area sports columnist, former Stanford University literature instructor

I saw everything I saw through his words, and what words they were. I was studying English at Stanford so I was into words and here was Bill who spoke in a kind of prose poetry. Every word was the right word, so vivid and perfect. And he was opinionated. Maybe I liked this the best. He had opinions on players and he sure had opinions on the refs. He was not afraid to put himself out there and be critical. He was so un-California in a sense and I always admired his courage and honesty.

BRUCE JENKINS

Jesus, him on the Warriors! What a pairing: Bill and Hank Greenwald on the Channel 2 telecasts. Incredibly tense moment, and here's Bill: "Rick Barry at the line. Warriors down by a point, twenty-three seconds to go — Rick has to make these." And there's a little pause and Hank goes, "Well, he doesn't have *to."*

TYLER BLEZINSKI, Athletics Nation

Bill King made it feel like I was watching the game with him.

He made me feel like I was sitting down next to him listening to him complain about having to spend a hot summer night in Arlington, Texas, or feel like I was celebrating another walk-off win. Bill never held back. When the team wasn't performing, he was the first to say it. But he also would celebrate the same way that we would when the team was at its peak performance. It would cheapen Bill's legacy to say that he was one of the fans simply because the man was brilliant. But that's how Bill made you feel. He made his listeners feel that every "Holy Toledo!" was a genuine cry of joy, shock or amazement. It wasn't a canned response or something that was unnatural. He was as genuine as they came and it came across in the pleasure he brought to his profession, which brought that same pleasure to A's fans.

STEVE BITKER, KCBS

When I worked alongside Bill, I would absolutely love *it when he threw in one of his patented "Holy Toledo" calls. I would bask in that, because I was, for a moment anyway, part of a "Holy Toledo" moment, albeit indirectly. A wonderful blast back to my past. You can imagine what it was like to grow up in the Bay Area listening to Bill and then play for the A's and have Bill calling the games. So many of the A's great stars had ties to the area, like Dennis Eckersley, Rickey Henderson and Dave Stewart.*

As exciting as the Raiders were, they almost were more exciting listening to the games on the radio, because unlike any other announcer I had ever heard as a kid and unlike any announcer I've heard since then, Bill allowed you to listen to the game and see the game through your mind's eye like nobody else. Even before that I had listened to him call Warriors games with Hank and for so many years, Bill was the connection, the conduit, on the radio.

RON TIONGCO, via the *Holy Toledo* Facebook page

Bill King ranks right up there in Bay Area sports folklore with the likes of Rick Barry, Rickey Henderson, and Kenny Stabler, especially to a young kid growing up in the East Bay in the '70s and '80s before the onslaught of media outlets now readily available to anyone with an internet connection or satellite. I think I spent more time growing up listening to Bill than I did my teachers or parents and I know I learned more about the game of basketball listening to Bill's broadcasts on KNBR *than I did watching it on* TV *or playing it in* CYO.

VINCE COTRONEO, A's and former Texas Rangers broadcaster

At The Ballpark in Arlington, the two team radio booths are separated by a pane of glass. The one thing that always caught my attention was Bill's enormous binder filled with sheet after sheet of information that he leaned his left arm on during every game. No doubt packed with stories and anecdotes from seasons gone by. And yet among Bill's strengths was his energy, play calling and immense knowledge of the language. Oh, I saw the nightly wardrobe change, too, and chuckled that he was always comfortable being Bill. But from my perspective, I especially saw in Bill the belief that preparation was his security blanket and it allowed him to give the listener unforgettable moment after moment.

DANIEL CHANIN, via the *Holy Toledo* Facebook page

Some baseball fans talk about muting a TV *broadcast so they can hear their favorite radio announcer. Bill King fans did it regularly. He often made me opt for the radio instead of the television. Growing up in an era (late '80s and '90s) dominated by* TV *you would think it would take a lot to pry a young kid away from the tube. All it took was Bill King.*

KEN MACHA, former A's manager, who joined Bill for an interview show before each game

They paid me a small stipend for doing those shows, but actually I should have been paying Bill for the education he gave me. He was a unique individual. He would come over before the show and he would have something about, for instance, Bastille Day, because that day might have been Bastille Day. He wasn't just a baseball announcer, he was involved in so many other aspects of life. The guy was giving me an education. I talked to him a lot about when he worked in the NBA, *I asked him a bunch of questions about Wilt*

Chamberlain and he was happy to talk about him. His vocabulary was off the charts, so if you really listened to how he formed his questions or how he talked, that was part of the education you were receiving. You were increasing the size of your vocabulary.

TONY LA RUSSA

The thing that our family connected with Bill on was away from the ballpark. He was really into the arts. Smuin Ballet, he was a big supporter. He really enjoyed the fact that our family, when we had spare time, we did theater or dance or even symphonies.

SUSAN FORNOFF

When I started covering the A's in 1985, it was still a little weird for a woman to be in the locker room and on the bus. I sat by myself a lot. One night Bill sat down next to me on the bus and made sure I knew that he believed I had the same rights as the men when it came to covering baseball. And then he started talking about some opera, so there went our common ground.

FRANK BLACKMAN, former *San Francisco Examiner* A's beat writer

Bill and I both enjoyed ethnic food (goulash in Cleveland, etc.) and once or twice a season we would go out to dinner. I avoided even mentioning the subject with him otherwise. With his habit of ordering multiple bottles of wine and generally living large, it would cripple my per diem for a month. I did break that rule once in Toronto because the restaurant was one I found with (fellow beat writer) Kit Stiers and subsequently introduced to Bill, who became a regular and favorite of the owner. Anyway, we went that night and I had a great time (Bill was a gifted raconteur), but as I also recall, my share of the bill was about $150. Safe to say, that was my last meal with Bill.

ROBERT KUWADA, former *San Jose Mercury News* A's beat writer

The one scene I always play back in my mind, we were in Chicago, where they used to put out this great spread before Sunday day games, and I was sitting at a table with Bill and Frank Black-

man, and Bill was going on and on about some Russian guy I had never heard of — might have been a poet or author or opera singer or someone sitting at the next table for all I knew. Anyway, we're all eating and I'm watching Bill eat and talk and Frank go through all these mental gymnastics trying to keep up with the conversation and Bill is way over my head - I'm sitting there wondering why I put so much syrup on my waffles. But I remember thinking two things. One: That guy can get after a plate of food. Two: I've never seen anyone eat onions like that.

PEDRO GOMEZ, ESPN reporter

Since moving to Arizona before the 1998 season, one of my absolutely favorite parts of every spring training was doing anything at Phoenix Muni, the longtime spring home of the A's, a club I covered on a daily basis from 1992 through 1997. The biggest thrill for me was always walking into the radio booth to catch up with Bill King. He never disappointed. There he would be, usually snacking on something unhealthy, wearing shorts he'd probably first put on his still-trim body sometime in the late 1970s and brimming with a joyous welcome unlike any in any MLB radio booth.

Having spent so many years traveling with Bill and gaining his respect and confidence meant you were instantly admitted into his inner circle. It was definitely a place you WANTED to be in because it meant you were rewarded with rich stories of him being tee'd up at the Cow Palace by the likes of Mendy Rudolph, watching Billy Martin mix vodka with MORE vodka, or regaled with even better stories from those dominant but renegade Oakland Raiders teams of Kenny Stabler, John Matuszak and Otis Sistrunk. There was simply no one who had more riveting tales nor told them better.

LOWELL COHN

One time when I was at the Chronicle *and was a stupid young man, I wrote a column which had some criticisms of Bill. Nothing major and I don't remember what I wrote, but it was critical. We ran into each other the next day or the day after that at the Oakland Coliseum on the field before a game, and I'll never forget this. He came over to me. I thought, oh boy, Bill's going to let me have it. But he asked how I was doing and shot the breeze and was simply lovely to me. Meanwhile, I felt guilty and knew I had been a real dope. Later, I thought about what Bill had done. He was such a dear man. He knew I felt bad and he was trying to make me feel comfortable. Can you imagine that? He was so far above the whole situation, and he showed me how a gentleman would act, how a mensch would act. I hope I learned from him. He was the ultimate mensch.*

NIC CACIAPPO, via *Holy Toledo* Facebook page

During A's batting practice in 1987, Bill King invited me to the broadcast booth after I told him that I was a radio DJ in Modesto who wished to learn baseball play-by-play broadcasting.

I spoke with Bill at the batting cage about his favorite symphony, Camille Saint-Saens' Symphony No. 3 with organ. He asked me how I knew this about him. I told him he had mentioned it on the air a couple of weeks earlier. I added that it was one of my favorite symphonies as well, and I explained that the station I listened to A's games on was an AM stereo station in Modesto that had a classical-music format.

"I don't believe it, an AM station in Modesto plays classical music and A's games?" Bill said. "Yes," I replied, "and their station ID includes "KBEE, the three B's, Bach, Beethoven and Baseball." Bill called Lon Simmons over by the BP cage.

"Tell Lon what you told me!" Bill said. I complied, and then Bill had an invitation for me: "Come on up during the second inning and sit behind us in the booth and watch, then you'll see if it's something you want to try,"

I arrived at the booth as suggested and Ray Fosse invited me in. I watched the masters in action. Paper with information was constantly flying around. After a couple innings, I didn't want to overstay my welcome, so I excused myself and thanked them very much. After the game I walked by Bill and Lon, and they asked me, "So, what do you think, are you going to go into baseball broadcasting?"

"No way," I said. "You guys are amazing. I couldn't possibly do that!"

JERRY HOWARTH, voice of the Toronto Blue Jays

I first met Bill at a Warriors game in Oakland when I was a young fund-raiser at the University of Santa Clara in their athletic department. I was interested in perhaps starting a broadcasting career. I called the Warriors and asked if I could visit with Bill and they said that would be fine as Bill did this with a lot of people interested in sports broadcasting. When I walked into the empty arena, there was Bill at the press table doing his homework and preparing for that night's game and broadcast. He couldn't have been nicer to me, a perfect stranger. He stopped what he was doing and we just talked — or should I say I just listened. Bill had a fantastic mind and shared a lot with me that evening that included his humor, too, and some things that did not go so well with his career and we both laughed. He made me feel so relaxed and comfortable. I never forgot that. I left that meeting after about an hour inspired by Bill, thinking that maybe I could do this, too.

LARRY YANT, former *San Francisco Chronicle* deputy sports editor

While researching the early years of the Warriors in San Francisco, I called Bill King for help filling in missing information. For the next forty-five minutes, one of my childhood heroes pulled out his media guides and more importantly, pulled amazing facts and stories from his seemingly endless memories. All the cracks in my research got filled and then some, because he took the time to help a newspaper type he had never even met.

KING KAUFMAN, Bleacher Report

My first experience around a big-league press box was in Oakland in the late '80s, as I did leisurely research for a magazine piece I was writing for the A's magazine. On one of my first evenings doing this, I was eating dinner alone in a media room, and various reporters and broadcasters were sitting around tables, eating, shooting the shit, passing the time before the start of the game.

Bill King bustled in, a sheaf of papers tucked under his arm. He quickly filled a paper plate with food, clapped another paper plate over the top of it and rushed back out. I remember him not saying

a word to anyone, though maybe he offered some quick greetings.

This may have been me, a twenty-five-year-old newcomer, pro-jecting attitudes that weren't there onto the older men — pretty sure they were all men — around me. But I had the distinct feeling that the guys in the room were all kind of smirking with each other: Get this guy — he's actually WORKING!

BRIAN MURPHY, KNBR host

I worked at the local movie theater in Mill Valley, Sequoia Twin Cinemas. We were showing Carmen, *the 1984 film version of the Bizet opera. One Sunday night, here he came: sports coat, handlebar mustache, unmistakable voice. "Two for* Carmen," *Bill King said to me in the ticket booth, and I nearly shook in my brown polyester coat, my clip-on bow tie no doubt askew. Of course he was coming to see* Carmen! *The game programs hadn't lied. He was an opera buff!*

I made sure to scurry from the ticket booth to the small refreshment stand in the lobby. Nobody was taking Bill King's order other than me. Bill King was coming to see Carmen, *and if he wanted a popcorn and a Sprite, I'd make sure the broadcaster who might as well been a sports deity would get his popcorn and Sprite. "I'll take a small popcorn, and a Sprite," he said. I would never forget the order, as Bill King and his lovely bride made their way up the carpeted steps into the darkened theater. I knew he'd watch the film with a critical and hopeful eye.*

NICO PEMANTLE, Athletics Nation

When my childhood friend, Gordon, shocked me with news of King's sudden passing, I was immediately struck with a realization: Outside of my immediate family, there was probably no one's voice I had heard more as a child than that of Bill King. Throughout my childhood, he accompanied me to all rooms of the house, to the car, the backyard and the nightstand by my bed. His voice was such a fixture in my life, as a young sports fan, that I can still replay its precise timbre clearly in my head more than seven years after his death.

VINCE COTRONEO

Imagine following that legacy. It was clear then and continues to this day — Bill was one of a kind and I felt the best way to honor him was to prepare and simply attempt to do the best job I could each and every game. It was difficult for A's fans because they could not honor Bill in a proper setting on his terms. My very first A's broadcast, from spring training 2006, I began with a short but heartfelt note about the fans' loss and appreciation of who Bill was from someone who admired him from afar. Ken and Ray embraced me, helped me on a nightly basis grow into the position. You cannot escape Bill's presence to this day, with countless remembrances about him both on and off the air in the booth that bears his name. It speaks to the impact that Bill had on the organization from the booth.

MARIA ESCORIO

I was so saddened by his death. It felt like losing a dear old friend. To this day, when there's an exciting play on the field I can still hear Bill's "Holy Toledo!" ring out loud and clear. What a shame today's younger fans can't have that same experience! As far as I'm concerned, Bill King was and still is the voice of Oakland A's baseball. He will forever hold an honored place in Athletics history!

TYLER BLEZINSKI

To me Bill's biggest legacy is that I will forever wonder how he would've reacted to each and every big A's moment.

MARCOS BRETON, *Sacramento Bee* columnist

Bill King is more revered today because we took him for granted when he was still with us. He didn't flaunt his excellence so we didn't praise him enough for it. Our memories are tied to his voice and his descriptions of indelible moments in sports history. But those memories wouldn't be as thrilling or indelible without Bill's voice and the spontaneous majesty he brought to each description of each game — year after year. Bill erased the distance between the listener and the action.

He made you feel the games in your gut, your heart and your mind. His basketball calls, perhaps his best sport, were like machine-gun blasts of raw energy. His football calls were brimming with drama to match the pulsating essence of NFL football as a violent chess match. In baseball, Bill was the storyteller, the wise sage, the brilliant uncle. Only now, in his absence, have we realized that no one else could match his peerless skills. His legacy lives in our memories. We can recite his calls years after he left us. He can make us smile, even now. I miss Bill, but I can still hear him and I will for as long as I live.

PEDRO GOMEZ

I remember grabbing the annual copy of the A's media guide one spring and opening to Page One and there was this wonderful black-and-white photo of Bill, under the announcement of he and the A's celebrating twenty-five years together. I have never, ever asked for an autograph of anyone in baseball. It's taboo in our industry. But if there was ever an exception, this was the one time I would make it. I walked into the booth and basically ordered Bill for an autograph. As usual, he did not disappoint.

"Pedro, What memories!" he wrote. Signed, "Bill King."

A pair of simple words but he captured perfectly what it was like to spend time with Bill. I still cherish that autograph.

ACKNOWLEDGMENTS

As I neared the end of doing the interviews for this book, I placed a call to Tom Flores. I had met Tom once but it was brief at Bill's memorial at the Coliseum. He was gracious when I asked if he had some time to talk about Bill but he told me that it wasn't a good time since he was leaving soon on a trip. Then he said: "Call me next week because I want to make sure I give you at least an hour to talk about Bill." And that was really the story of doing the research for this book.

We've all known people who've passed through our lives but don't make a big impression. With Bill it was: "I want to make sure I give you an hour."

There were two things I realized in working on this project that were necessary to complete a book: Number 1, I had to have a passion for the subject. And Number 2, I needed a push. Writing about Bill was easy. The hard part was knowing when to stop.

Steve Kettmann brought his dad out to the last game of the 2012 regular season in Oakland, when the A's beat the Texas Rangers to win the American League West. I think being back in the States and spending time with his dad rekindled Steve's love of baseball, and while they were enjoying the game from the stands, I did something during the sixth inning of the game that was completely unplanned.

I never dared use Bill's signature "Holy Toledo" on a broadcast.

Those were sacred words, although I thought if the A's ever won a World Series maybe that would be an appropriate time to break it out. Well, the crowd was whipped into a frenzy and the drama of the end of the season had built to such an incredible crescendo, that it just came out. In the sixth inning, when the A's basically put the game away, I screamed that Brandon Moss' hit that broke the game open and the subsequent delirium was "worthy of a Holy Toledo!"

Steve and I had talked over the years about how I had thought about someday writing a book about Bill. Steve and his dad were listening to the postgame highlights on their drive back to San Jose and I think the "Holy Toledo" exclamation ignited something in Steve. It wasn't more than a few days later that he called me. His thought was for me to write a memoir that would be part of a mentor series that Steve figured would be a great way to introduce Wellstone Books and pay homage to Bill. He figured maybe a short book, somewhere around twenty thousand words.

The fact that Steve, who is such an accomplished writer, was so enthusiastic provided the impetus I needed to seriously pursue writing the book. The passion for the subject — well, Bill and I worked for ten years together but my journey with him really was one that lasted almost my entire lifetime.

It was more than symbolic that our first interview was with Hank Greenwald. That lunch at Perry's in San Francisco kicked off the project, but also led me to an immediate crossroads. Steve pushed me, for good reason, to make the book as personal as possible. But listening to Hank, I was already expanding my focus. Not only was he eloquent in talking about his close friend, but the stories were so insightful and colorful that I thought a Bill King book had to also be told through the voices of the people who knew Bill best.

So Steve and I had a little creative tug-of-war. He pushed me toward my personal reflections and I went in search of interviews. It became a little humorous. I'd call Steve and tell him about talking with Scotty Stirling or John Madden or Billy Beane or Al Attles or Dave Henderson, and he would tell me about how many words

I had already written. It was like, "we're at forty thousand words," and then a little later it was up to fifty thousand and finally I think he just gave up.

It wasn't as if I was writing just to fill pages so I could say I had written a two hundred-page book. It was simply that everybody had a great story. I'd get off the phone energized about writing because the people we interviewed had a passion for talking about Bill that mirrored his own zest for life. The interviews were also like a trip down memory lane for someone like me who spent hundreds of hours listening to Bill and following sports in Northern California. I owe Steve and the book's editor, Pete Danko, a huge debt because the book took much longer to write than we had originally planned but they never wavered in their support.

That first day when we had lunch with Hank was very important because the day wouldn't have been complete without our dinner with Bill's stepdaughter, Kathleen Lowenthal, and her husband, Barry Lowenthal. Like any loyal and loving family member, Kathleen carefully looks out for Bill's best interests, even though he is gone. Asking for her blessing on the book was a little like asking for permission to marry. That's how thrilled Steve and I felt to have her support. Kathleen's brother, Johnny Stephens, was also very helpful getting us going and filling in many of the blanks.

A project like this couldn't have come to fruition without the help of so many people who cared about what we were doing and about Bill.

There were many people who would have been great choices to write the foreword to this book, but it took me about two seconds to settle on Jon Miller. Jon's career speaks for itself — it doesn't get any better than the Frick Award — and his friendship meant the world to Bill, as it does to me.

My good friend Marty Lurie opened his library of interviews to me during a memorable day at his home in Mesa, Arizona. I had heard of Tom Spencer because of his work with CBS, but we had never met. Tom's email offer of the key points from his 1999 interview with Bill proved invaluable. I shared many wonderful days and nights on the A's radio broadcasts with Steve Bitker. I can't thank him enough for providing the old cassette recordings of his broadcast with Bill at Rohnert Park Stadium in 1996 and for his help in arranging the interview with John Madden. The interviews with Roy Eisenhardt and my old friend Scotty Stirling were numbers two and three on the "must talk to" list — a list that kept growing and growing.

Also, thanks to the writers, broadcasters, former players, executives, friends and fans of Bill and those who worked with him. Lon Simmons, Rich Waltz, Jerry Howarth, Pedro Gomez, David Feldman, Susan Slusser, Steve Vucinich, Bruce Macgowan, Jason Giambi, Mike Lefkow, Jay Alves, Glenn Dickey, Sandy Alderson, Andy Dolich, Blez, Nico, Ken Pries, Shooty Babitt, Mickey Morabito, Greg Papa, Rich Marotta, The Legendary Gary Hughes, Monte Poole, Lowell Cohn, Curt Smith, Barry Horn, David Bush, Dave Henderson, Murray Olderman, Bob Welch, Marty Brennaman, Dennis Eckersley, Mike Marquardt, Bob Rose, Randy Adamack, Mike Baird, Paul Olden, Wally Haas, Gary Radnich, Scott Hatteberg and Billy Beane. Thanks to the Bay Area Radio Museum for keeping the legacy alive and for being a valuable source of information.

Special thanks for being so generous with their time and insightful in their reflections to Rick Barry and Tom Meschery — not a bad combination of NBA forwards. And to John Madden, whose comment that "Bill was a good get-away guy," pretty much summed up much of what a friendship with Bill meant. Alvin Attles, Ken Macha, Art Howe and Tom Flores are, like John, part of the Bay Area coaching and managing fraternity and the book wouldn't have been complete without the generous sharing of their time.

I've spent eighteen wonderful years on A's radio with Ray Fosse. His friendship and his amazingly insightful commentary have meant the world to me. I still look forward to the "Fosse days." Vince Cotroneo has been a great broadcast partner for the last eight years with the A's. We also sit next to each other on the team flights, but I was pretty quiet during the 2013 season because I was writing most of the time. The Oakland A's, by the way, have been the greatest employer anyone could possibly hope for.

Our days at the Coliseum are always spent with Mike Baird

at the controls in the Bill King Broadcast Booth. Mike worked his audio magic converting many of the interviews into files and saving us a ton of time. John Trinidad is a genius with his production work and very special thanks go to Ken Pries, Robert Buan, David Don, Bruce Macgowan and John for their help in finding many of Bill's radio calls. And thanks to Niall Adler for stopping by the Coliseum with an old cassette interview with Bill from 1999.

Steve Kettmann not only is the publisher of this book, but he is a good friend as well. His heart is behind his brainchild known as Wellstone Books and he is going to make a huge contribution and do important work with Wellstone. I didn't know Pete Danko when we started this project, but eventually we spent hours exchanging emails and talking on the phone. Pete's editing was so good and his dedication so impressive that now I look back and feel that he knew Bill and me from the start. I'll never be able to repay Pete for all of his hard work on this book. Thanks to Adam Candee and Drew Goldstein, AKA Boy Wonder, for their help with transcribing many of the interviews. I don't know much about social media, but I do know that Drew and Steve were diligent and creative in developing and updating the Facebook page for the book: facebook. com/HolyToledoBillKing.

To my wife, Denise, and daughter, Emilee — I know they think I'm crazy and they are probably right because of my tunnel vision when I get involved in an endeavor like this one, but without their love and support none of this had any chance of happening. Emilee was also a huge help and a creative force behind the Kickstarter effort.

I had a small family as a kid, just my dad, mom and me. But thanks to my Dad's marriage to Janet our family has grown to include Janet, Mark and Lisa and their families as well. They have always been a great source of inspiration as have my in-laws, who go all the way back to my first year broadcasting San Jose State football and basketball.

The Boys know who they are and how much they have meant to me. My golf buddies are looking for my pitching wedge as I am writing this.

Finally, I can't thank my dad enough for all the times I tagged along when he was coaching or we were going to games. And, well, for the guidance and love of a father — all I can say is that I've been very fortunate.

As I did at Bill's memorial, I'll break one of the three rules he gave me when we had dinner for the first time. Thanks.

—Ken Korach

THE NEXT BILL KING

I t wasn't the first thing that crossed my mind or the second, but it had everything to do with my saying "yes." This was 1994 and, despite hoping never to end up working full time as a sportswriter, I'd just spent a long season covering the San Jose Sharks for the *San Francisco Chronicle*. Sports editor John Curley wanted to promote me and called me into his glass-walled office to give me the good news that I was being moved up to the baseball beat. I met the announcement with an uneasy blank stare. For one it was the middle of the season and the beat guy he wanted me to replace, David Bush, deserved respect and deference, not a midseason switch. I thought of Roger Angell, one of my favorite writers, and how he had shown that writing on baseball could be both the ultimate challenge and a springboard to timeless story-telling. Then I thought of Bill: Bill King, whose voice I'd heard on the radio so often growing up in San Jose, Bill King, whose love of language planted a seed that sprouted when I went to Berkeley thinking I'd get my Ph.D. in theoretical astrophysics but wound up a would-be writer instead.

I'm deeply thankful to Bill for inspiring me and later, in my years covering the A's for the *Chronicle*, for becoming my friend, but I'm even more thankful to Ken Korach for agreeing to my suggestion to write this book and in the process teaching me more about life and writing than I thought one book project could teach me. Ken, like Bill himself (and like yours truly), can be difficult, I discovered in the work on this book, and here's to Ken for always fighting hard for his vision. Sometimes it seemed too great a challenge, trying to do right by as unique a figure as Bill, but thanks to Ken and the editor on the book, former *Riverside Press-Enterprise* sports columnist Pete Danko, yet another who grew up listening to Bill in awe and amazement, we were able to keep in mind that what mattered was passing on as much of Bill to readers as we could. Our first Wellstone Books intern, Drew Goldstein, has a natural ear for language and talent to burn and helped the project forward in essential ways as well. Ken inspired me because he always had faith we'd get where we wanted to go and he inspired me because he wrote so beautifully and honestly about what Bill meant to him and about the art of broadcasting. When I left the Bay Area in 1999 to go live in Berlin for most of a decade, Ken was an excellent broadcaster; when I moved back to California in 2012 to start up the Wellstone Center in the Redwoods along with co-founder Sarah Ringler and once again tuned Ken in on the radio, I found to my pleasure that Ken had become a great broadcaster in his own right.

Now Ken has also established himself as a wonderful writer, in my view, but you be the judge, please. The point is: Ken went from never having written a book to commanding the stage like an old hand. He was a natural, it's clear enough, but I think the revelation in these pages of a fresh voice also speaks to an exciting trend in publishing: Small publishers like Wellstone Books can stand shoulder to shoulder with the great houses in New York, at least now and then. We can focus on giving voice to unpublished writers. We can emphasize personal writing that is not afraid to inspire and along the way tell some good stories. We believe that writing matters more than ever and that books are here to stay in whatever form they are published. We also believe that if you focus on greatness, some of it can rub off. This book can be read by anyone and enjoyed, but we will be especially pleased if some young broadcaster of tomorrow picks it up and feels some of the Bill magic. There will never be another one like Bill, that goes without saying. But who knows what talent of tomorrow Bill might inspire? Who knows how Ken's graceful portrait might shape and inform that unfolding talent?

The *Holy Toledo* book project has been a labor of love for many people, starting with Ken Korach and Pete Danko and the whole Wellstone Books team, and we've been very lucky to have so many great contributors. A special thanks to Dale Tafoya and David Beach for their helpful push in getting out the word early on our *Holy Toledo* Facebook page, at *facebook.com/HolyToledoBillKing*. Everyone involved with the book has been energized by the strong following we've enjoyed via Facebook, and we pay our respects by including quotes about Bill in the book from many of you who checked in with us via FB. The Facebook page also brought us our interior designer, Alvaro Villanueva, who brought energy and talent and good cheer to the project and made a huge contribution to improving the book in ways both obvious and subtle; we could never have brought the project home without Alvaro. Thanks also to Mark Ulriksen for his wonderful portrait of Bill for the cover of the book. We've all been Ulriksen fans for a long time — no one does sports better — and we're deeply thankful he would lend his talents to the project. For the fantastic cover lettering, our lasting gratitude to Mark Matcho, and a big shout-out as well to our creative and resourceful web developer Dave Kettmann, whose work gives *www.holytoledo.info* its distinctive look (check it out!); he too grew up listening to Bill call the Warriors.

Our following at FB made launching a Kickstarter campaign much easier, and thanks again to Emilee Korach for her great video of Ken to announce the project. It's still online, if anyone wants to go back and enjoy it now. Our Kickstarter backers truly did kickstart this project, turning this into a full-length book, and we're thankful to all of you:

Rusty Abernathy, Miriam Aguilar, Jim Anderson, Mike Andersen, Zach Anderson, Ken Arneson, Russell Atkins, Jeffrey August,

Phillip Avalos, Mary Baca, Anne Baker, Mark Baker, William Barnes, Gil Batzri, David Beach, Todd Becker, Ed Bellah, Deena Benton, Cheryl Bethe, Seth Blair, Nick Bohlender, Aron Borok, Randal Brandt, Bill Bretag, Greg Brower, Dan Brown, Tom Burke, Linda Burnett, Susan Camarillo, Denise Canadas, Paul Chamberlin, Wesley Chang, Stephen Chen, Yea-Hung Chen, Nels Christensen, Niall Coppinger, Jennifer Cornet, Neil Darin, Josh Deitcher, Debbie Downs Delgros, Adam Dolci, Tony Dorie, Gabriel Doss, Steven Douglas, William Drobick, Daniel P. Duggan, Conn Dunning, Ken Egel, Brian Ehrich, Steve Fainaru, Nick Fanelli, Charles Fannin, Aida Fisher, Matthew Fockler, Richard Fong III, Deanna Fountain, Lanny Freeman, Joseph Freitas, Dave Friedman, Matthew A. Gabel, Erika Garcia, Michael Gaskins, Bob Gonsalves, Marc Gougeon, the Grossman Family, Guy Haberman, Dan Hagen, Paul Hallaman, Mark Halling, Dan Hamman, Audrey and Richard Hausman, Mike Headley, Greg Heilner, Marc Hershman, Amirali Hifai, Wesley Hofmann, Stephanie Hopkins, Catherine Howard, Larry Huffstutler, Aaron James Hutchison, Martin Imahori, Lisa Marie Intravaia, Kevin Johnson, Stephen G Johnson, Molly Jones, Margie Kahn, Stephen Kay, Matthew Kerns, Nancy Kettmann, King Bag Company, Stuart James Kitchen, Peter Klabunde, Janette Klingner, Kevon Knudsen, Lynette Kruger, Courtney LaBree, Thomas (Tate) G. Lacey, Samuel Lam, Tiffany Lam, Steven Lavoie, Jason Leary, Adam Lerios, Brian Lewis, Jr., Michael Liedtke, Dave Linn, Sean Lovens, Marc Anthony Lugo, Greg Lundblad, Brian McCarthy, Tom McDonald, Matt McDonell, Sean McGarvey, Dennis and Lynda McGee, Mike McGee, Rachel McKissick, Sean McKissick, Steven McIntire, James McManis, Brian McMillin, Matt Mackay, James Manion, Dennis Marsh, Charlotte Martinez, Jennifer Maxwell, David Mendelsohn, Ross Meyerson, Michael Miller, Thomas Miller, Robert Mon, Lucas Morrison, David Mortenson, Rhamesis Muncada, Kevin Murphy, Eyleen Nadolny, Tike Narry, John Nassar, Eric Nelson, Amy Nelson Smith, Bryanne Ningas, Emily Nolan, Sherryl O'Neill, Teresa O'Rourke, Carrie Olejnik, Andrew Oliveira, Megan Oliveira, Marisa Ong, Francisco Orosco, Robert Palassou, Padmini Parthasarathy, Mark Pelzner, Shelley

Perreira, David Peters, Lori Petrini, Michael Petrocelli, Mike Pettigano, Mike Pionus, Eugene L. Placencia, David J. Ponte, Julianna Pratt, J.G. Preston, Mary Purdey, Wayne Purves, Tim Quinn, Michael Ravina, Richard Reising, Bruce Reyes-Chow, Elias Reynoso, Jeff Rubenstein, Aric Rubin, Dan Rubin, David Saidian, Jarrett Sanchez, Justin Sanchez, Ross Sanderson, David Schaefer, Julie Pestka Schardt, Roberta and Don Schiller, Paul Schroeder, Eric Schuerman, Matthew Scott, Rupesh Shah, Ferris Shahrestani, Greg Shaver, Mike Silva, Peter Silva, Richard Silva, Susan Slusser, Robert Slye, Jr., Alexander Smith, Sara Somers, David Spencer, David Spencer Bloch, Keith Stanley, Lisa Stanley, Robert S. Steinberg, Carl Steward, Daniel Stewart, Josh Suchon, John Taber, Gary Teves, Mayank Thanawala, Ryan Thibodaux, Nina Thorsen, Ceil Tilney, Ron Tiongco, Mike Tonsing, Jr., Anna-Lisa Ulbrich, Jake Unguren, Larry Valderrama, Erich Valo, John Valva, Pete Vaz, James Venes, Andrew Viloria, Mark Violich, Michael Visser, Marlene Vogelsang, Jean Walker, Kevin Walters, Tom Wheelock, Brendan Williams, Ronald J. Wilson, Nick Wong, John Yap, Jim Yoshii, Jonathan Zucker, Scott Zumsteg and Lynn M. Zboyovsky.

—Steve Kettmann

INDEX

COMING SOON FROM WELLSTONE BOOKS
FALL 2013

One Body
Massage

by
Grace Ku

If you are irritated by every rub,
how will your mirror be polished?
~Rumi

The body speaks.
If we quiet our mind, we can hear its wisdom.
~Grace Ku

Grace Ku, an artist as well as a massage therapist at Google, was living her own version of the familiar story: too much stress, too many hours hunched over a keyboard with no break, too much pain. She broke away from that life to become a full-time massage therapist and in this book, coming this fall from Wellstone Books, she distills the insights she's gained into the art of massage — and the art of better living through massage — and also presents a wealth of "tricks of the trade."

"Every massage session is an opportunity to be in a calm, peaceful, suspended space where one is enveloped between heaven and earth, connecting with one another," Grace says. "It's beautiful."

Grace has developed this book in tandem with her preparation for her regular couples massage weekend workshops at the Wellstone Center in the Redwoods, beginning this fall. For more information on those workshops or other activities at the Center, visit *wellstoneredwoods.org*.

THE ART OF FIELDING — CHAD HARBACH — LITTLE, BROWN

SHOELESS JOE — W. P. Kinsella — MARINER

BERNARD MALAMUD — The Natural

HIGH AND INSIDE — Russell Rowland — BP

CASTRO'S CURVEBALL — TIM WENDEL — BALLANTINE BOOKS

MARK WINEGARDNER — THE VERACRUZ BLUES — ISBN 0 14 02.6026 5

COMING SOON FROM WELLSTONE BOOKS

SPRING 2014

WELLSTONE BOOKS'
TOP 100 BASEBALL NOVELS OF ALL TIME

Despite what a *New York Times* columnist kept writing at the time, Jose Canseco's best-selling steroid tell-all *Juiced* was not a "novel." It was a work of nonfiction. The true baseball novel can take many forms, at its best using the medium of fiction to explore larger truths or just to have fun. From Peter Lefcourt's frisky *The Dreyfus Affair* (a double-play combination hooks up) to Chad Harbach's deft and ambitious *The Art of Fielding*, from Malamud's *The Natural* to Kinsella's *Shoeless Joe*, the baseball novel can add depth and feeling to anyone's baseball imagination, the lens through which real fans of the game take in the sport.

Wellstone Books will mark the start of the 2014 baseball season with a guide to the top 100 baseball novels of all time and we want your help: Send us your ballot, listing your personal top ten favorite baseball novels and tell us what you liked about the books you're picking — and we might quote you in the book. If you're an author and want to send us your baseball novel for consideration, feel free!

SNAIL-MAIL US YOUR LIST, IF YOU LIKE. SEND IT TO:
BALLOTS, 858 Amigo Road, Soquel, CA 95073

OR EMAIL IT INTO:
ballots@wellstoneredwoods.org

ALSO, IF YOU'RE ON GOODREADS, YOU CAN VOTE THERE:
goodreads.com / list / show / 41820.Best_Baseball_Novels_of_All_Time